IMAGES
of America

BOATS AND PORTS OF LAKE WINNIPESAUKEE
VOLUME II

IMAGES
of America

BOATS AND PORTS OF LAKE WINNIPESAUKEE VOLUME II

Dr. Bruce D. Heald

ARCADIA
PUBLISHING

ISBN 978-0-7385-6437-1

Published by Arcadia Publishing
Charleston, South Carolina

Printed in the United States of America

Library of Congress Catalog Card Number: 2003106998

For all general information contact Arcadia Publishing at:
Telephone 843-853-2070
Fax 843-853-0044
E-mail sales@arcadiapublishing.com
For customer service and orders:
Toll-Free 1-888-313-2665

Visit us on the Internet at www.arcadiapublishing.com

To my loving daughter Allyson and the
New Hampshire Antique & Classic Boat Museum.

Contents

Acknowledgments

Special thanks are extended to the following individuals, towns, and historical societies for their contribution to this volume:

The Appalachian Mountain Club, Gladys Bickford, Joanne and Dick Binette and Handy Landing, C.T. Bodwell, The Boston & Maine Railroad, William J. Buchanan, Joseph Bush Sr., The Center Harbor Historical Society, The Concord & Montreal Railroad, Merrill Fay and Fay's Boat Yard, William H. Genne and the Geneva Point Center, The Granite State Monthly, Holy Trinity School, Al Horne, Warren D. Huse, Irwin Maine, James Irwin, Jack Irwin, The Lakes Region Association, Beth Lavertur, Bob Lawton and The Weirs Publishing Co., Don Minor, James Morash and The Winnipesaukee Flagship Corporation, Mark Morris and The New Hampshire Antique & Classic Boat Museum, New Hampshire Profile, New Hampshire Troubadour, New Hampshire Planning and Development Commission, Harold Orne, E.D. Putnam, Thomas Quinn, Charles Whitten and The Weirs Chamber of Commerce, Lake Winnipesaukee Historical Society, and all those unsung contributors who have made this historic publication possible.

Introduction

Lake Winnipesaukee, the largest and most beautiful water-sheet in New Hampshire, is one of the country's most popular vacation resorts.

How vividly one may picture the marvelous panorama of nature bursting suddenly upon the view of the roving American Native as he breasted the crest of the hill; how easy to imagine the majestic figure outlined against the setting sun, one hand shading his eyes, and the other upraised in a gesture of amazement and admiration. Little wonder that his words were addressed to the Deity and that today, when the waters are dotted with the pleasure craft of the vacationers, the beautiful lake in the hills still bears the name Winnipesaukee, meaning the "Smile of the Great Spirit."

The Merrimack River, the source of the aborigines' favorite highways, was a convenient halting place for native inhabitants on their return from Canada.

This picturesque body of water is cradled among several mountain ranges—the Ossipee Mountains to the east, the Belknap Mountains to the west, and the White Mountains to the north. The lake is 25 miles long and 12 miles wide at its widest point with an area of 72 square miles, and a mainland shoreline of 186 miles. This vast body of inland water is dotted with 274 habitable islands. Fortunately, the merits of this lake have warranted the existence of the famous *Mount Washington* and many other sailing craft. These boats have enabled all visitors to witness the panoramic beauty of Lake Winnipesaukee.

On a bright summer afternoon, when the hours seem to pause for a while, the pleasure fleet of humanity, clad in gallant array, wends its way from bay and cove, from isle and mainland, out into the clear mirroring surface of the peaceful waters. Steamboats, excursions boats, motorboats, sailboats, canoes, and rowboats all join in the daily pageant.

There is practically no limit to the diversity of outdoor recreation at the disposal of the visitors. Even in the winter the region offers the enticements of ice-boating, skating, and fishing. Many who view it fall love the region so devotedly that even during the season of frost and snow it draws them back like a magnet.

The queen of all New England lakes, Winnipesaukee still reigns with undimmed glory over an annually increasing host of loyal subjects. It is through this glorious vestibule that a majority of visitors pass to their smiling haven of rest and recreation. Indeed, there is no section of this vast New England summer playground that has more to commend it to the casual traveler.

Through this rare photographic journey in time, I have attempted to capture some of the lake's charm and character and to preserve in print the spirit of a legacy so dear to many who return to this region year after year.

This second volume has been assembled through the generosity of the New Hampshire Antique & Classic Boat Museum, and the many friends who wished to share with you the romance and heritage of the boats and ports of Lake Winnipesaukee.

Bruce D. Heald, Ph.D.

One

Lake Winnipesaukee

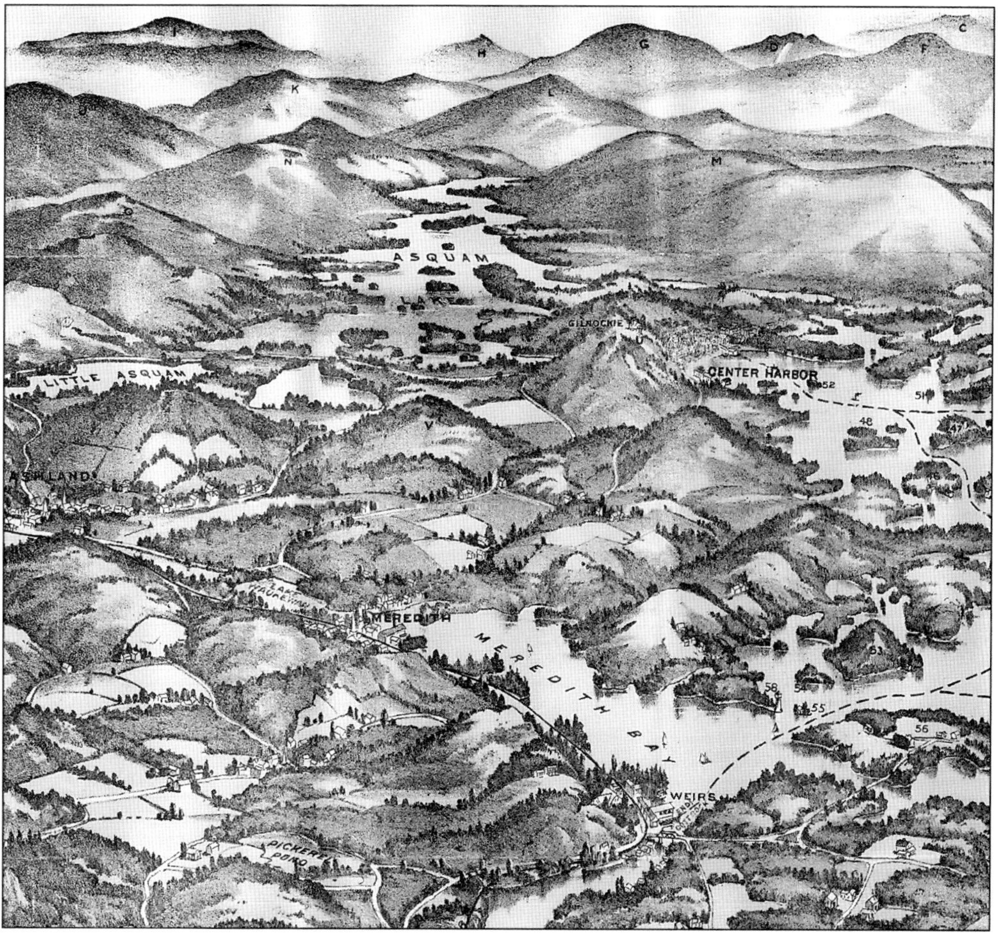

A sectional map of Lake Winnipesaukee and its surroundings, issued by the passenger department of the Boston & Lowell Railroad, 1909.

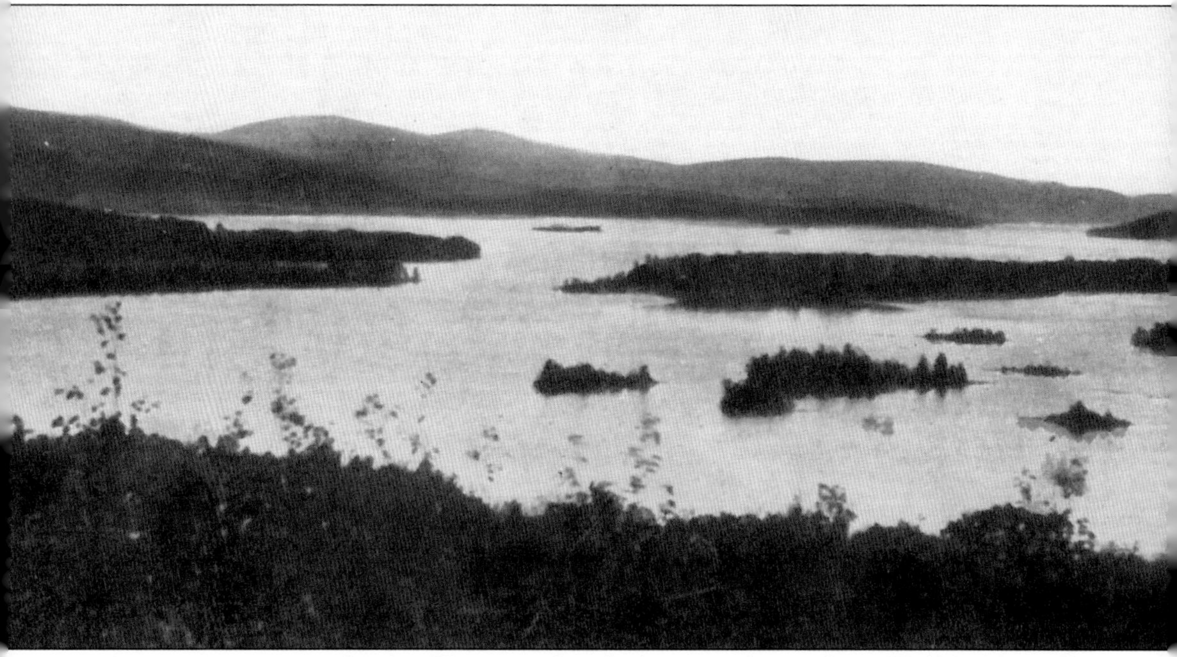

A panoramic view of Lake Winnipesaukee looking northwest from Wolfeboro. In the background is Rattlesnake Island with the Belknap Mountain Range on the far left. This lake is one of the three largest freshwater lakes in the continental United States that lies wholly

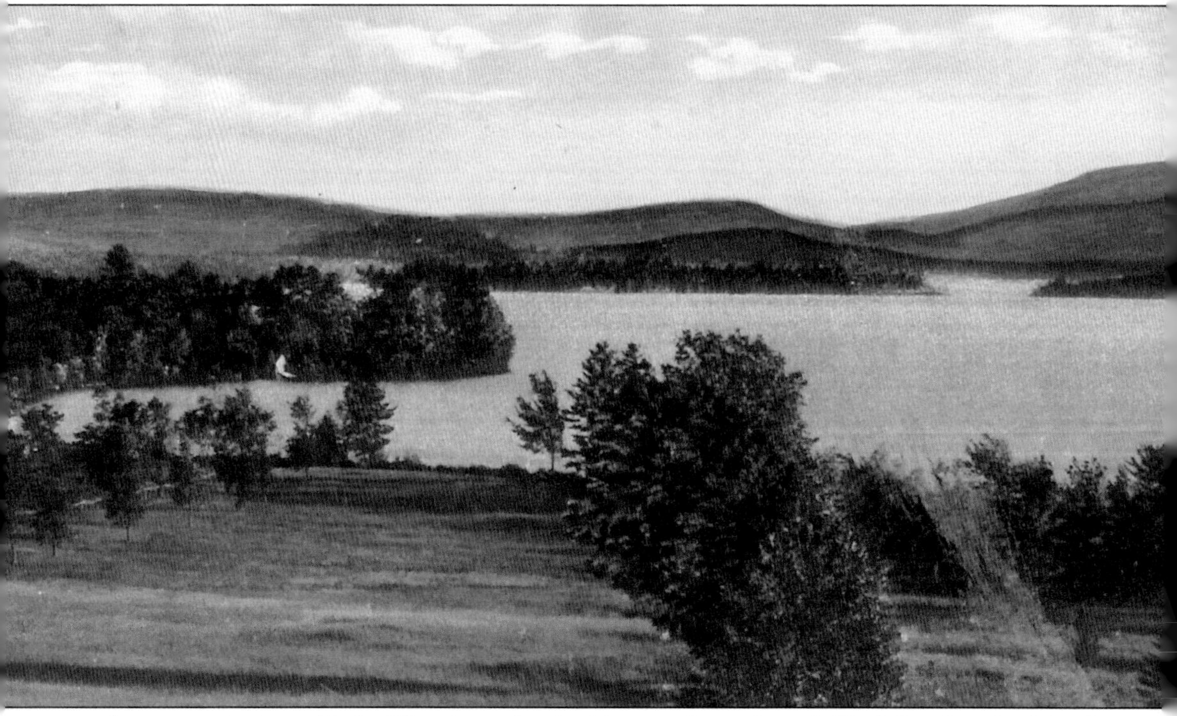

A panoramic view of Lake Winnipesaukee looking northeast from Gilford. Rattlesnake Island is on the right with the Ossipee Mountain Range in the background. Nothing can exceed the beauty of the mountains on the north shore; they are the Ossipee, Sandwich, and Presidential

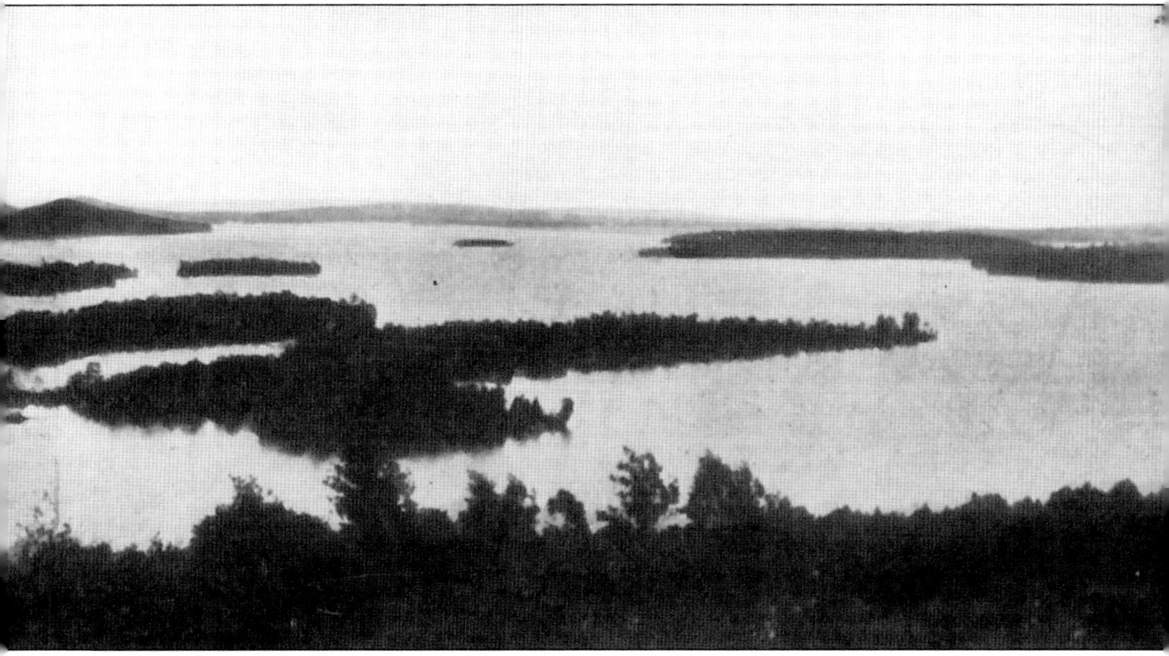

within the borders of one state. Winnipesaukee, New Hampshire's largest lake, with an area of 72 square miles and a mainland shoreline of 186 miles, is dotted with 274 habitable islands and surrounded by the foothills of the White Mountains.

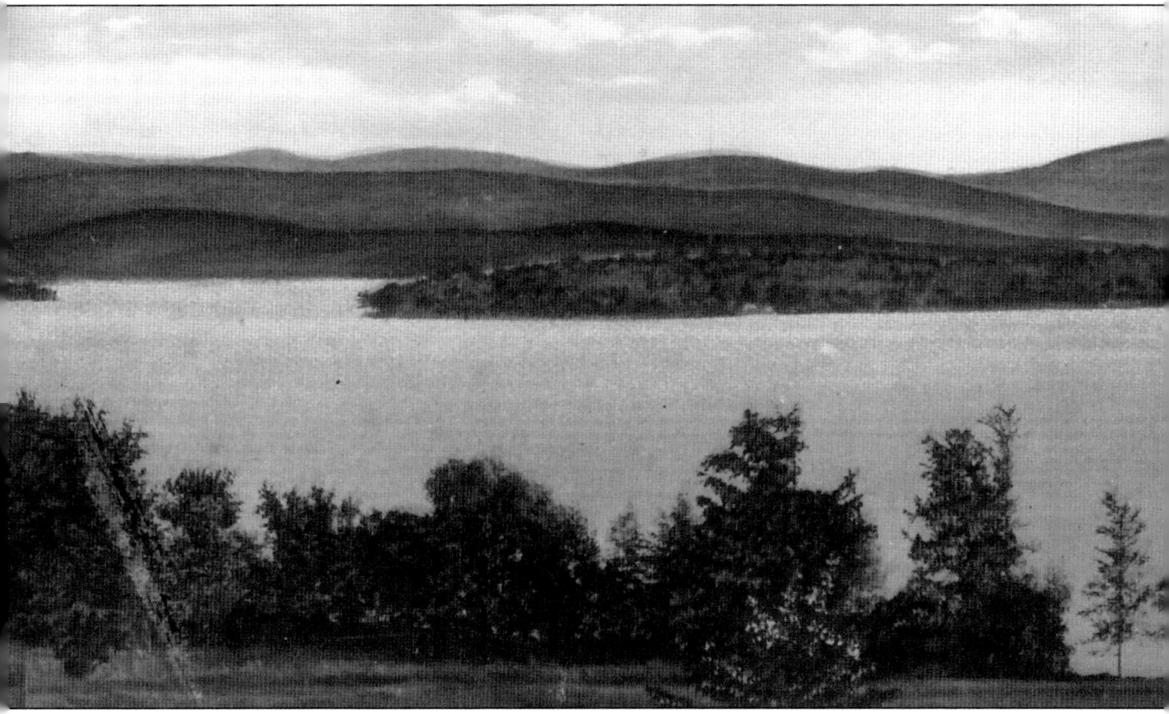

Range in the White Mountains framing the water's edge. The water of this lake empties into the Winnipesaukee River, which soon forms a junction with the Pemigewasset River; the two rivers unite making the Merrimack River at Franklin Falls, New Hampshire.

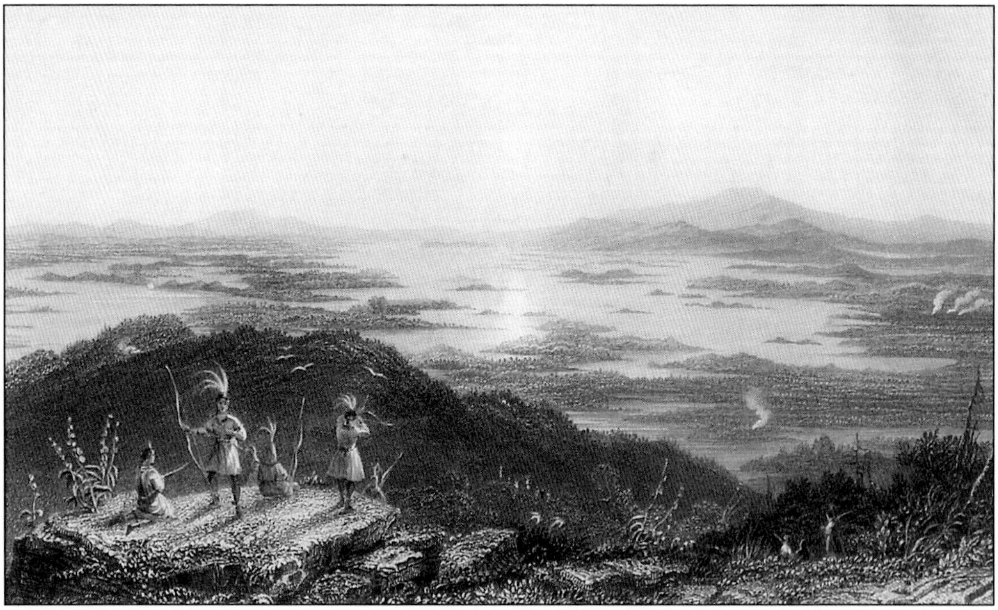

Lake Winnipesaukee looking southwest as seen from Red Hill, 1836. This lake is one of the most beautiful water sheets in the world with islands ranging in size from 1,000 acres down to tiny dots of rock and turf which are scarcely large enough to hold a small summer camp. The "Smile of the Great Spirit" was aptly named by the Native Americans, although a more proper translation of the name means "Beautiful Water in a High Place." Today, this lake is home for thousands who have come to cherish it as much as the Native Americans did hundreds of years ago. (A William H. Bartlett print.)

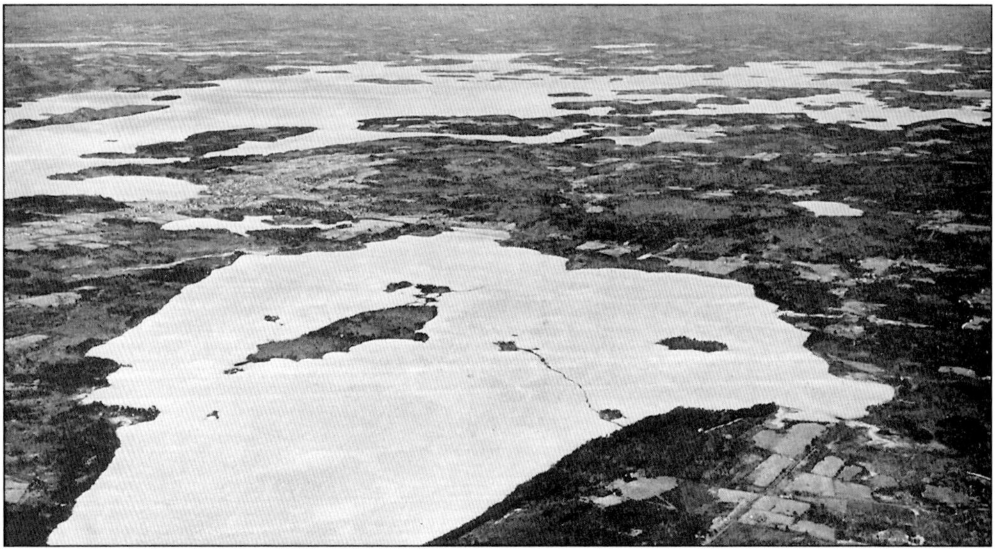

An aerial view of the Lake Winnipesaukee quadrangle looking to the west with Lake Wentworth in the foreground and Wolfeboro village center left. Lake Winnipesaukee was glacially formed. At one time the Belknap and Ossipee Mountains, located on either side of the lake, were active volcanoes. The lake is very deep, ranging in depth up to 200 feet, and is mostly spring fed. Many of the cottages around its shores take their water directly from it without any treatment.

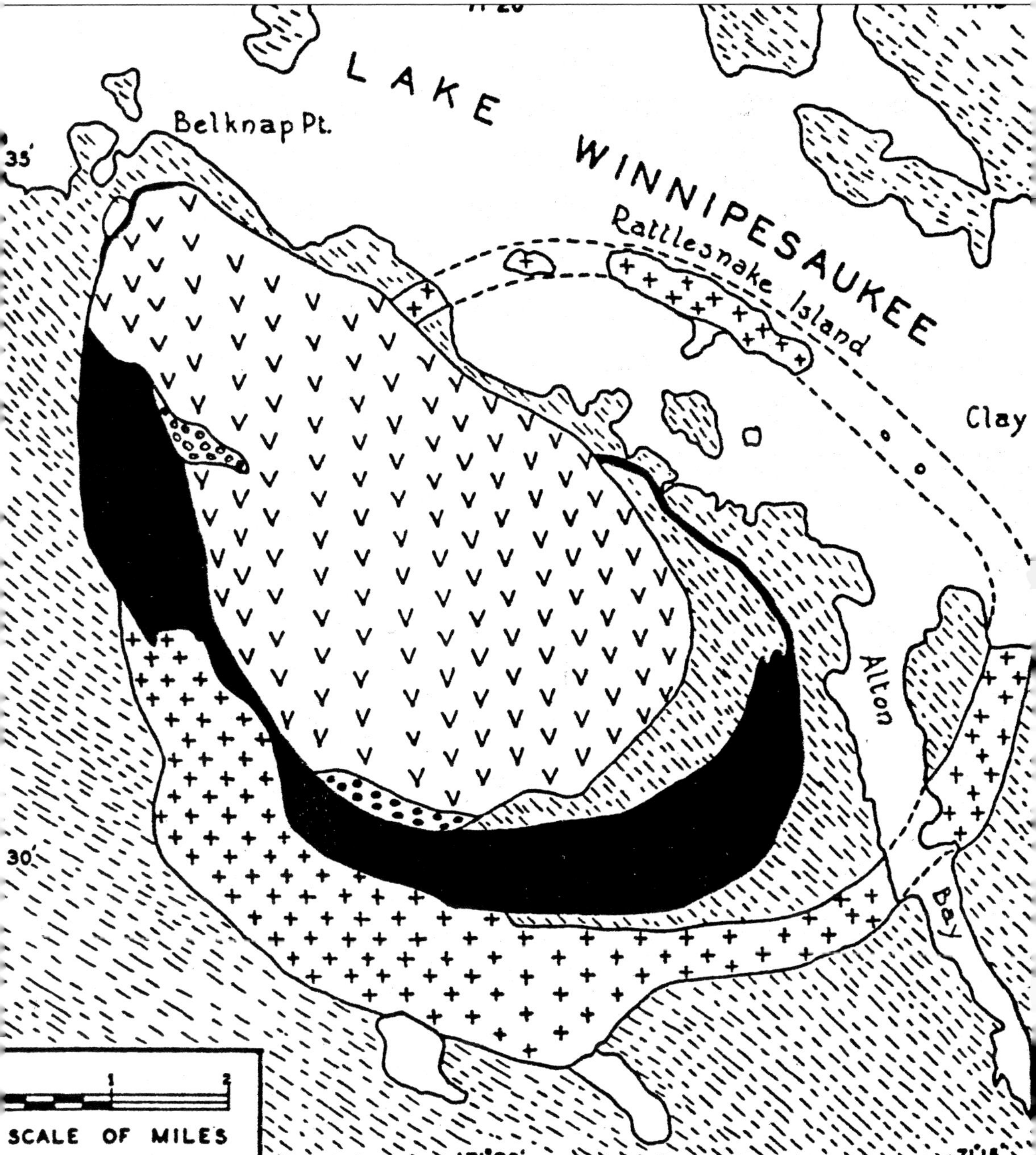

A simplified geological map of the Belknap Mountains and vicinity. In the Belknap Mountains there exists a large and spectacular variety of rocks as in the other areas of the White Mountain magma series. Spectacular exposures of the contact of the Albany quartz syenite and the Meredith porphyritic granite may be found on the top of Mt. Major and the hills which are 1.3 miles east of Round Pond.

This range shows superb examples of a peculiar type of geological structure known as a "ring-dike." Only part of the Belknap Mountains lies in the Winnipesaukee quadrangle; the rest are in the adjacent Gilmanton, Alton, and Wolfeboro quadrangle.

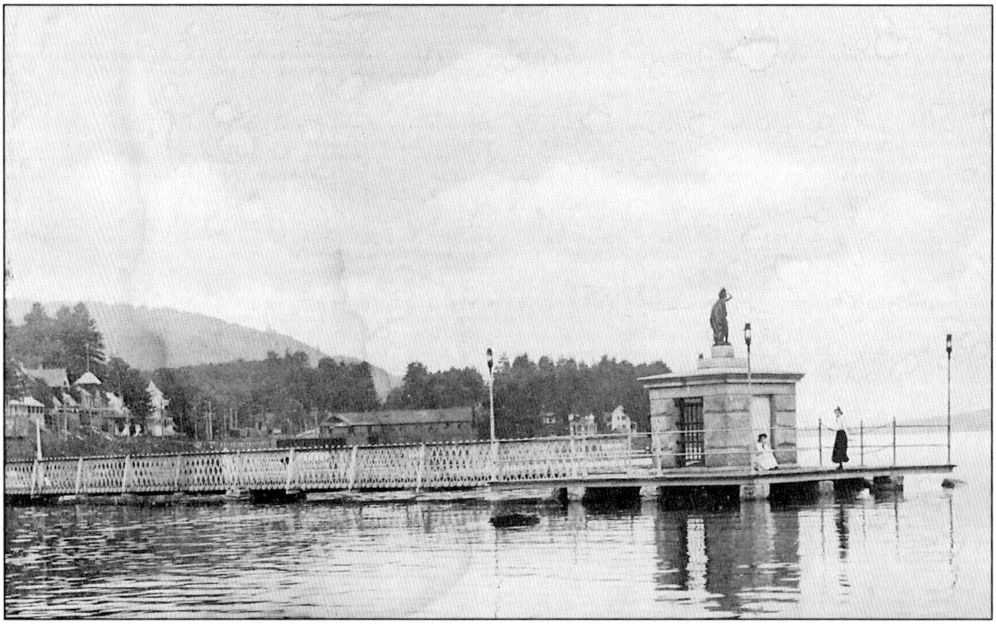

The Endicott Rock Monument in the channel at Weirs Beach, 1900s. In 1652 the Massachusetts Bay Colony sent a delegation to ascertain the northernmost boundary of its territory. They chiseled the name of Governor Endicott on a large, round-topped boulder at the river mouth of the outlet of Lake Winnipesaukee. For 181 years this was apparently forgotten. In 1833 it was rediscovered and in 1892 the State of New Hampshire erected, as a memorial, a granite structure enclosing it.

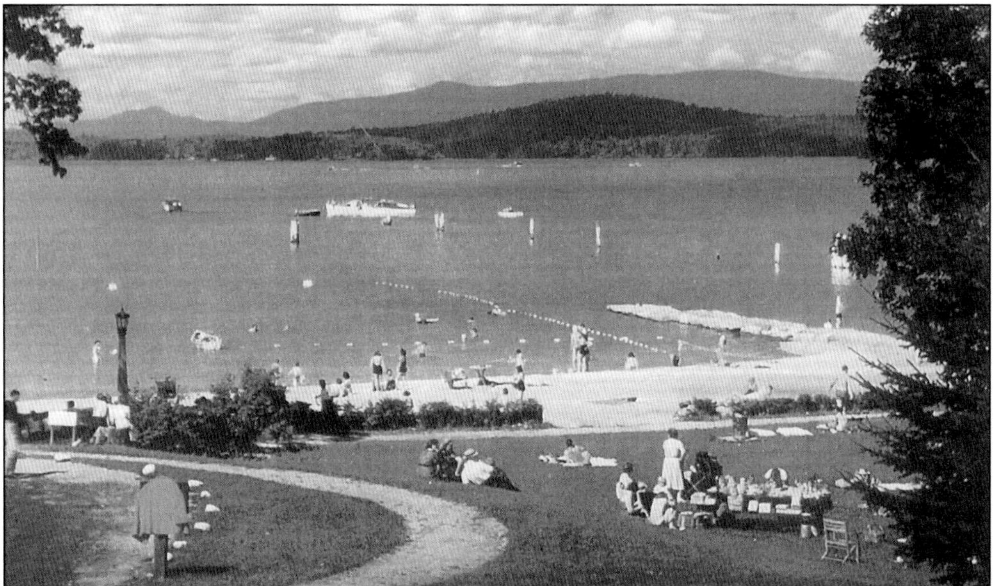

The Weirs Beach and picnic area next to the Endicott Rock Monument, *c.* 1950s. The beach has continued to be very popular with summer bathers. This beach and channel serve as the outlet of Lake Winnipesaukee to join Lake Paugus, the Winnipesaukee River, Lake Winnisquam, and finally, the Pemigewasset River in Franklin to form the Merrimack River.

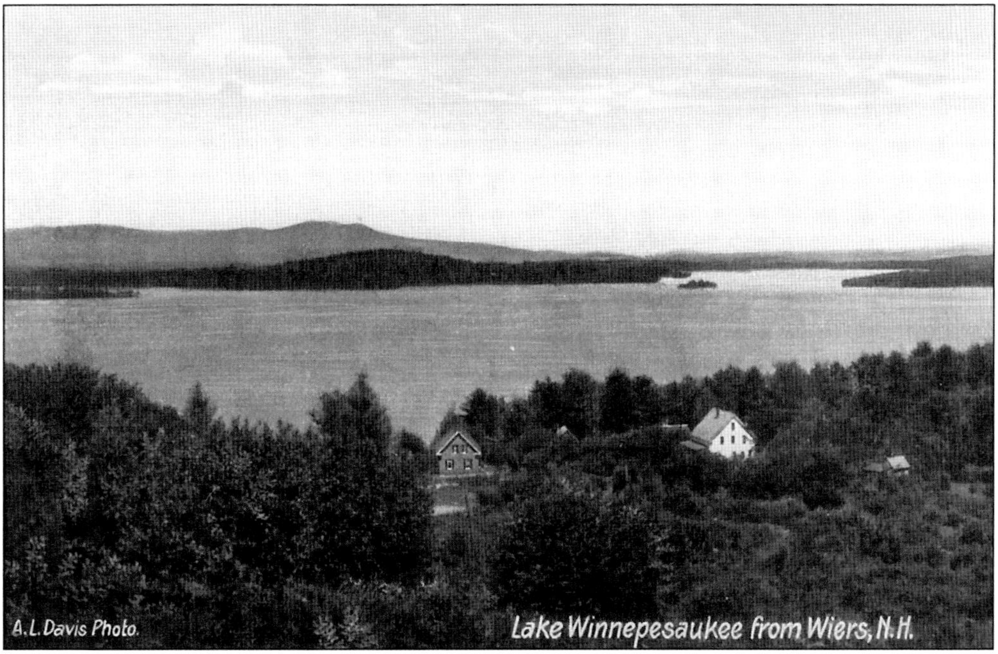

The Meredith and Weirs Bays from Winnecoette Hill looking south. Mount Shaw, in the far distance, dominates the horizon. To the right is the northern tip of Governors Island and to the far left is Spindle Point. The small island in the center is Eagle Island.

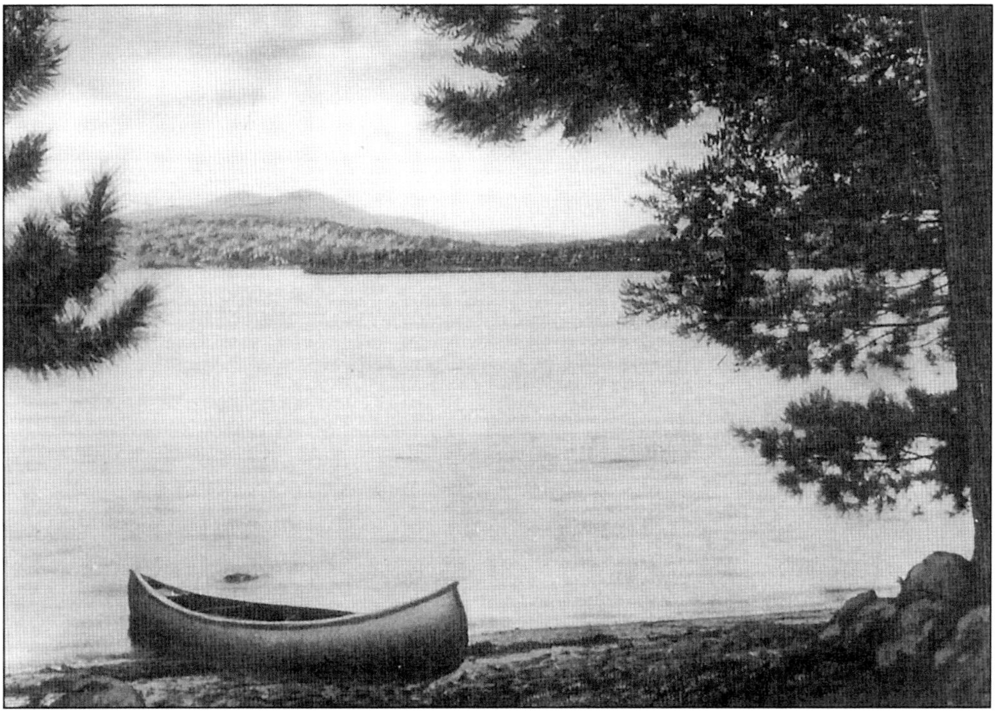

Mount Belknap and Mount Gunstock as seen from Meredith Neck on the shore of Lake Winnipesaukee. The mountain range is renowned for its recreational areas, particularly among ski and camping enthusiasts, who flock to it during winter and summer months.

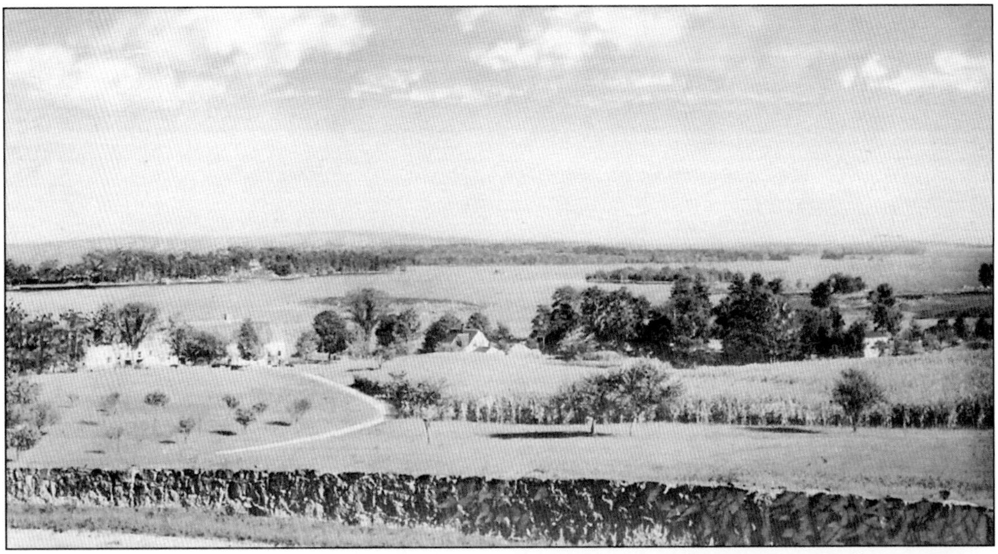

Lake Winnipesaukee as seen looking east as seen from Garnet Hill in Center Harbor, 1920.

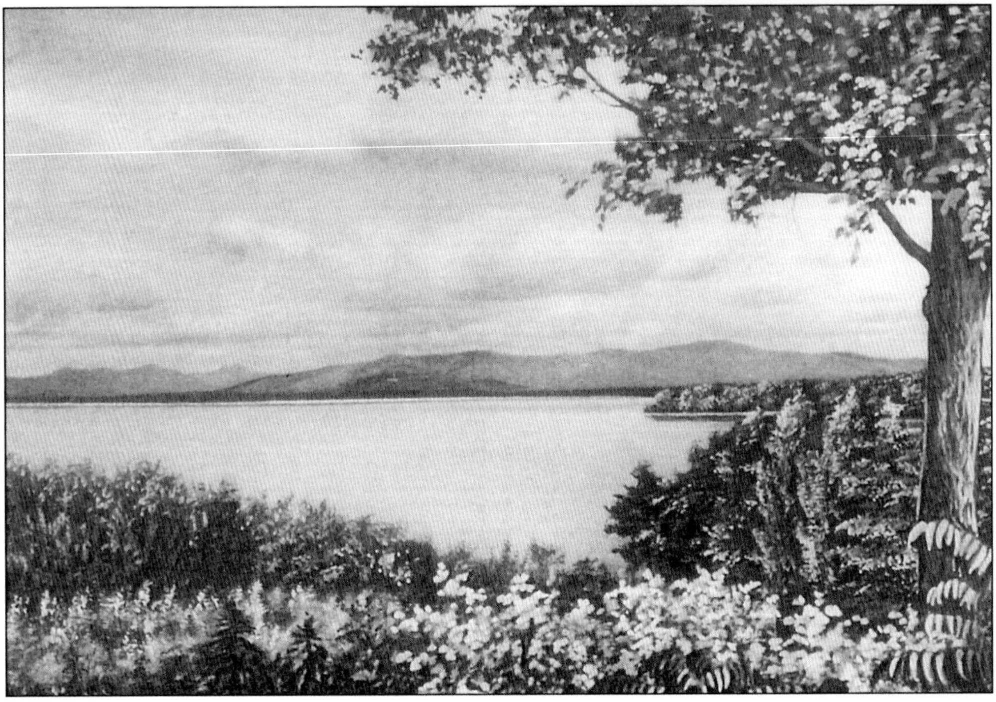

Lake Winnipesaukee and the Ossipee Mountain Range.

"The shadows round the inland sea
Are deepening into night;
Slow up the slopes of Ossipee
They chase the lessening light

Tired of the long day's blinding heat
I rest my languid eye
Lake of the Hills! Where cool and sweet
Thy sunset waters lie!"

—John Greenleaf Whittier

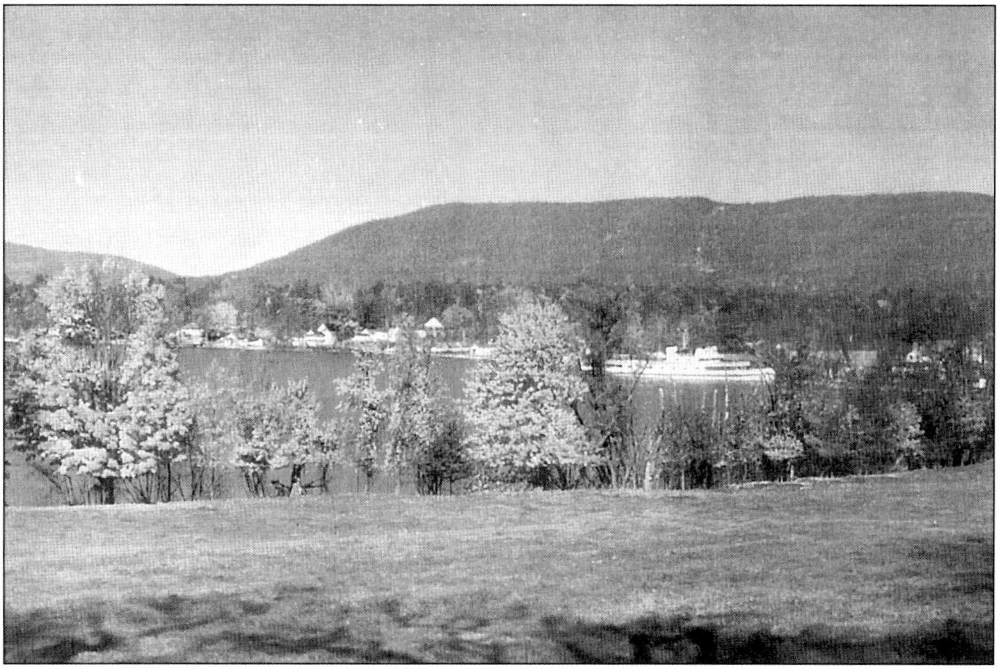

Center Harbor looking north with Red Hill in the background and the *Mount Washington* in the bay, 1950s. This hill of gray syenite, 3 miles long and 2,043 feet high, is indeed red in autumn. It rises nobly over the Sandwich plains, and the view from its summit has won enthusiastic praises from all who visit its flowery exuberance.

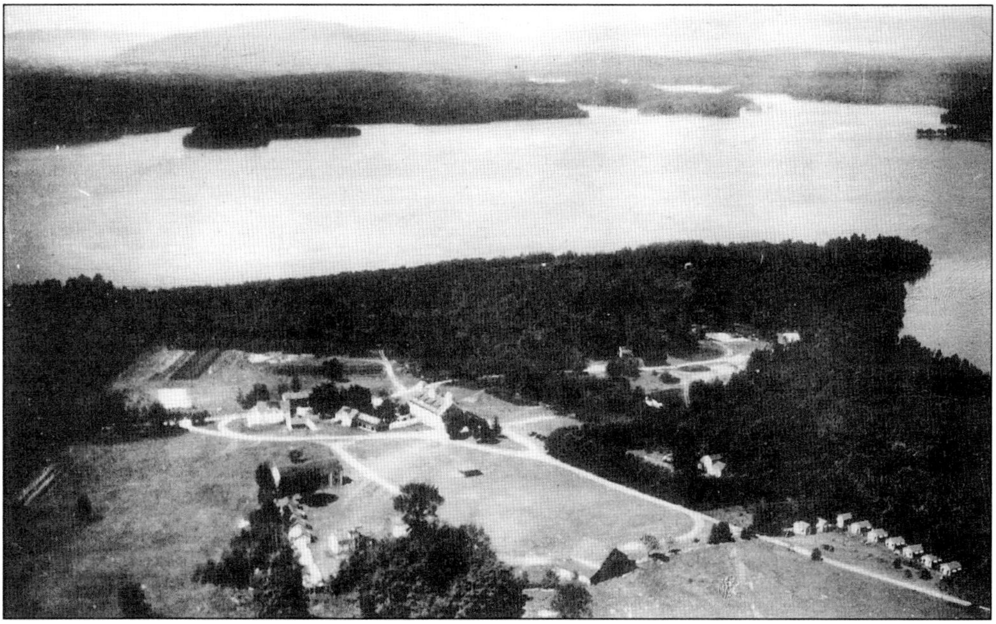

The Geneva Point Camp in Moultonboro, New Hampshire, with Winnipesaukee in the background, 1942. The beauty of this center has been retained and for thousands of people it has become a place where they have found it easy to communicate with their Creator in body, mind, and spirit.

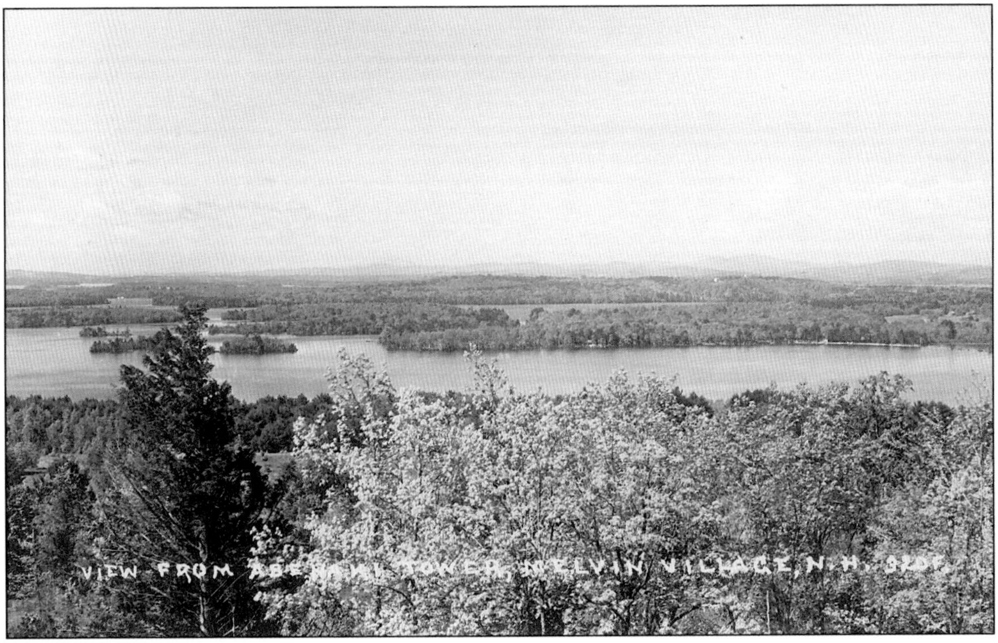

A view from the Abenaki Tower in Melvin Village, New Hampshire, looking west.

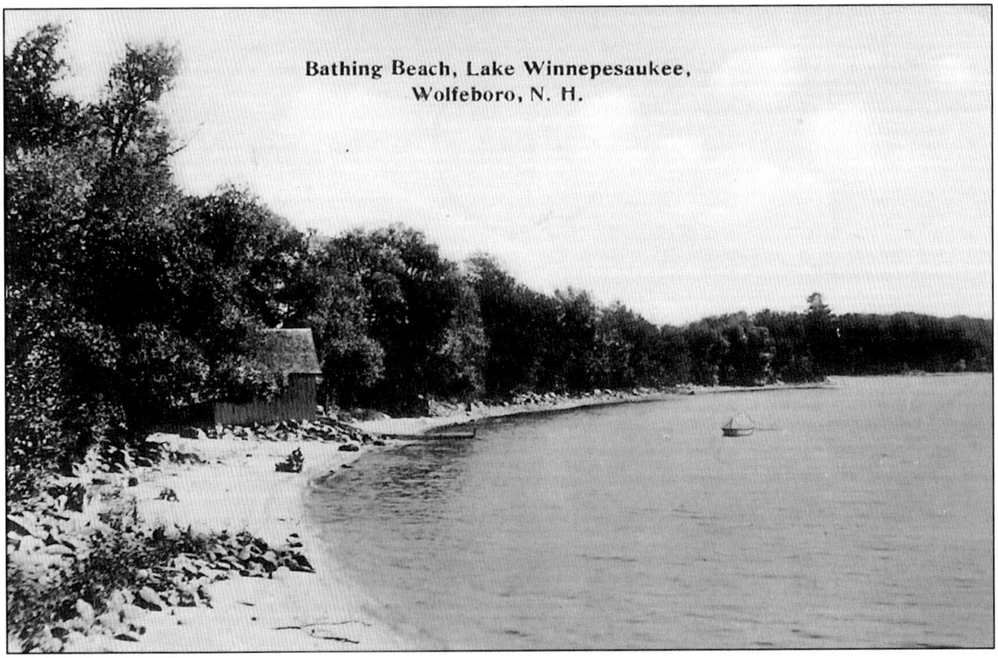

The Bathing Beach on Lake Winnipesaukee in Wolfeboro, New Hampshire, 1912. For years this has been a favorite bathing beach for thousands of visitors to the area.

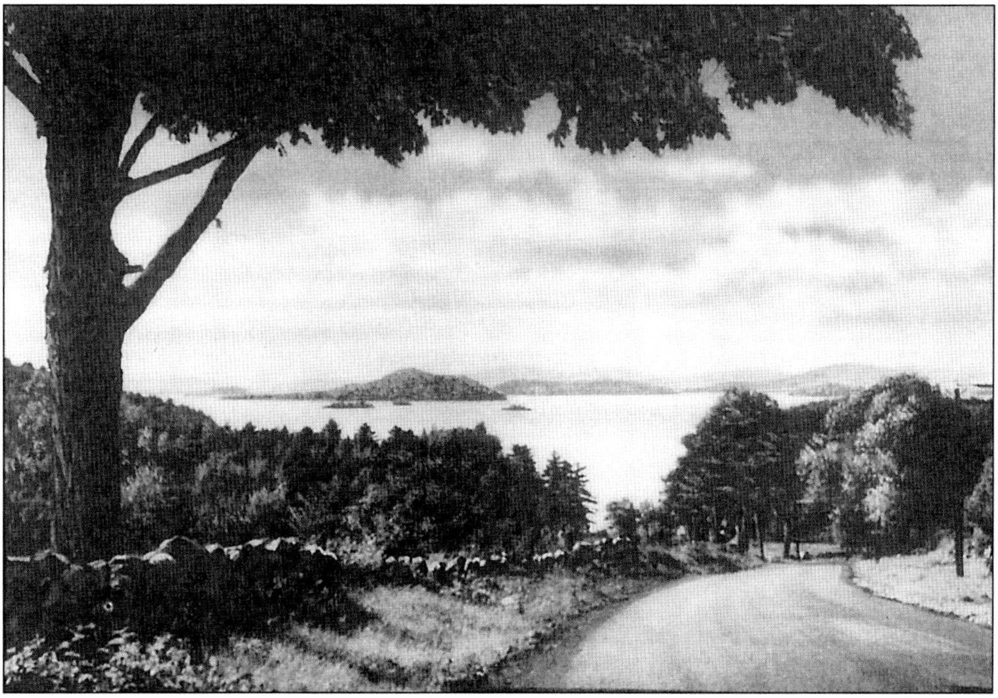

A vista of Lake Winnipesaukee from the highway between Alton Bay and Wolfeboro, New Hampshire. The view overlooks Roberts' Cove. Rattlesnake Island (center) rises 390 feet above the lake, making it the highest island on Winnipesaukee. A legend passed down by generations still holds that at one time rattlesnakes inhabited the clefts and rocks of its mystic contours.

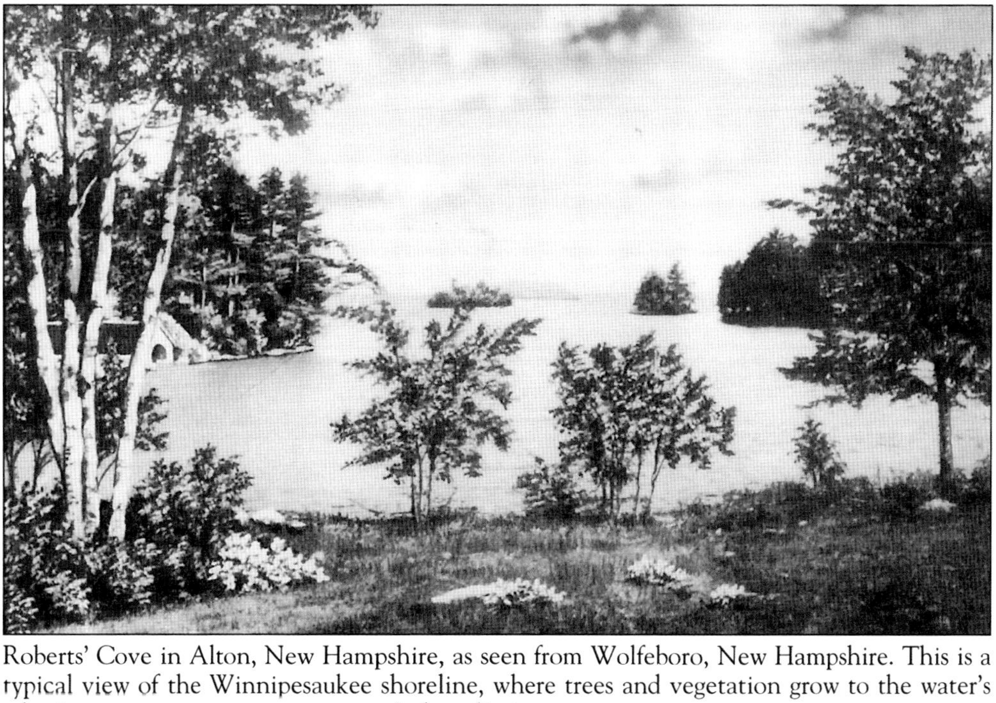

Roberts' Cove in Alton, New Hampshire, as seen from Wolfeboro, New Hampshire. This is a typical view of the Winnipesaukee shoreline, where trees and vegetation grow to the water's edge in constant supremacy over man's despoliation.

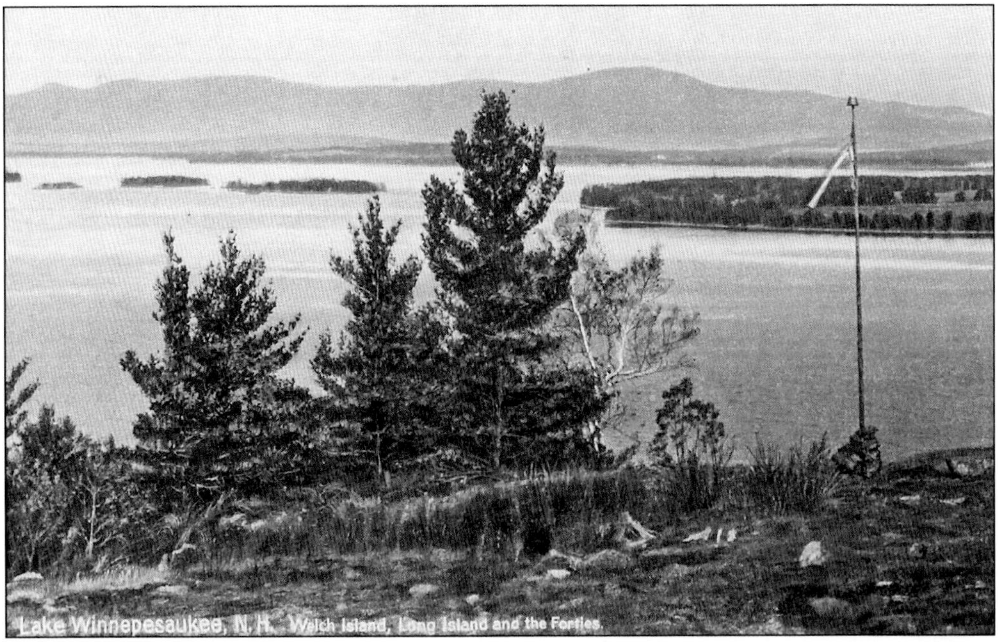

A lake view looking north with Welch Island on the right, The Forties (a group of islands) on the left, and Long Island in the distance. The Ossipee Mountains frame the eastern horizon.

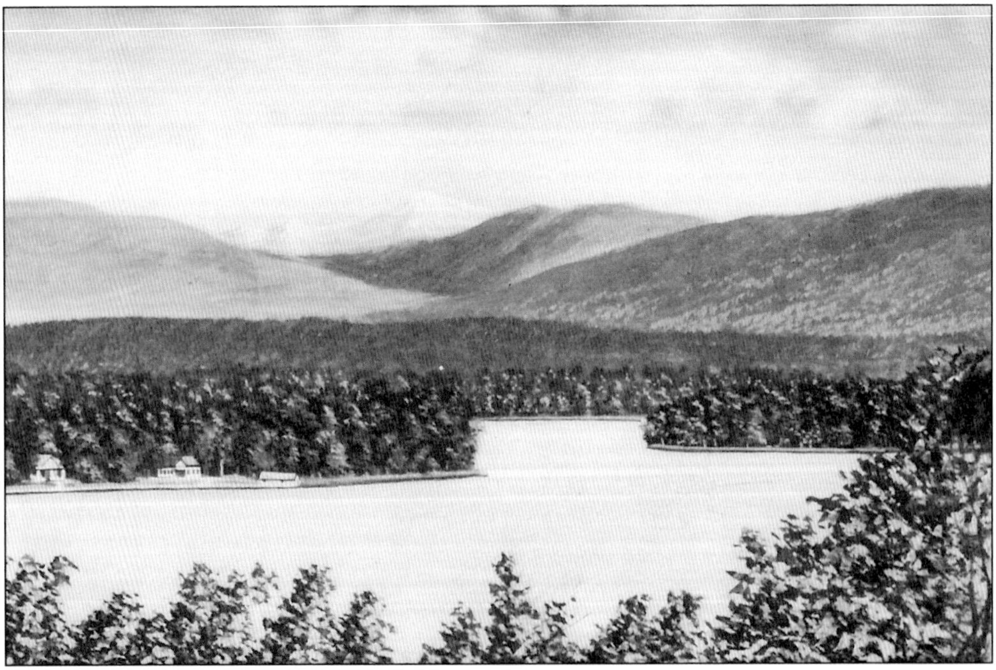

Mount Washington, with Lake Winnipesaukee in the foreground. The distance to the mountain, as the crow flies from the west shore of the lake, is approximately 50 miles. Mount Washington, of the Presidential Range in the White Mountains, is the highest peak east of the Rocky Mountains and north of the Carolinas rising to a height of 6,288 feet above sea level. In April of 1934, the highest wind velocity in the world was recorded on the summit of this mountain. The wind reached a speed of 231 miles an hour.

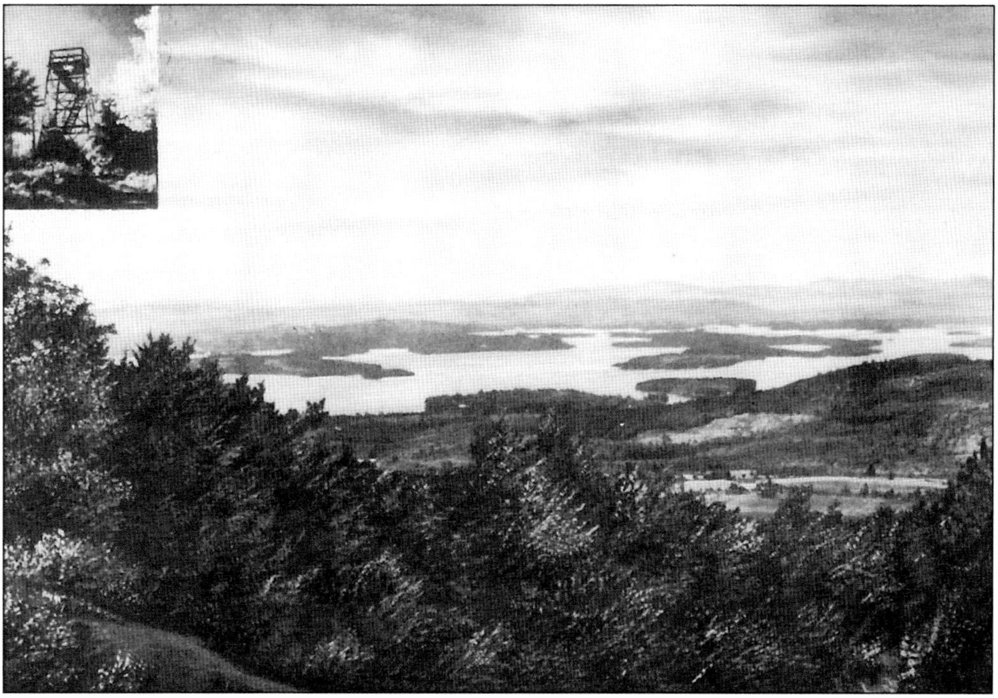

A lake view from the Belknap Recreation Area, 1940s. The fire tower, inserted in the upper left, is one of the many lookouts stationed at strategic points for quick fire control. Belknap Mountain is the highest of the Belknap Range. Lake Winnipesaukee's 44,586 acres sprawls over the landscape from the slopes of Gilford. In the distance the Sandwich Mountain Range proudly frames the northern horizon.

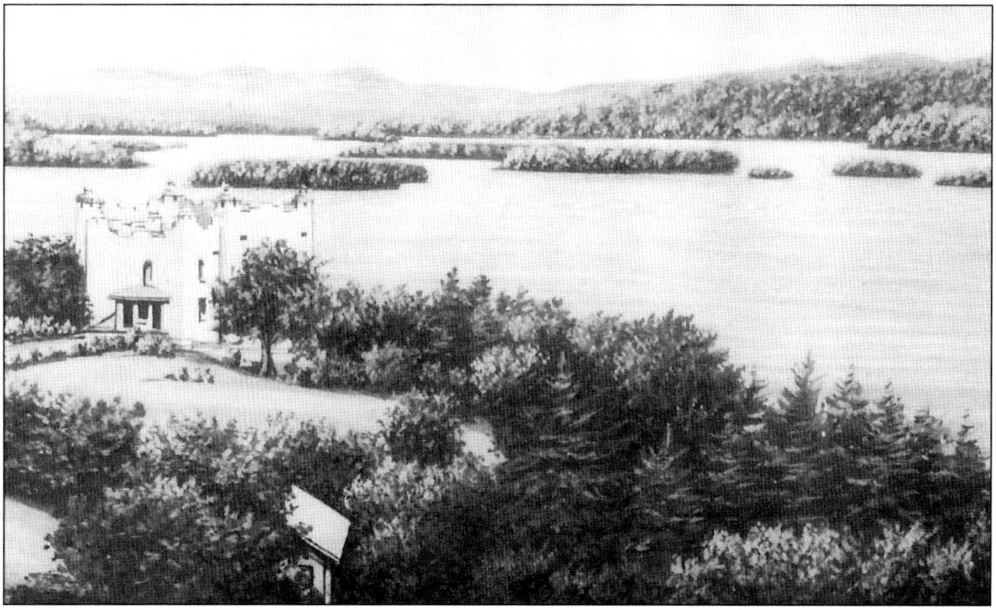

The Forties from Kimball's Castle on Belknap Point in Gilford, New Hampshire. This is one of the many interesting groups of islands dotting the lake's blue surface. There are not forty islands in the group, actually only thirteen. The largest island among them is known as Round Island.

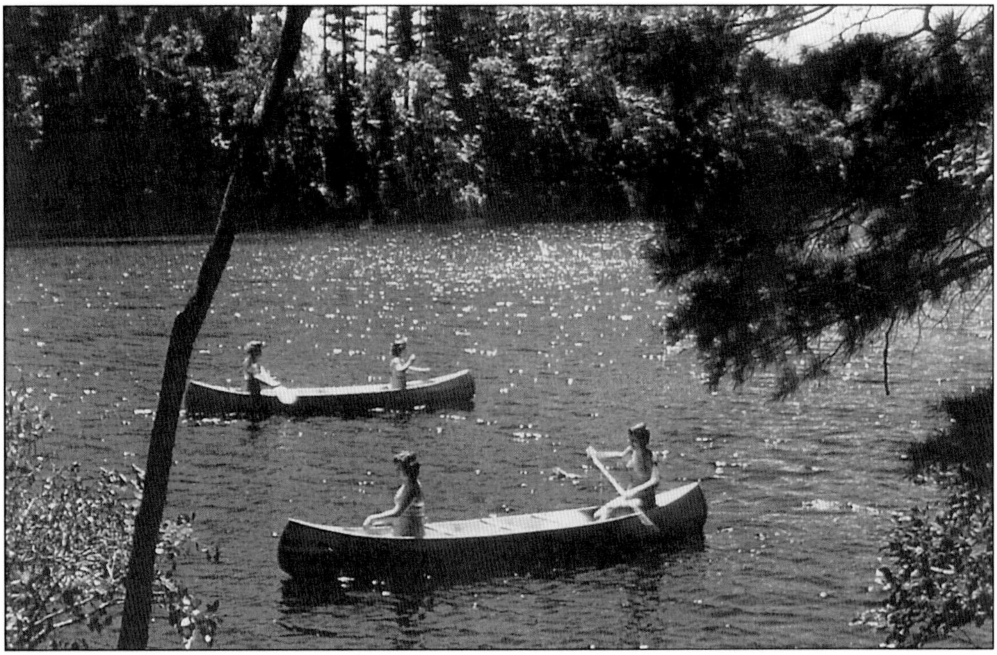

A quiet moment of relaxation on the tranquil waters of the lake.

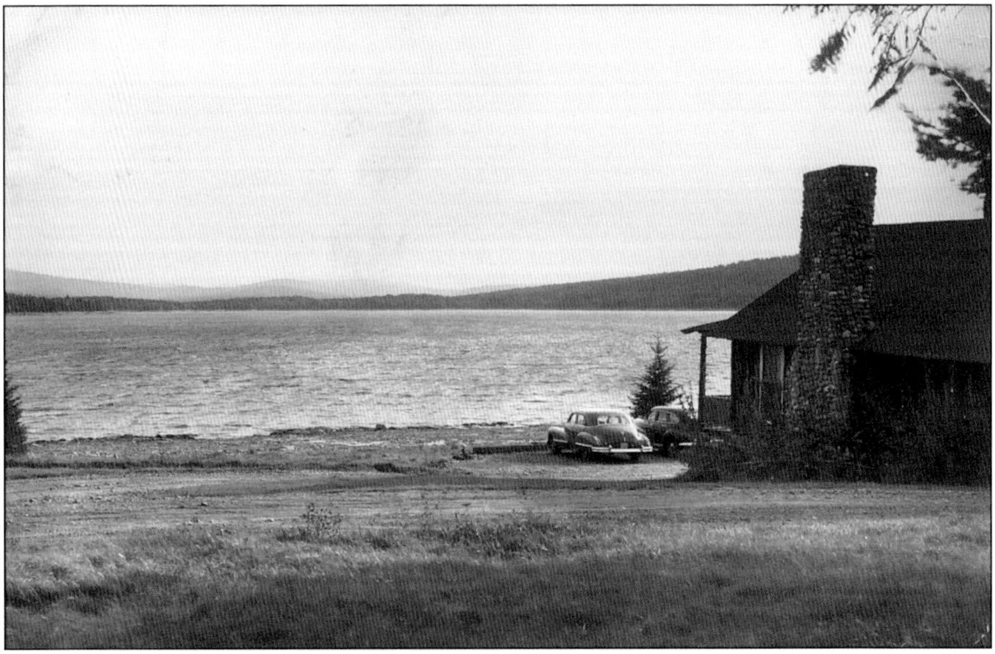

An autumn morning on the northern shore. Another season has passed and it's now time to close camp for the winter.

Two

Islands and Camps

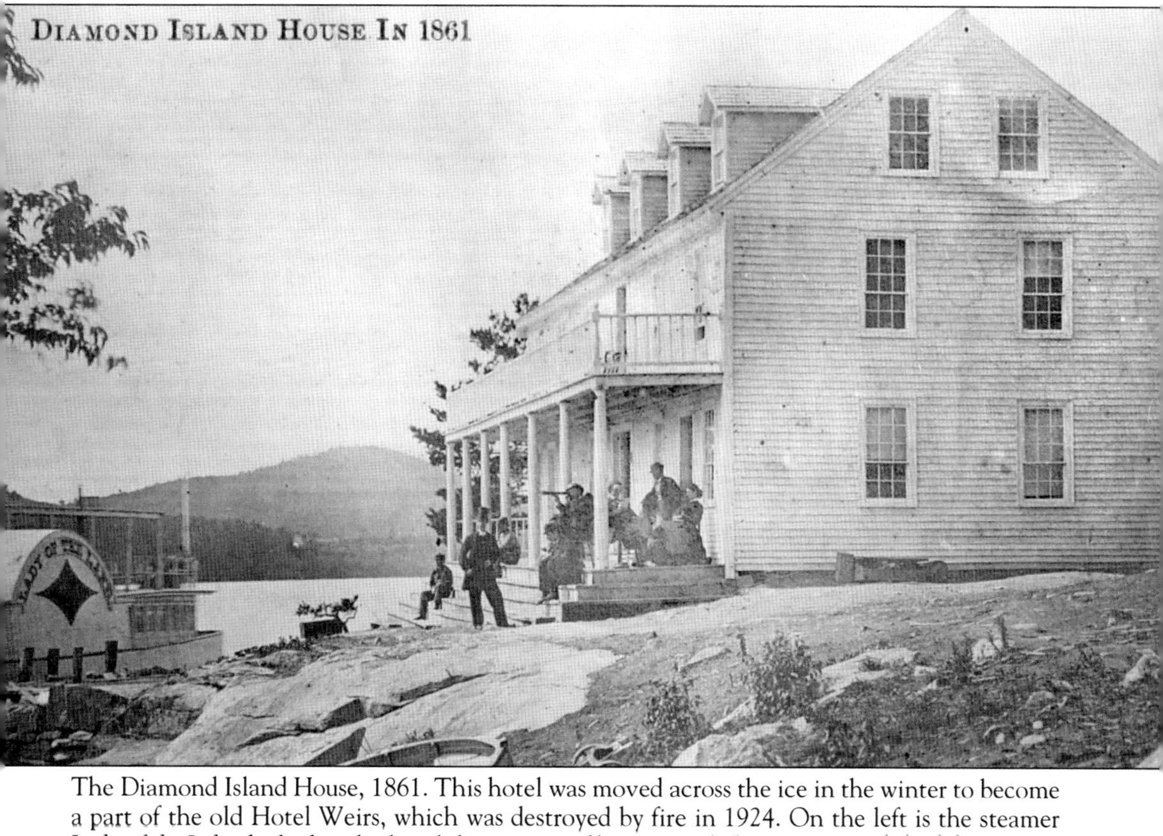

The Diamond Island House, 1861. This hotel was moved across the ice in the winter to become a part of the old Hotel Weirs, which was destroyed by fire in 1924. On the left is the steamer *Lady of the Lake* docked at the hotel during one of her many daily stops around the lake.

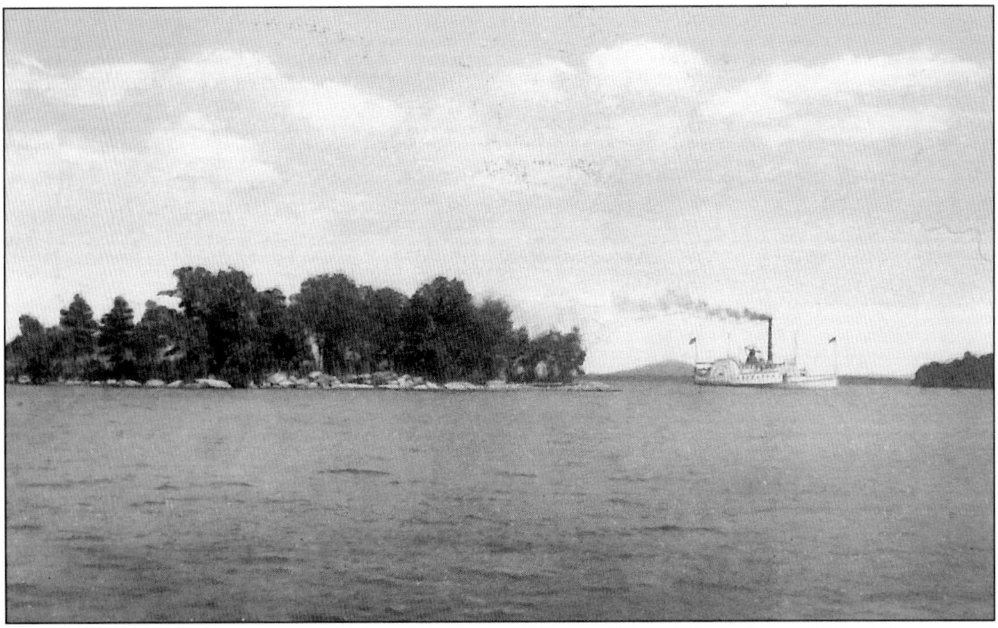

Eagle Island and the steamer *Mount Washington*, Weirs, New Hampshire, 1917. This island was once owned by the late Jack Wright, a noted Boston attorney. During his ownership of the island, his wife planted 42 varieties of shrubs and trees here.

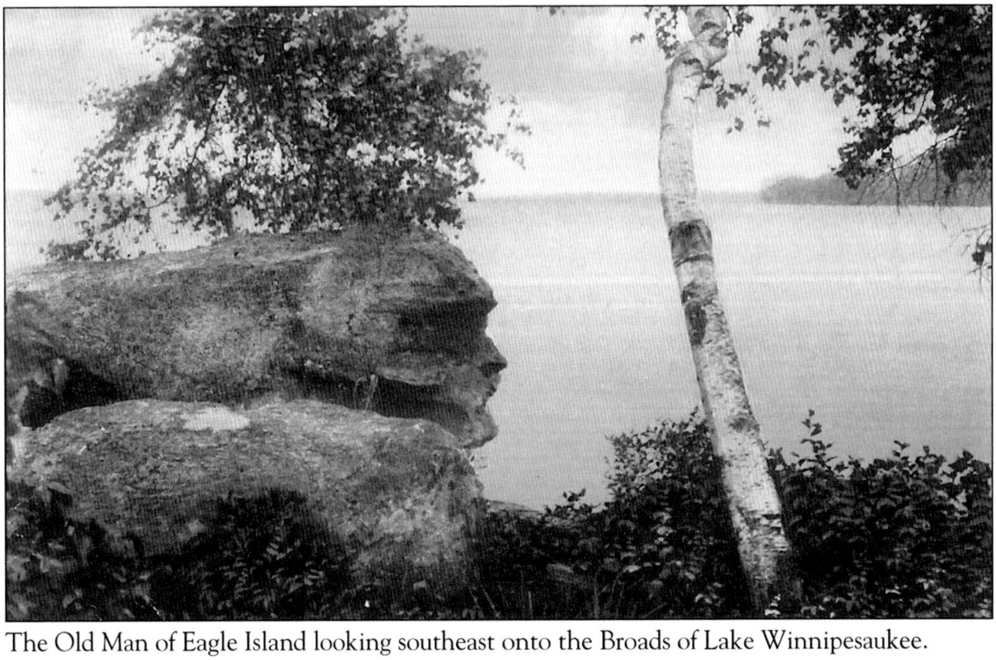

The Old Man of Eagle Island looking southeast onto the Broads of Lake Winnipesaukee.

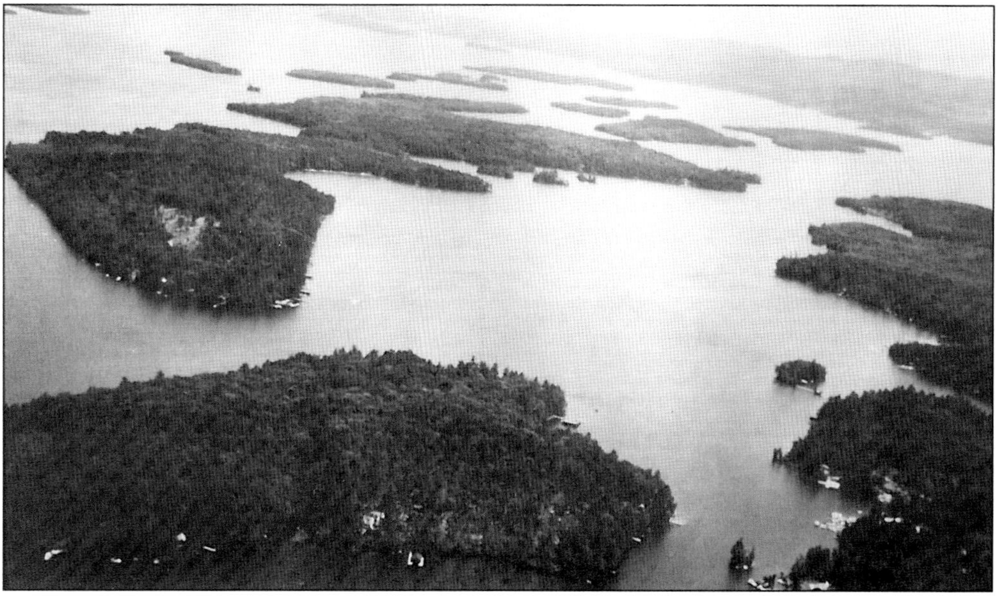

An aerial view of a southerly exposure of Lake Winnipesaukee, featuring Bear Island in the center and The Forties in the distance. Bear Island is the second largest island on the lake. It is quite thickly populated and is the only island that has its own church and post office. Some idea of the size of Bear Island may be gained from the fact that it has approximately 8.5 miles of shoreline.

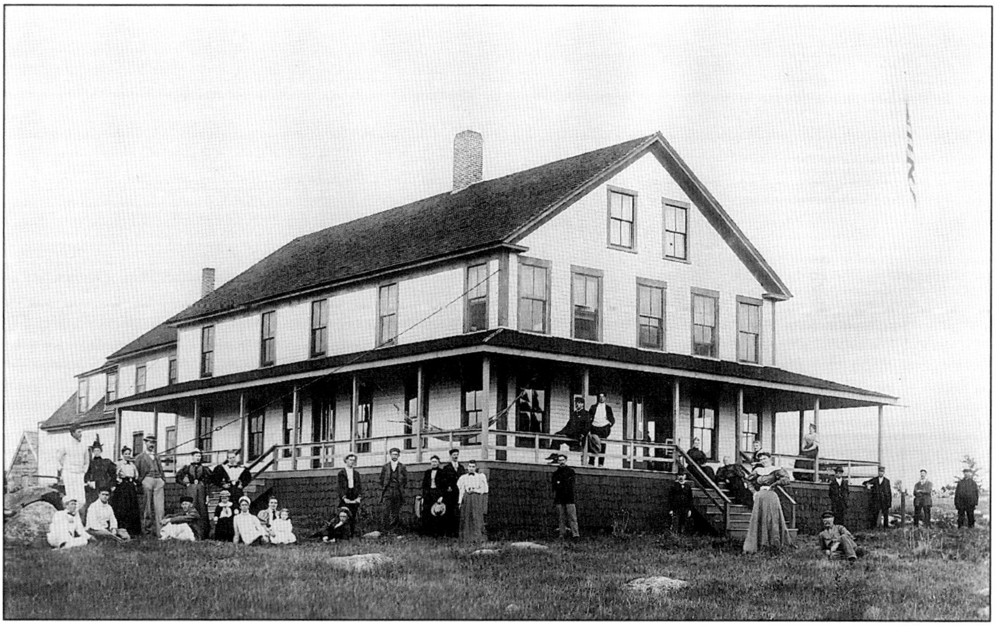

The Bear Island House, early 1900s. Originally this house was started as a boarding house by Mr. and Mrs. Leonard Davis in 1879. For many summers the fine hotel accommodated tourists from far and wide. In October 1934 it closed, and on November of that same year it burned to the ground. Its cellar hole can still be seen, about 1/4 mile inland from the P.O. dock on the north end of the island. During its heyday, the hotel was operated by Grana Hatte Fay; Merrill Fay also ran this fine seasonal hotel for a time.

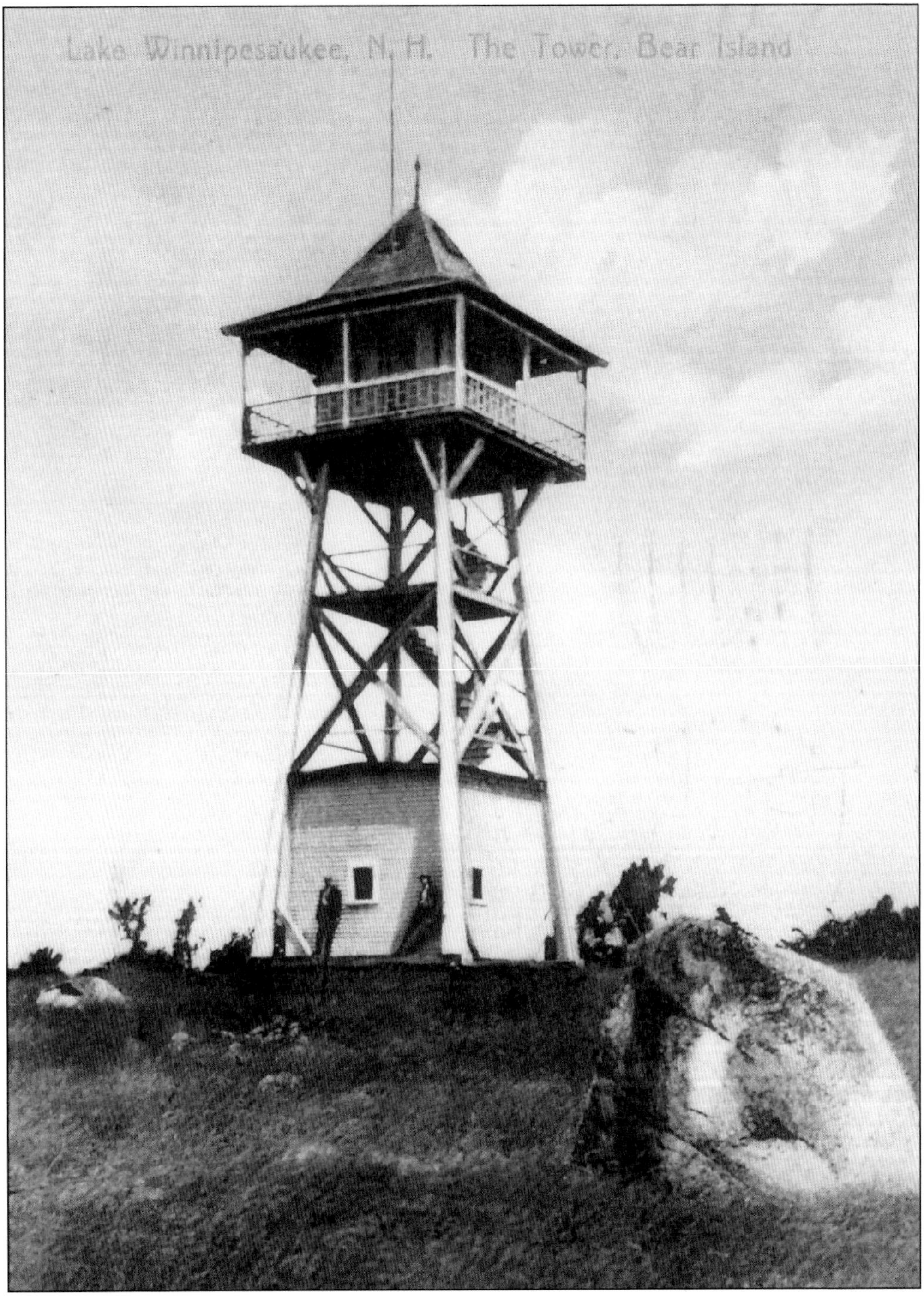

The Bear Island Observatory Tower. This tower was built around 1900 by Ellery Channing Mansfield. In 1926, the Rt. Rev. John T. Dallas purchased the property for the Episcopal Diocese of New Hampshire. The tower was repaired and enclosed, and a sanctuary built of local stone was erected between May and July of 1927. On July 31, 1927, the chapel was dedicated by Bishop Dallas in memory of Bishop Parker.

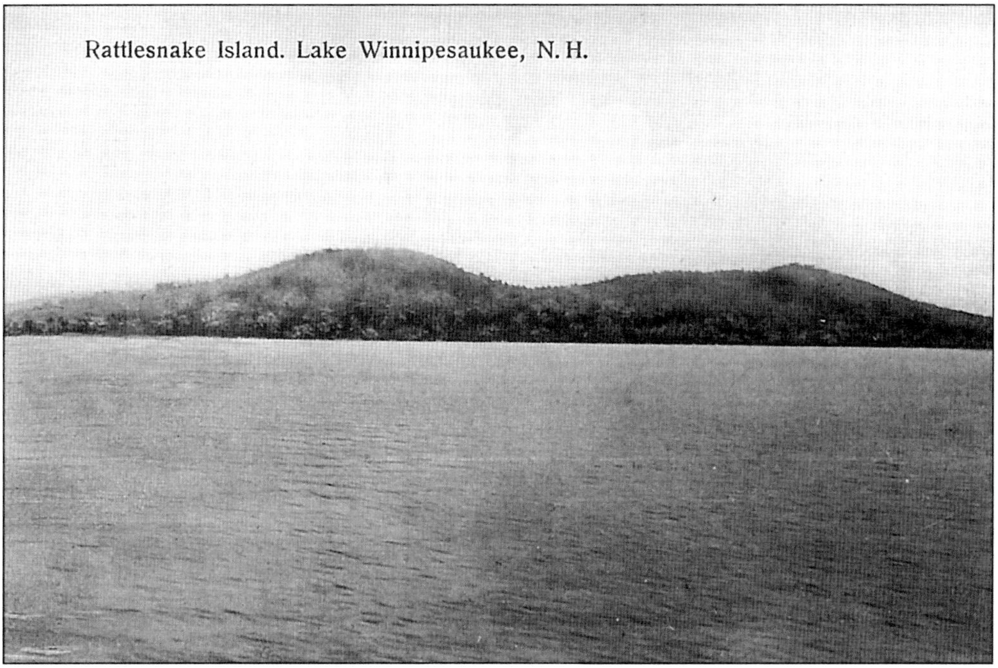

Rattlesnake Island. This island is one of the largest in the lake and has the highest elevation, rising 390 feet above the lake level. Rattlesnakes were actually found on the island as late as the 1940s. The skins and remains of some of these snakes can be seen at the Libby Museum in Tuftonboro, New Hampshire.

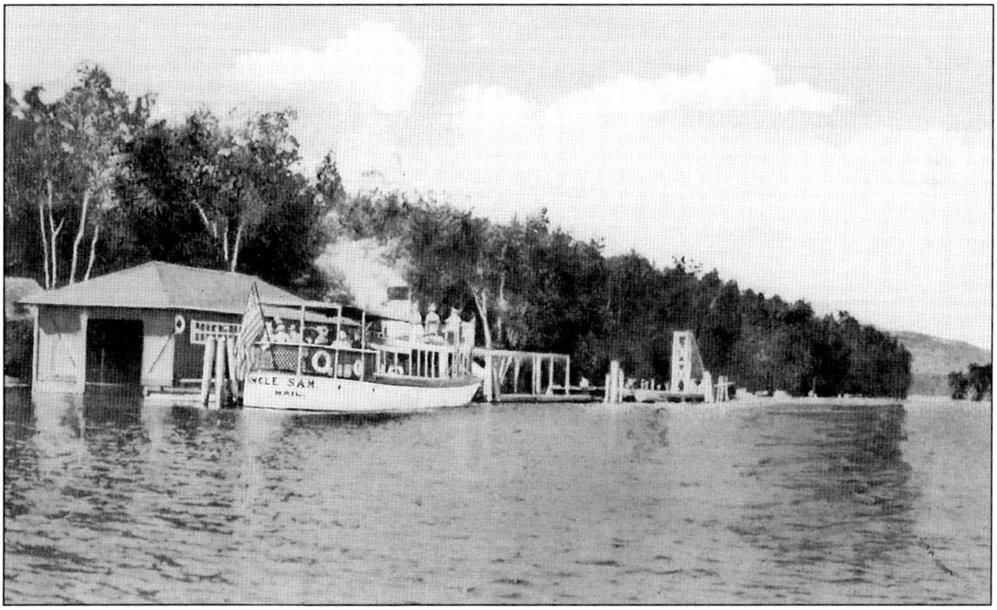

The U.S. mail-boat *Uncle Sam*. The Three Mile Island landing is one of the many stops the mail boat makes daily during the summer months.

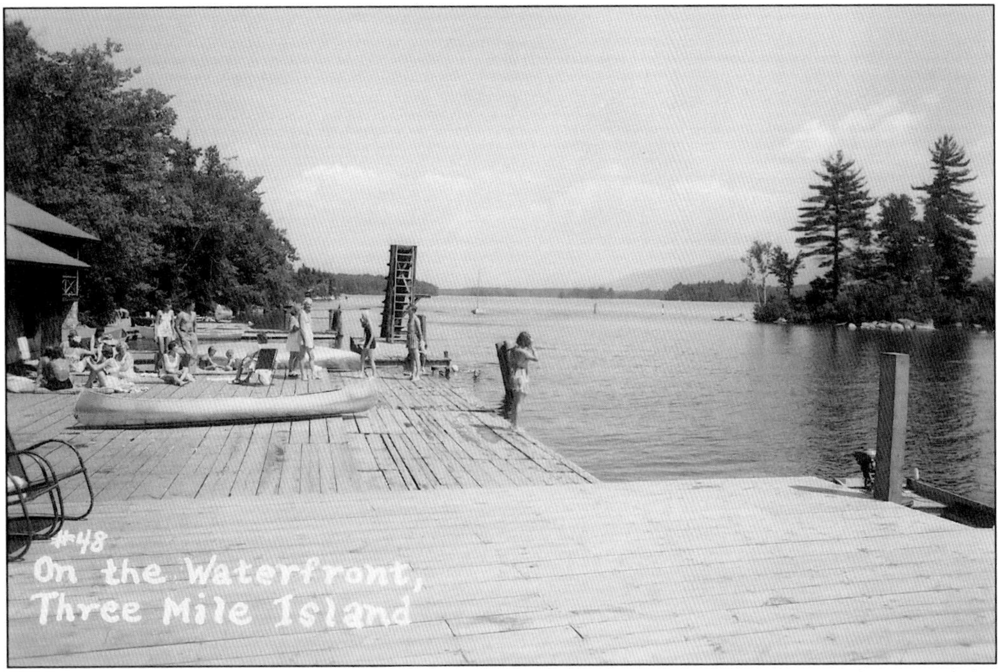

The main dock at Three Mile Island. This island has been one of the summer homes of the Appalachian Mountain Club since the year 1900. Originally, they summered here in tents, but they have expanded their facilities to the point where they now have about 50 cabins around the shore with a central dining and entertainment hall.

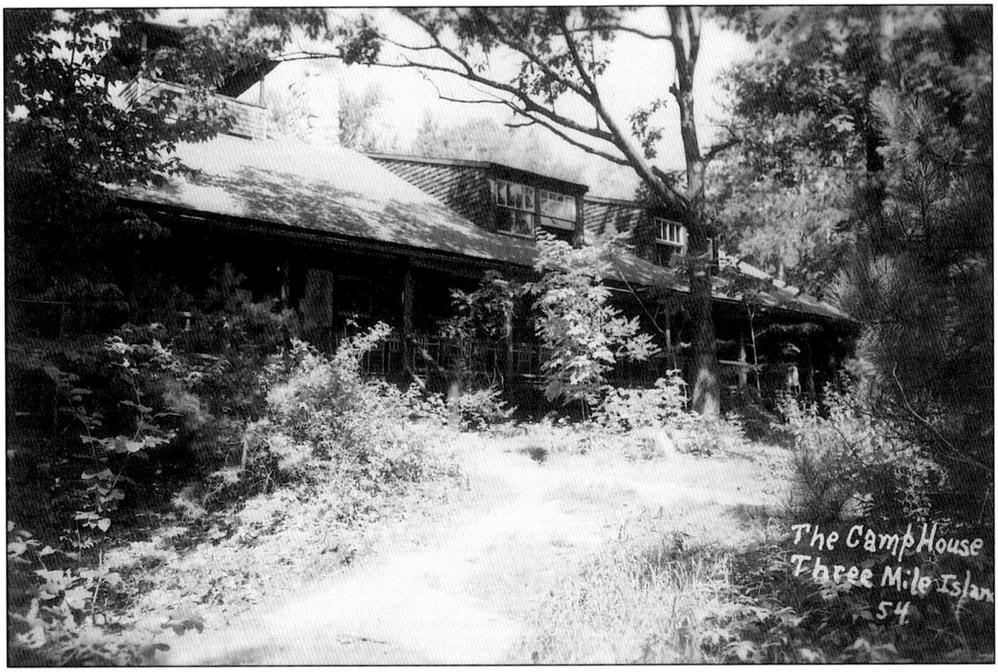

The "Camp House" on Three Mile Island. This island is a 1/2 mile long, rising to a height of about 50 feet as a ridge running north and south in the center, and less than 1/4 of a mile wide. Even though there are some very fine beaches the shoreline is mostly rocky.

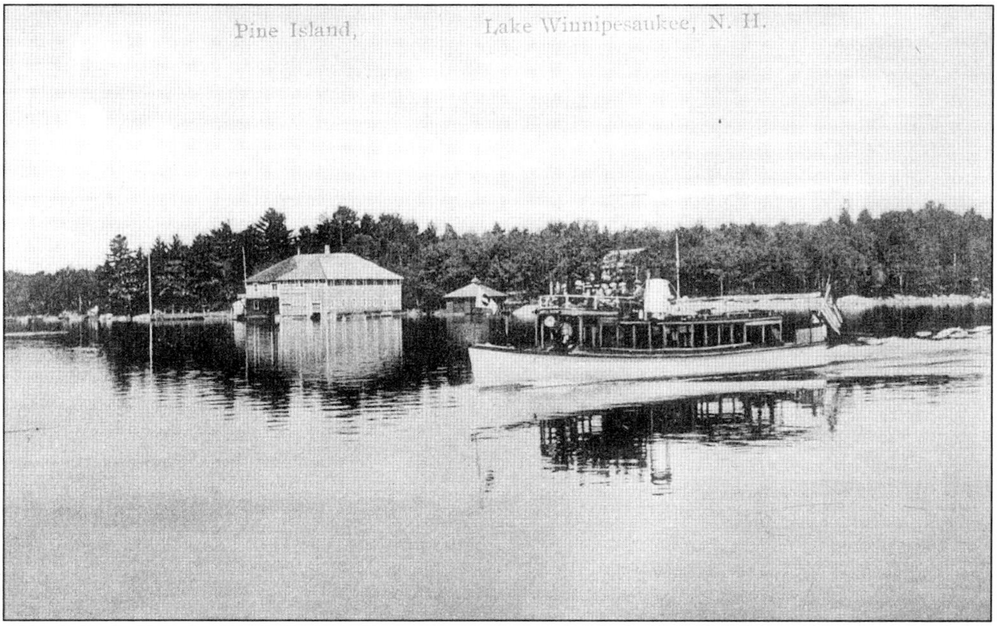

Pine Island with the *Uncle Sam* in the foreground, Meredith, New Hampshire, 1913. In the center of this island there are two small ponds that were used by Mr. H.O. Whitney to raise frogs. He used to enjoy eating their legs at his dinner table.

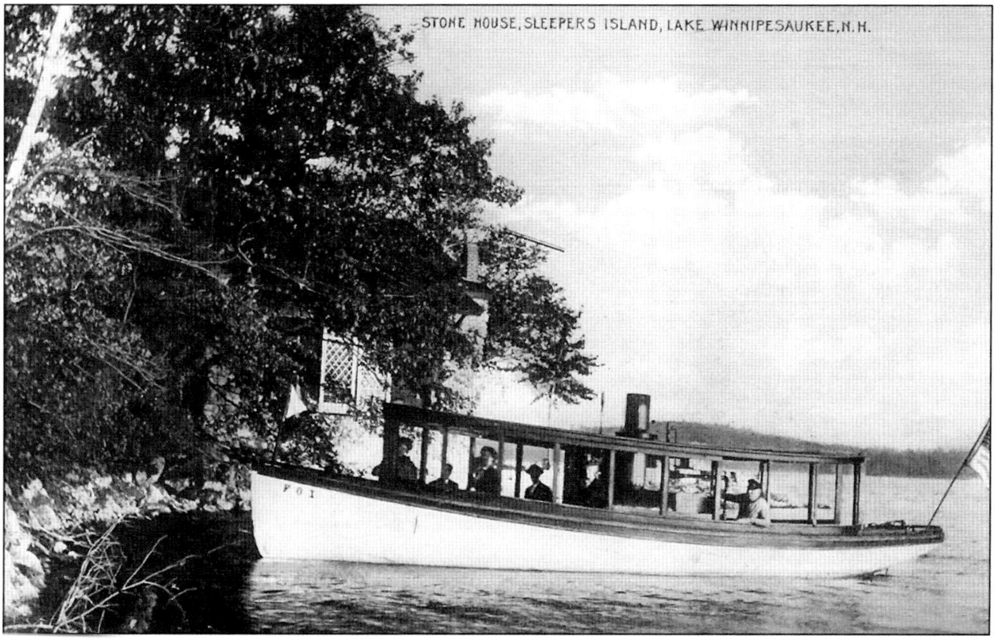

The steamer *Fox* docking at the Stone House on Sleepers Island in West Alton, 1916.

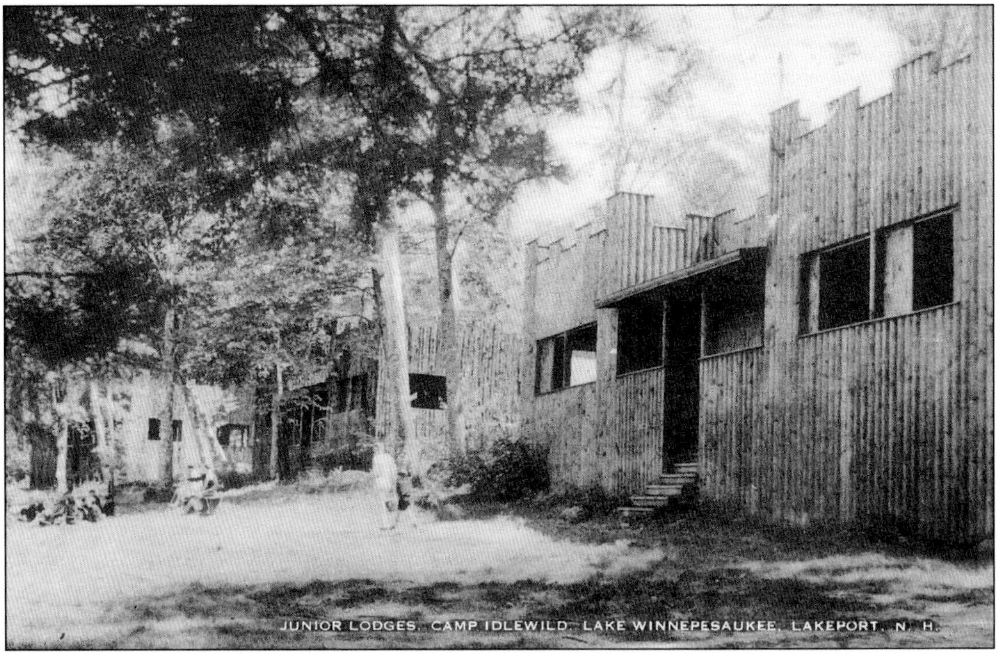

The Junior Lodges at Camp Idlewild on Cow Island, Tuftonboro, New Hampshire, 1950s. Camp Idlewild was established in 1892, and for over 60 years it was operated as a private boys' camp. Cow Island is shaped like a pair of spectacles, and the camp had the entire west lens for hiking and horseback riding privileges. The island has now been taken over by private cottages.

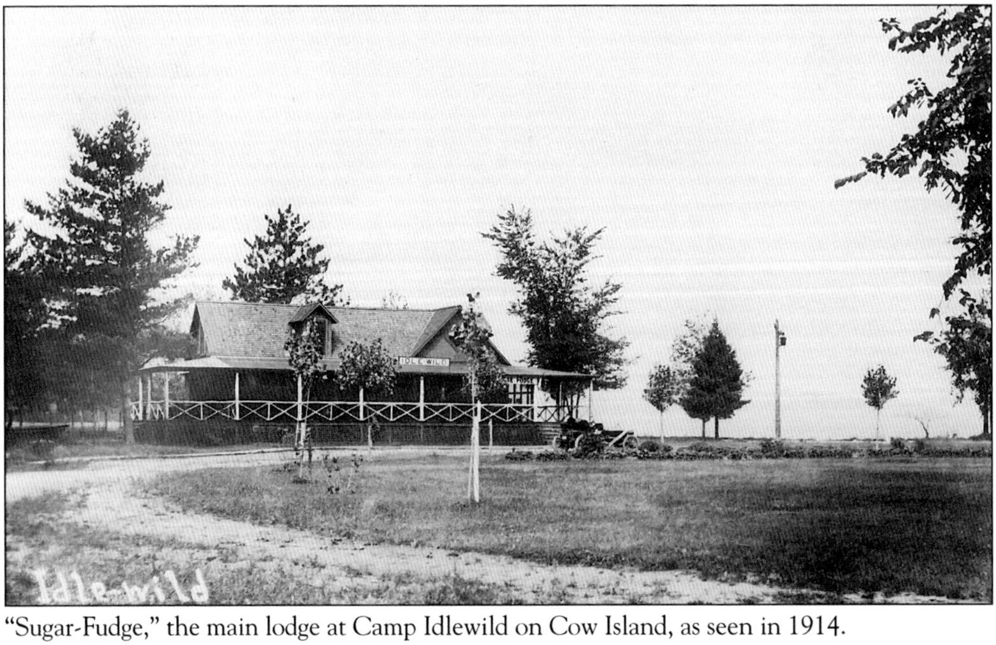

"Sugar-Fudge," the main lodge at Camp Idlewild on Cow Island, as seen in 1914.

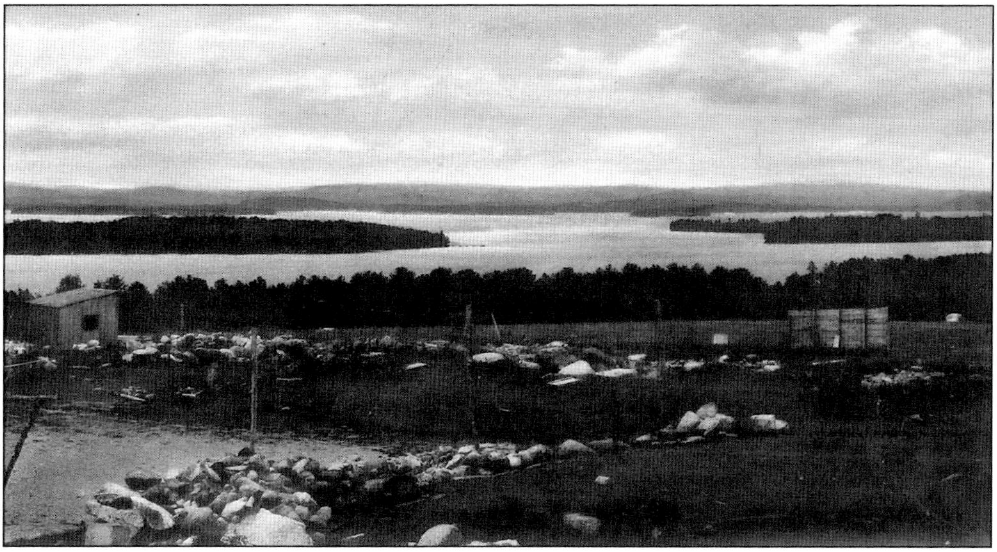

A view from Cow Island looking southwest to the center of the lake, known as the Broads.

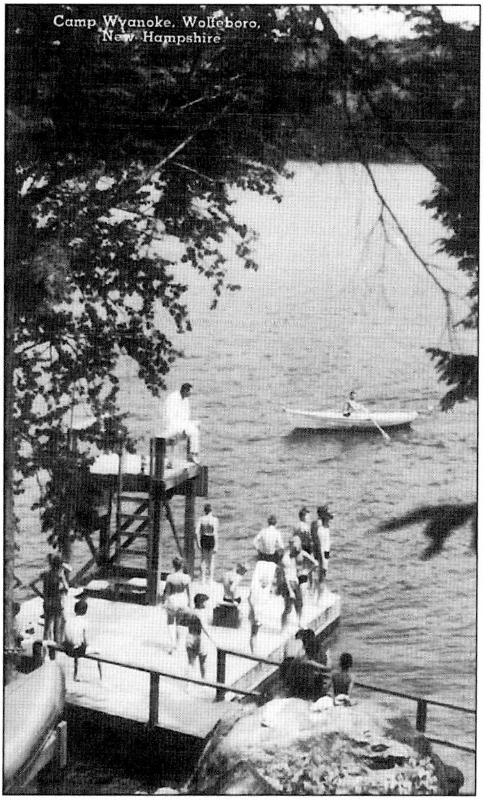

Camp Wyanoke in Wolfeboro, New Hampshire, 1949. Campers enjoyed afternoons of swimming and boating under close supervision from the dock.

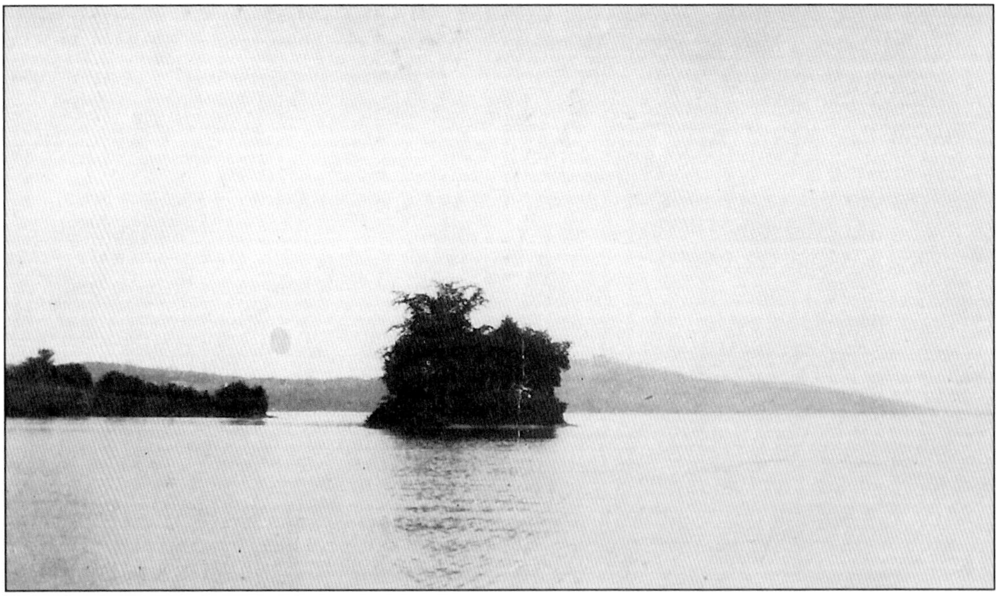

Lingsley Island and Pinnacle in Meredith Bay, New Hampshire, 1900s.

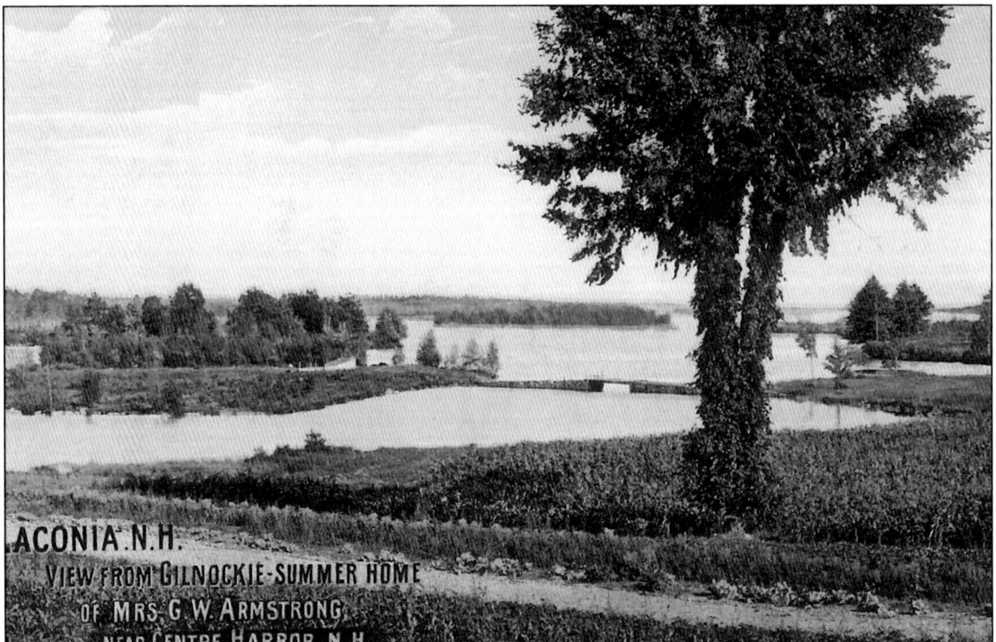

Half-mile Island (owned by Mrs. G.W. Armstrong, located in Center Harbor) as seen from the Gilnockie summer home, 1916. Note the connecting bridge to the island.

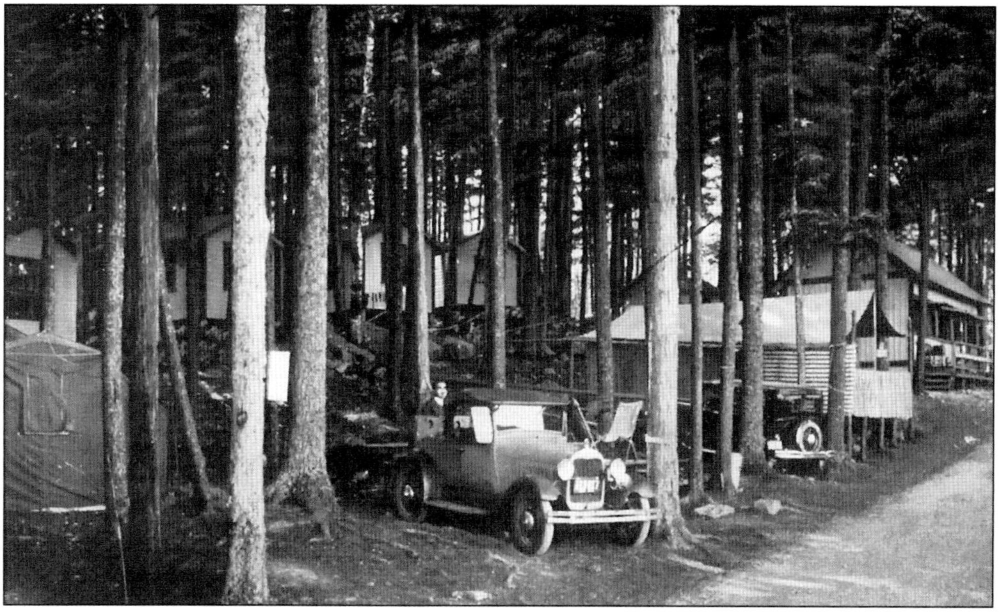

A cluster of cabins in the pines at Lake Shore Park, Gilford, New Hampshire, 1920s. Lake Shore Park is one of the most popular summer retreats in the region and has one of the largest bathing beaches on the lake.

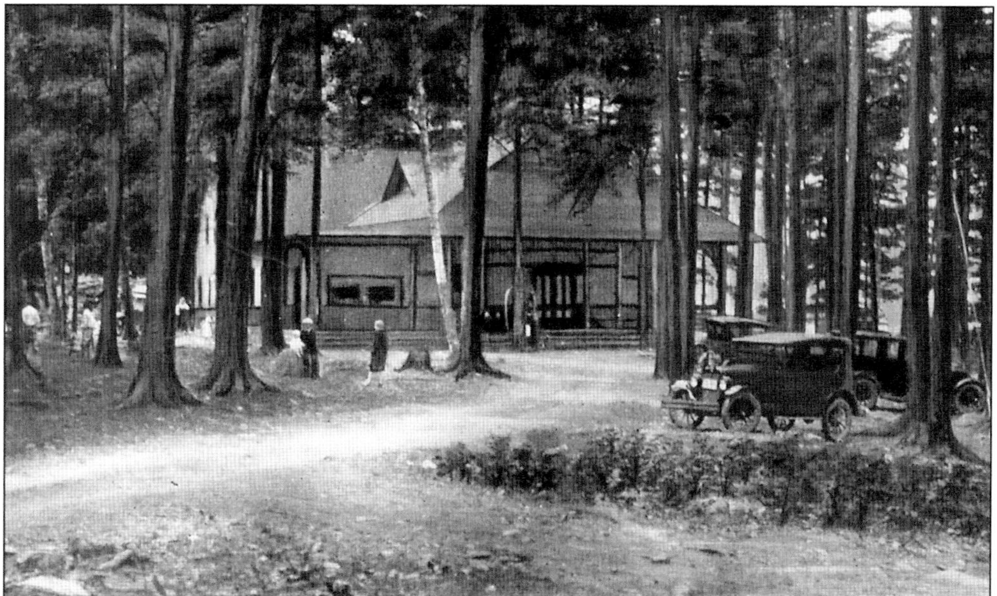

The Pavilion at Lake Shore Park. This was a popular recreation hall for campers and visitors alike. It is shown here at some point in the 1920s.

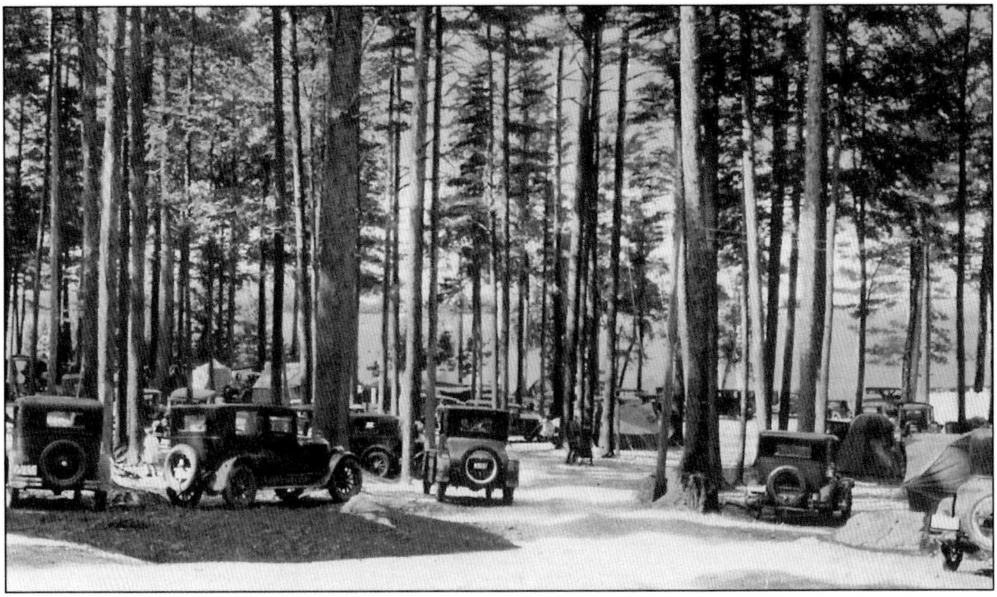

The beach at Lake Shore Park. This beach is one of the largest and most beautiful on the shore of Lake Winnipesaukee. It is seen here in the 1920s.

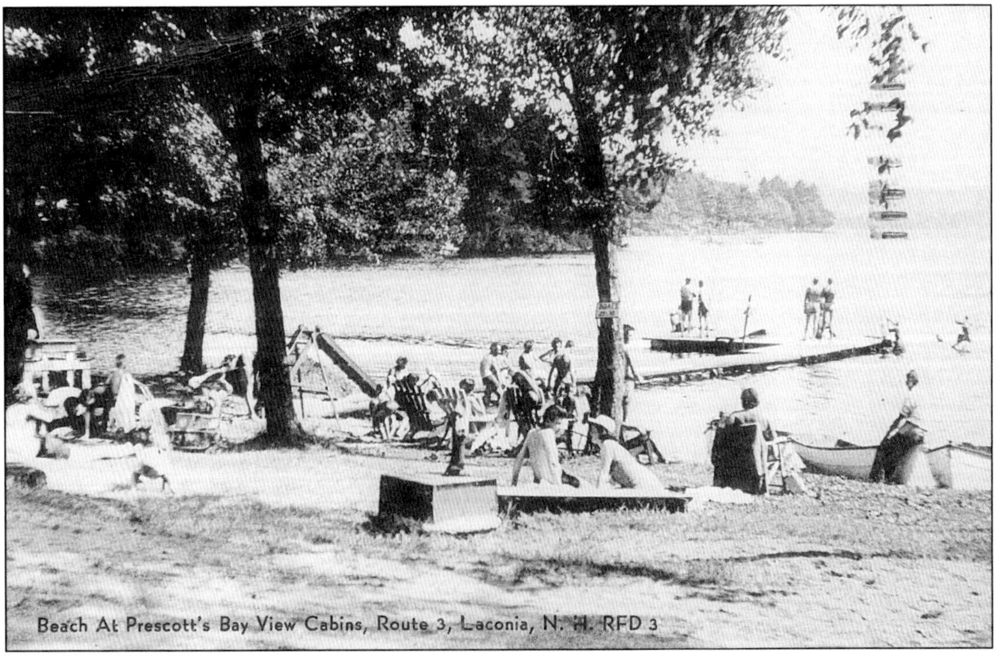

The beach at Prescott's Bay View Cabins, Route 3, Laconia, New Hampshire, 1955. This colony of cabins was located between Lakeport and The Weirs on Paugus Bay.

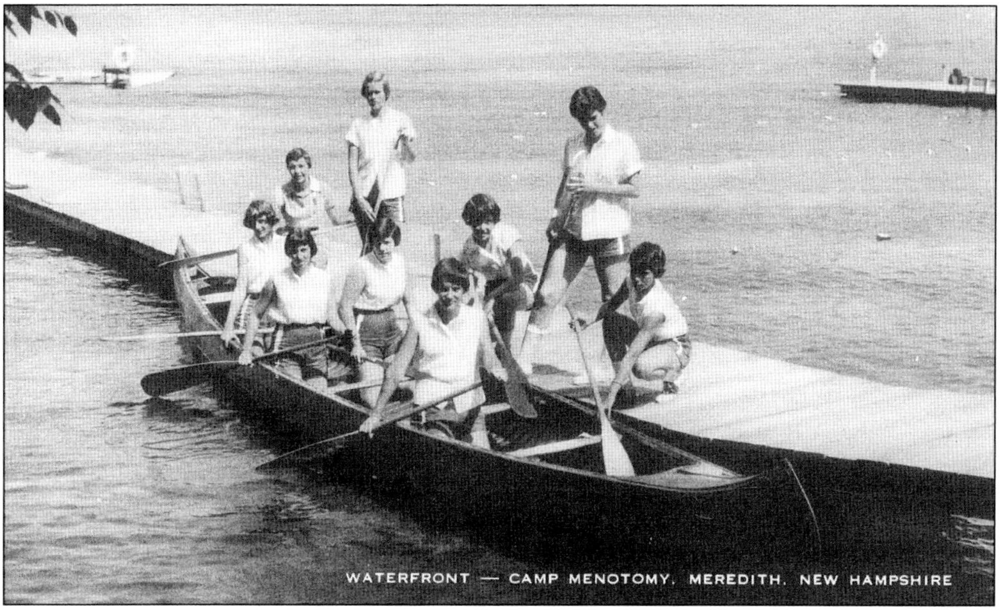

The waterfront for Camp Menotomy, a very popular girls' camp on Meredith Neck, New Hampshire, 1950s.

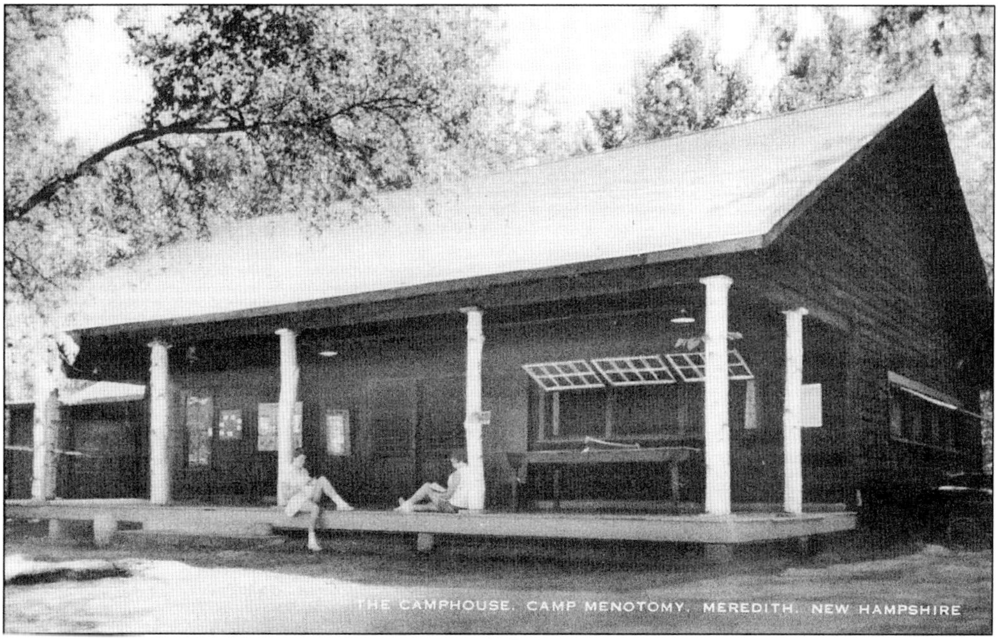

The Camp House for Camp Menotomy, Meredith Neck, New Hampshire, 1950s.

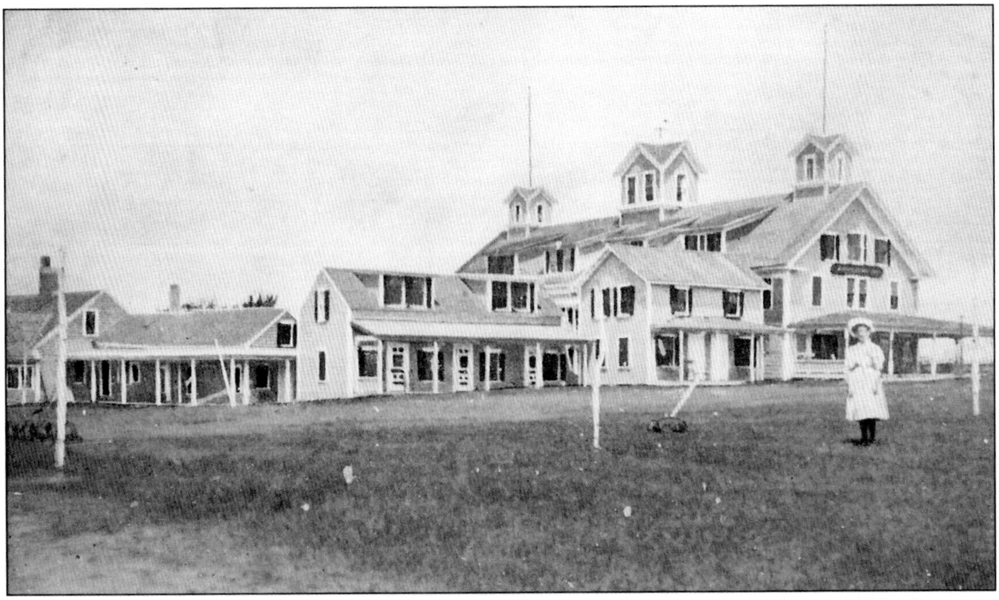

The Winnipesaukee Inn and Cottages, Moultonboro Neck, New Hampshire, 1906. At some point between the 1870s and 1880s, this structure was built as a barn for Roxmont Poultry operations. In 1896 this operation ceased, and the barn was converted into an inn by Dr. Alonzo Greene, to take advantage of the growing tourist business.

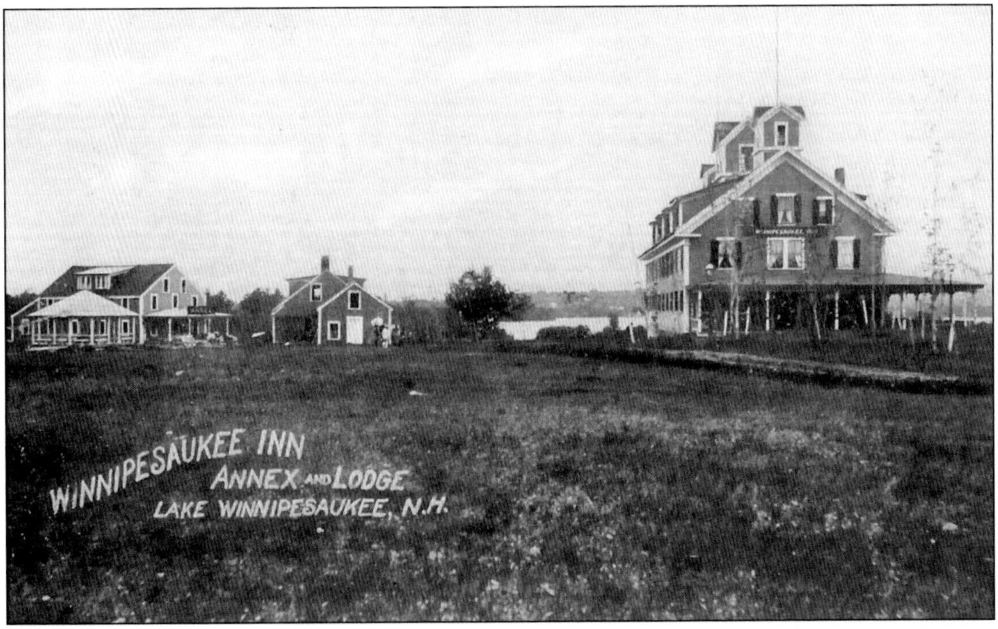

The Winnipesaukee Inn Annex and Lodge, Moultonboro, New Hampshire, 1911. During World War I the tourist business suffered; as a result, the land and buildings were sold for $30,000 in 1919, to the International Sunday School Association. At that time there were 236 acres; today there are only 200 acres.

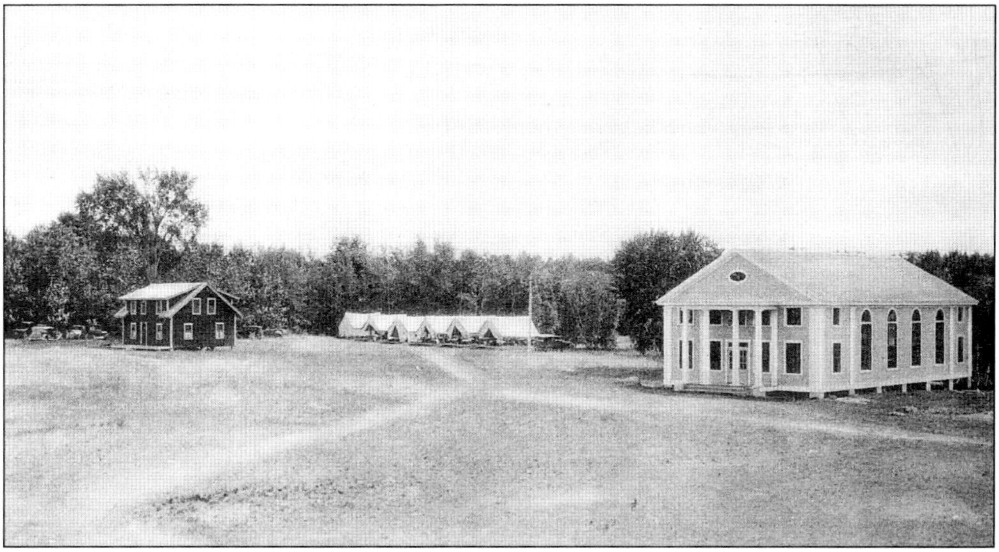

Geneva Point Camp's Tent Line, Chapel, and Malden Cottages, 1950s. As Geneva Point grew, improvements were gradually made. Campers and staff stayed in the inn and some of the cottages that were on the farm property. There were several tents with wooden floors. Electricity, however, did not reach the inn until 1926, and then only to the kitchen, dining rooms, and meeting rooms. Kerosene lamps were used in all of the sleeping quarters.

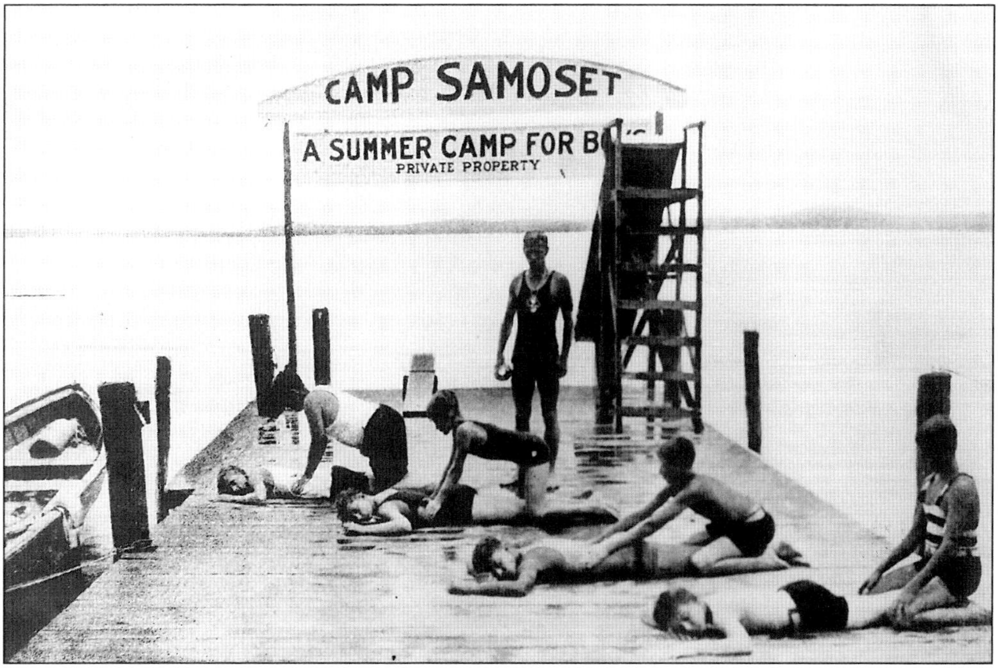

Camp Samoset in Gilford, New Hampshire, 1937. Water safety was always an important activity at camp. Here the life guard is seen conducting a safety class on the camp's dock. In 1939, Camp Samoset, founded by Thomas E. Freeman, celebrated its 25th anniversary. The camp was later sold to Manny Winston, who operated it from 1944 to 1968. Samoset was named after the only red-headed Native American ever known to have existed in this area. Today this is the site of the Samoset Condominiums on Route 11, Gilford, New Hampshire.

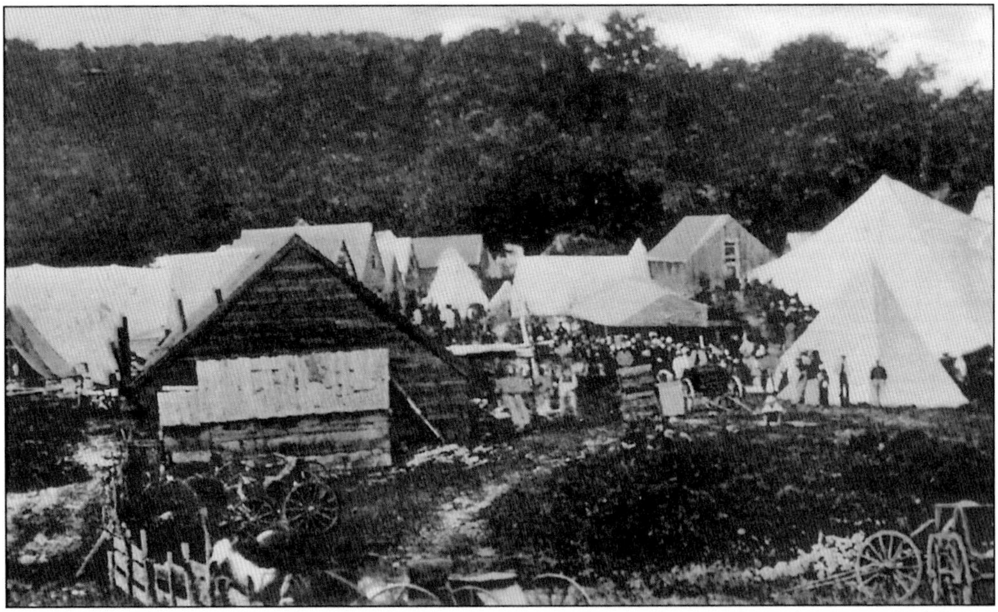

The Christian Campgrounds in Alton Bay, 1865. On September 7, 1863, the Second Advent Campmeeting held its first meeting here overlooking Alton Bay. The first campers lived in tents. The Alton Bay Campmeeting Association was incorporated in 1876, and over the years several permanent building have been erected. Unfortunately, on August 23, 1945, fire spread throughout the campgrounds. No one was injured or killed, but three chapels, the tabernacle, the seated grove, the bookstore, and 260 cabins were destroyed.

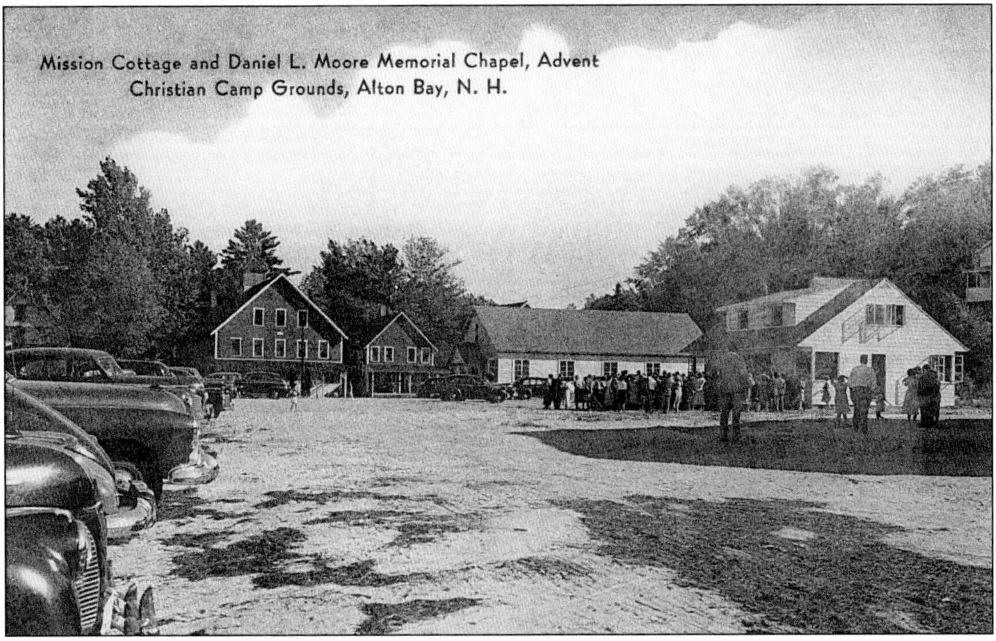

Mission Cottage and the Daniel L. Moore Memorial Chapel, Advent Christian Campgrounds, Alton Bay, New Hampshire, 1940s. Today the campground continues to grow and prosper hosting summer camp meetings and retreats for people of all ages as the Christian Conference Center.

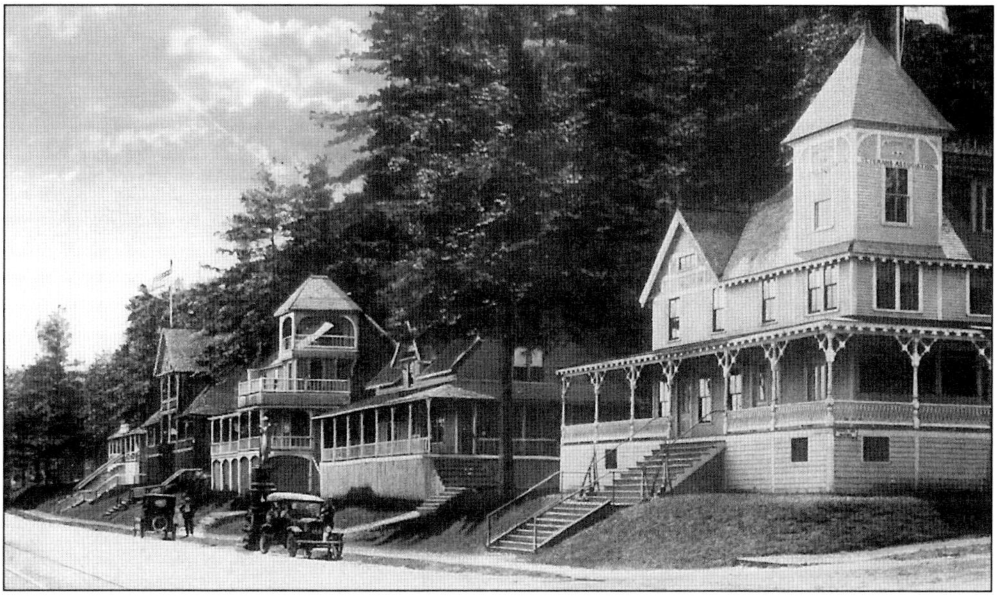

The Camp Meeting Grounds for the Veterans' Association on Lakesside Avenue at The Weirs, 1900s. Shortly after the Civil War, the New Hampshire Veterans' Association purchased property in The Weirs from the Concord & Montreal Railroad Company and established a campground for the purpose of holding their annual reunion during the last week of August. Each regiment established their own headquarters in the Veteran's Grove and along Lakeside Avenue in The Weirs.

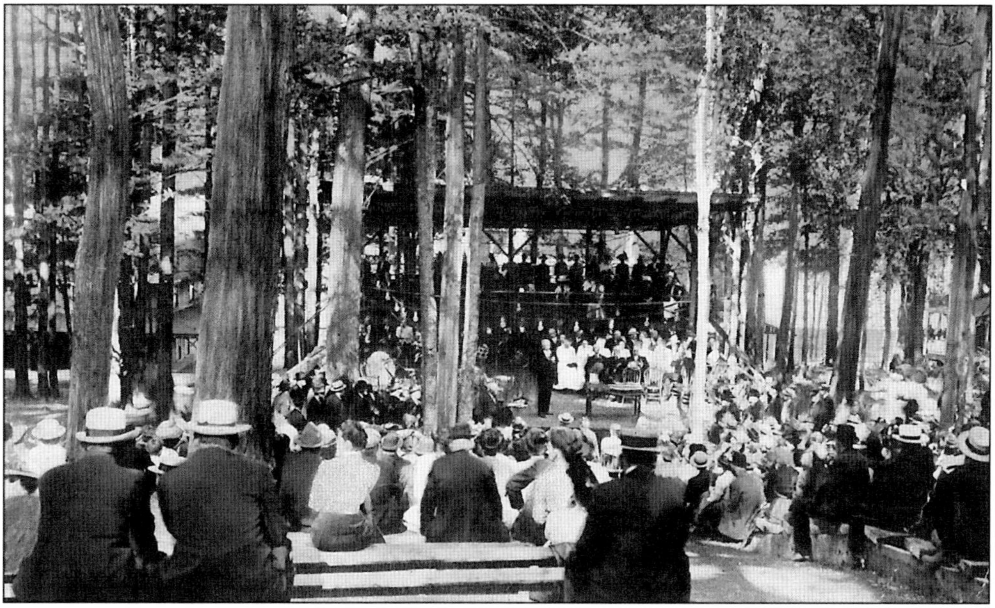

The GAR (Grand Army of the Republic) Encampment Grounds at The Weirs, 1900s. Today, a very fine display of memorabilia may be seen at the Veterans' Headquarters building at the corner of Veteran's Avenue and Lakeside Avenue in The Weirs.

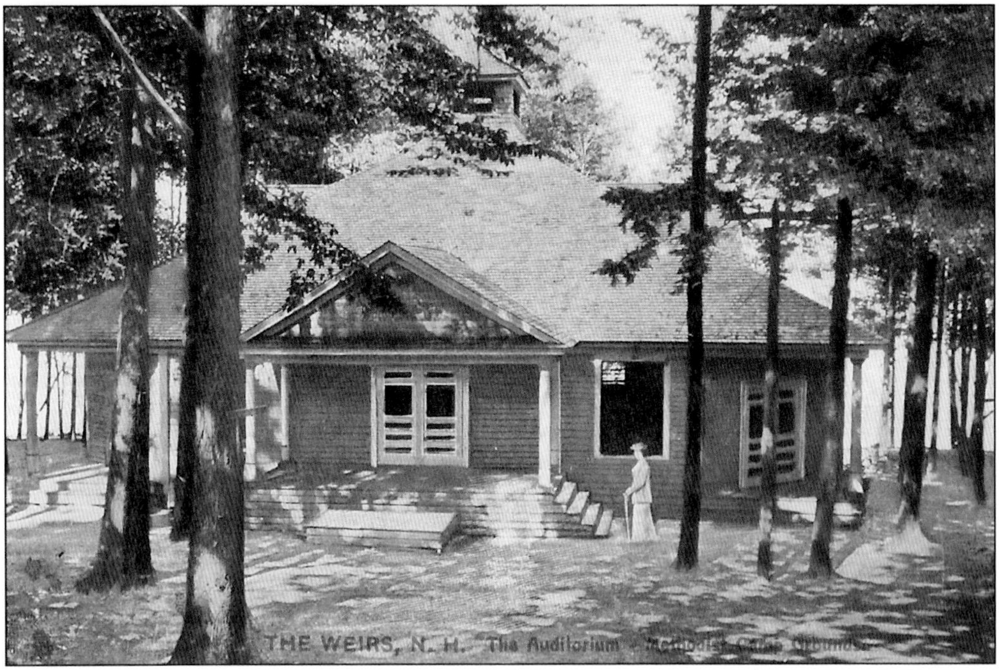

The auditorium at the Methodist Campground, Weirs, New Hampshire, 1929. When the Methodists were not using the campground, other denominations were invited to use the facility for their camp meetings.

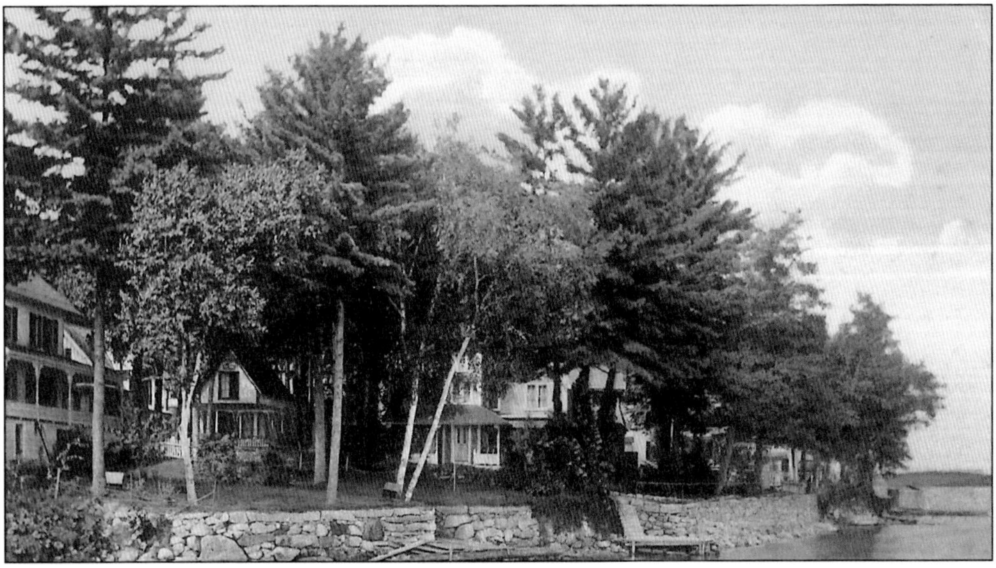

The Camp Meeting Grounds at The Weirs, 1900s. These cottages may still be seen on the shoreline just north of the Weirs railroad station.

Three

Early Pleasure and Commercial Boats

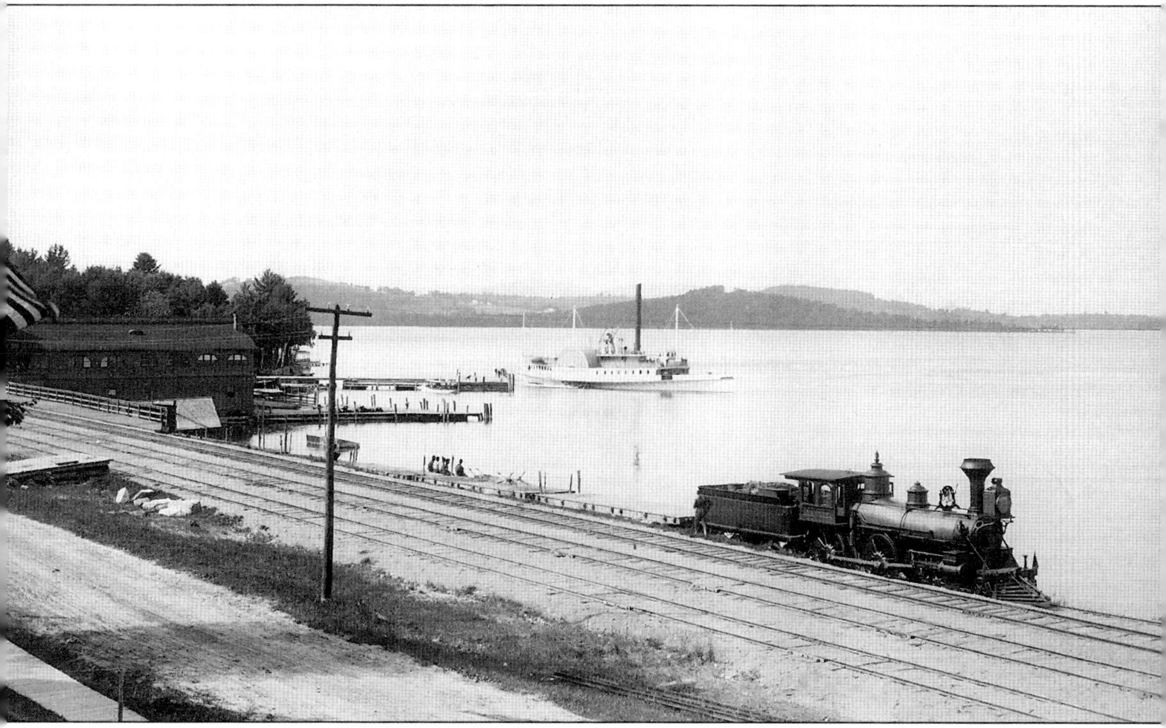

The *Lady of the Lake* docked at The Weirs Railroad Station, early 1880s. The launching of this vessel marked the beginning of an epoch in the history of steam navigation on Lake Winnipesaukee. She was 125 feet long with a beam of 35 feet; the largest steamboat yet to sail on the lake.

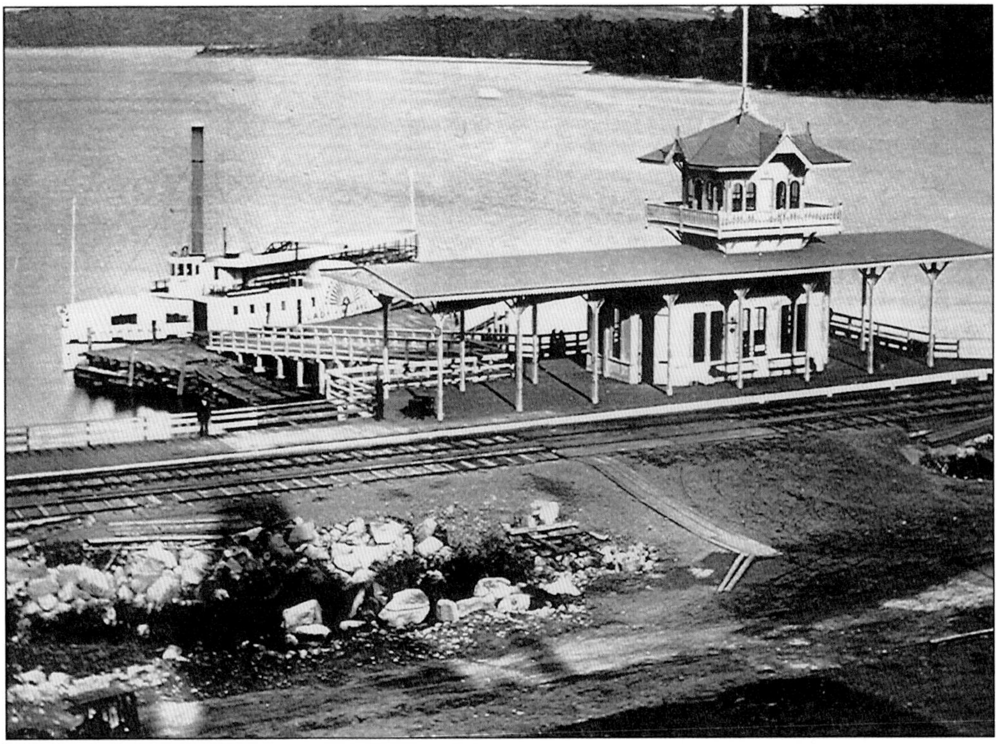

The *Lady of the Lake* docked at The Weirs Railroad Station, 1880s. The *Lady of the Lake* was a most durable steamboat which sailed for almost five decades on the lake. Today, her hull still remains in excellent shape in 40 feet of water on the bottom of Glendale Bay, where she was given an honorable burial. In the distance is Governor's Island; Interlaken Park is on the right.

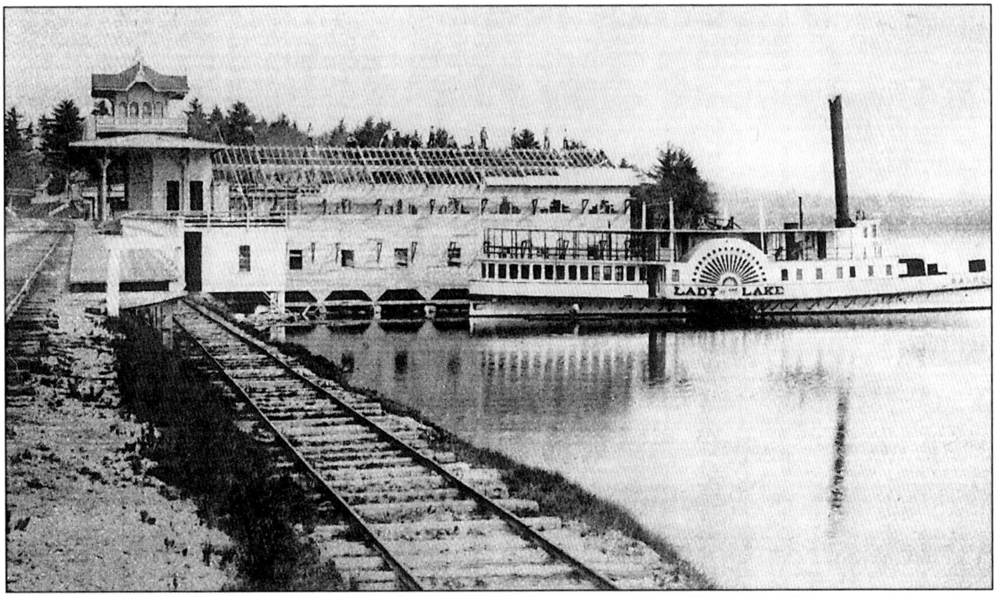

The *Lady of the Lake* docked at The Weirs Railroad Station. In 1885, the Weirs Cafe building was added to the rear of the station extending some 100 feet from the boardwalk out into the lake. Note the spur track going under the station.

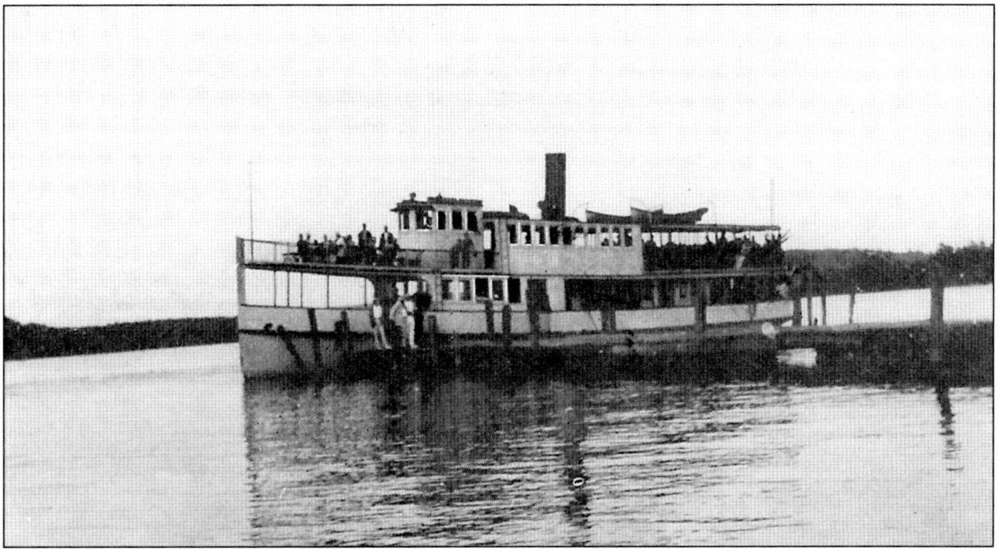

The *Governor Endicott* docked at Geneva Point Camp in Moultonboro, New Hampshire. The *Governor Endicott* was launched in 1905 and was owned by the Winnipesaukee Transportation Company. It was 100 feet long with a beam of 19 feet. Her first captain was Leander Lavallee. In 1922, Captain Lavallee sold the vessel to his son, Edward Lavallee, who operated it until 1927, when he sold it to the Reddington Interests. After two years of service, it was dismantled. She was the last steamboat of any competition to the *Mount Washington*.

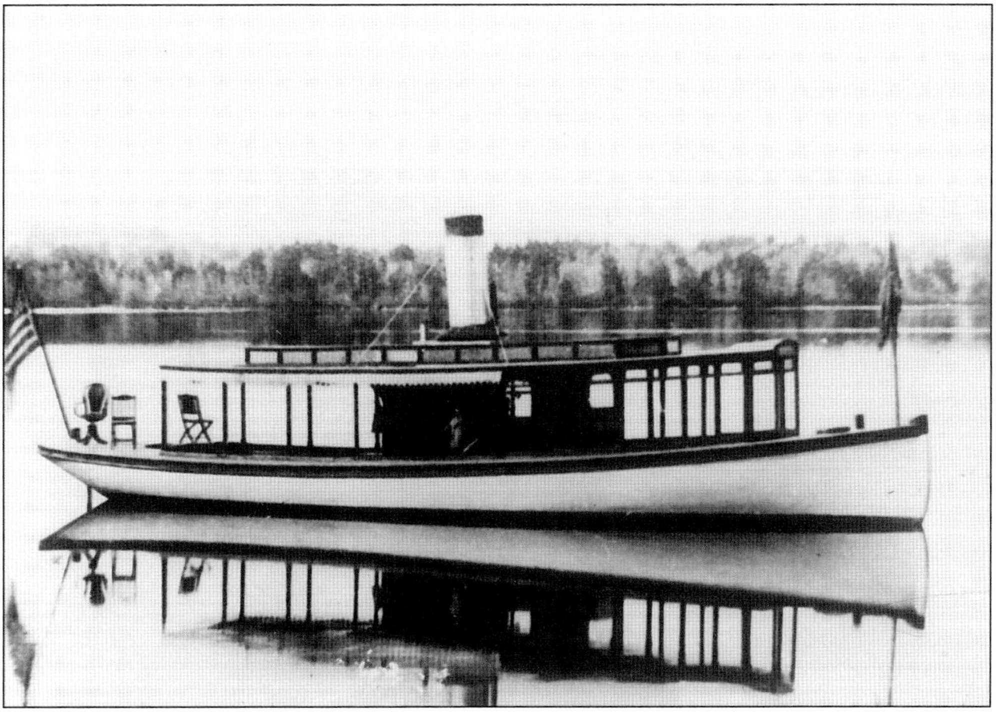

The *West Wind*. This vessel was built in 1891 and was owned and operated by Dr. Henry F. Libby of Wolfeboro, New Hampshire, early 1900s. The boat was considered a twin to the *Windermere*.

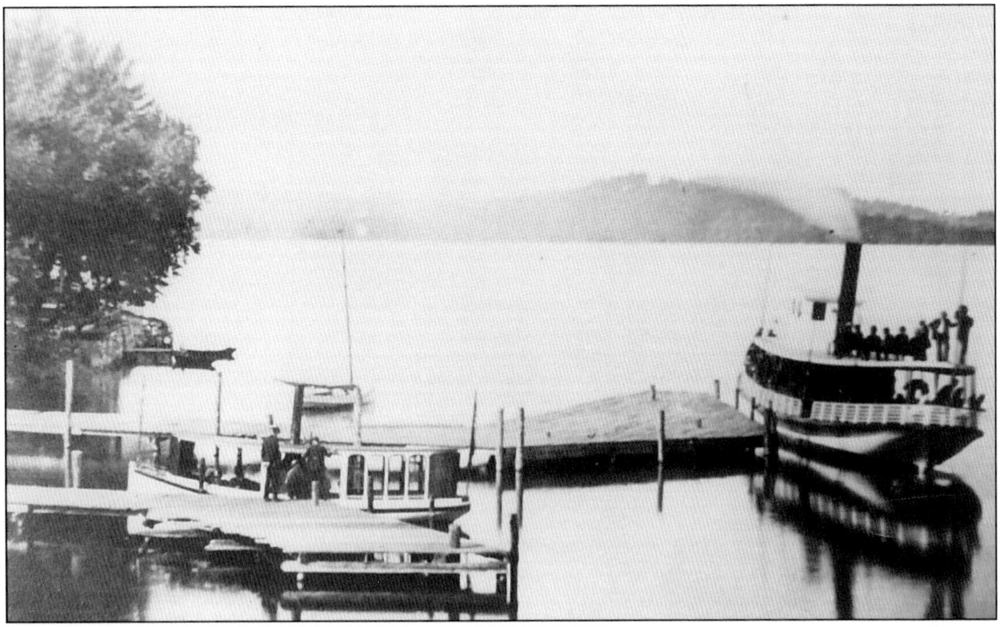

The *Swallow* at The Weirs dock, Nat Goodhue, pilot. The vessel was built in 1890 in Four Rivers as a flagship at Marblehead, Massachusetts. It was first brought to the lake in 1897 by Louis R. Spear; it was later purchased by Captain John Goodhue, who ran it as a party boat until he sold it to Mr. and Mrs. Herbert Dumaresq—a fitting addition to the estate known as Kona Mansion in Moultonboro. This vessel was probably one of the last commercial steamboats running on Lake Winnipesaukee.

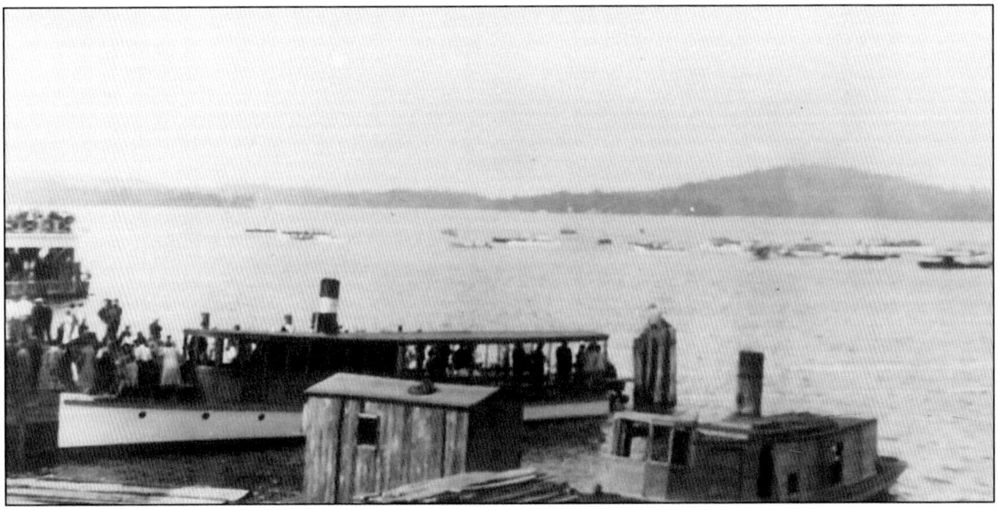

The *Marshall Fosh* at The Weirs dock. This vessel was originally owned by Dr. F.E. Greene. It was built for Col. Albert Pope of Hartford, Connecticut. She was brought to Lake Winnipesaukee and named *Windermere*. Following the death of Dr. Green, this vessel was purchased by Captain Leander Lavallee; it was remodeled and renamed the *Marshall Fosh*.

In 1932, Edward Lavallee had been awarded the contract for the marine mail route from Lakeport. Following the award of the mail route, Captain Ed purchased the former mail boat and reinstated her on the mail run in place of this vessel. In 1941, her career ended and she was dismantled.

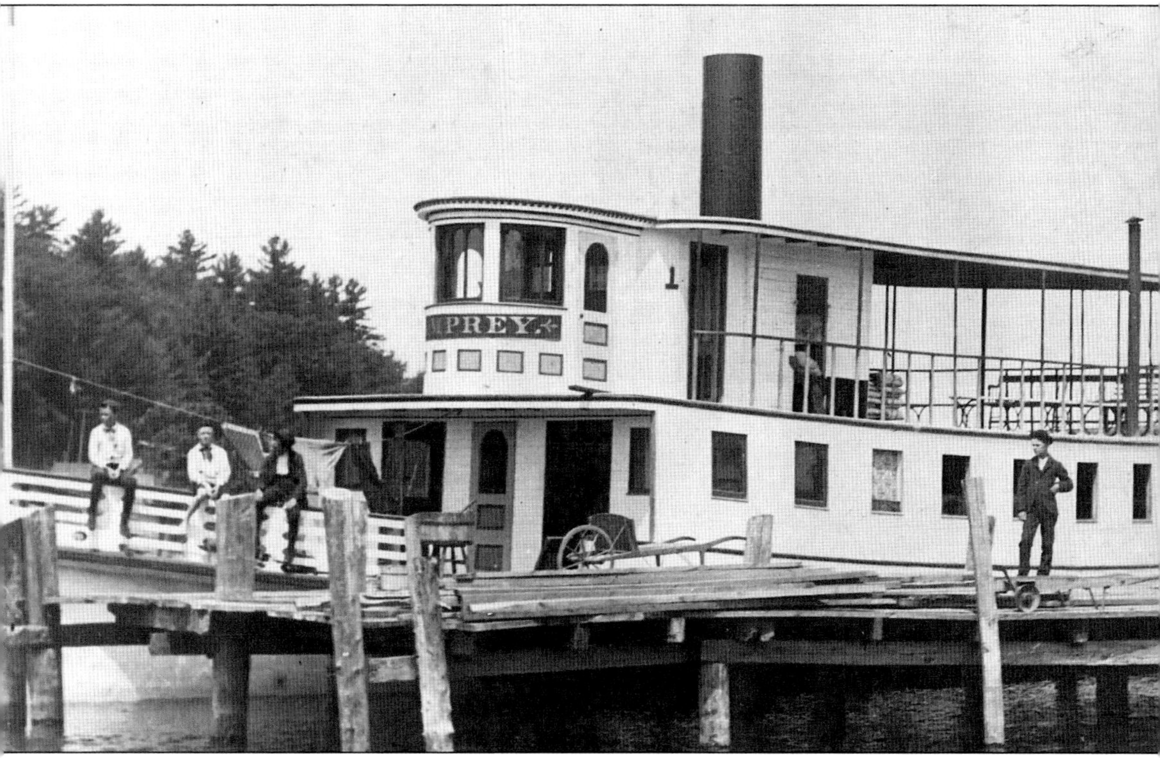

The *Lamprey* at Lakeport, New Hampshire, 1880s. This vessel was built in 1882 at Long Island in Moultonboro, New Hampshire, by Robert and Riley Lamprey. This vessel was 74 feet long with a beam of 18 feet. It was originally built for the freight and logging business on the lake. It finally burned in 1882 at the Moultonboro Wharf.

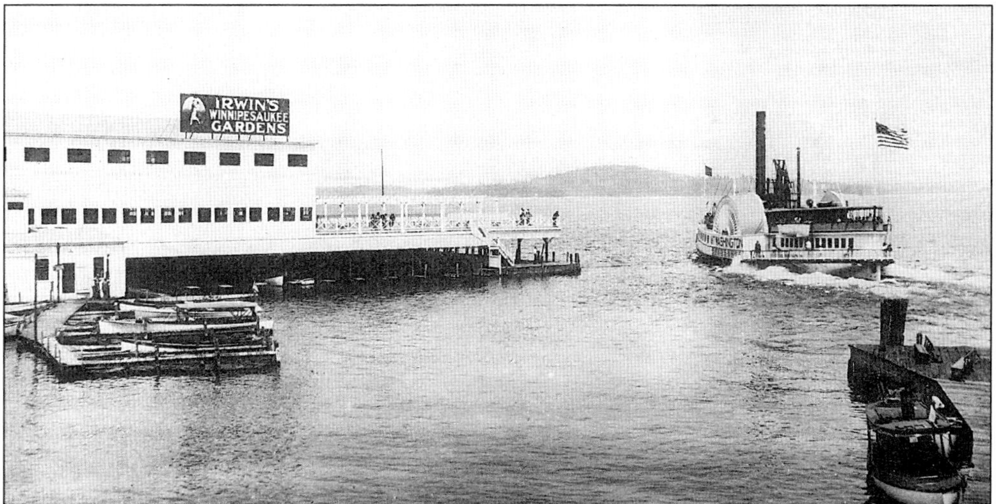

The steamer *Mount Washington* leaving The Weirs dock. Its daily trip was 65 miles around the lake during the early 1900s. On the left is Irwin's Winnipesaukee Gardens, one of the finest ballrooms in all of New England, where many of the big bands once performed. This dance hall was built in 1925 by Jim Irwin of Laconia, New Hampshire.

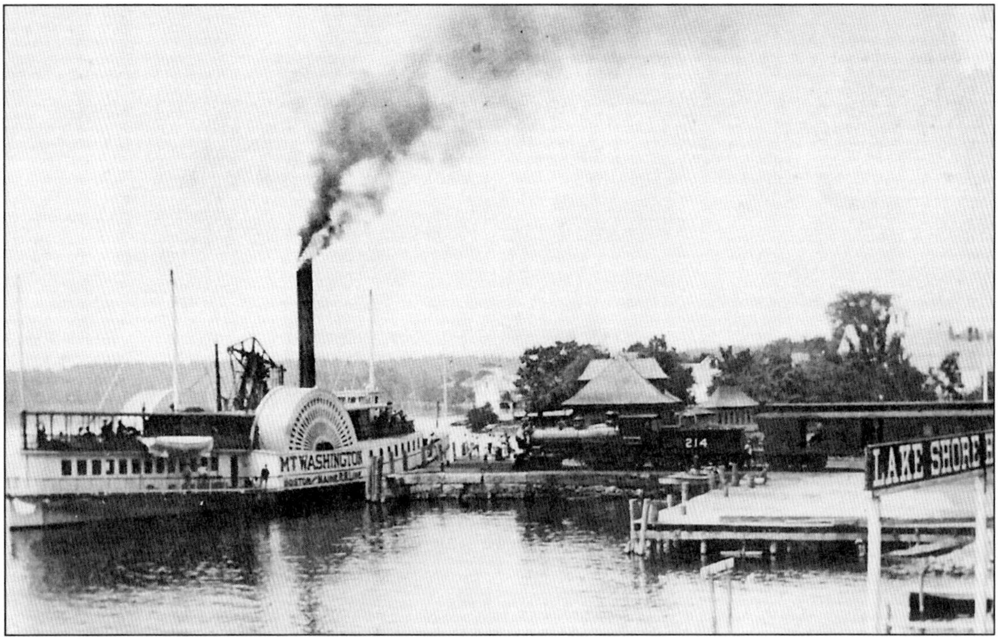

The steamer *Mount Washington* at the Wolfeboro Dock Station, 1910. The Boston & Maine train is seen meeting the steamer *Mount Washington* at the new station, which replaced the original building that burned in 1899. Note the hotel sign Lake Shore House on the right.

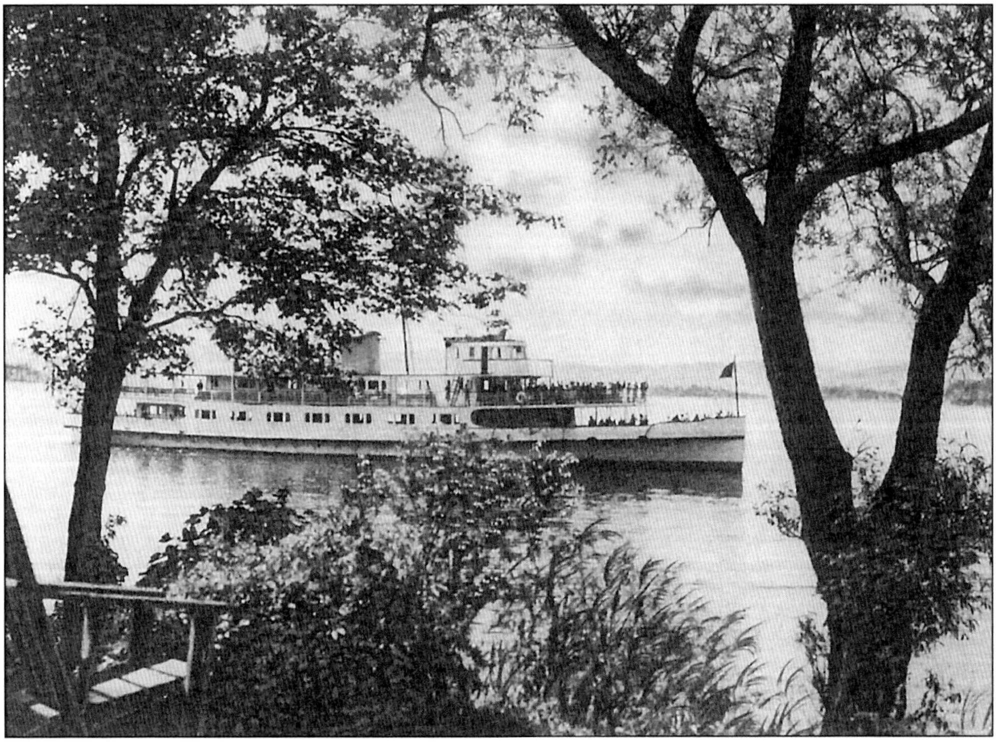

The M.V. *Mount Washington* as seen from the shoreline as it approaches the Wolfeboro dock, 1946.

One of the M.V. *Mount Washington*'s time tables, 1948.

DON'T MISS IT!!

New Hampshire's Famous Scenic Cruise on the Modern Diesel Powered

MOUNT WASHINGTON

Capt. BRYAN AVERY

DAILY TIME SCHEDULE

EFFECTIVE THIRD SUNDAY IN JUNE TO SUNDAY FOLLOWING LABOR DAY, INCLUSIVE — DAYLIGHT SAVING TIME

LV. WEIRS	9:00 A.M.	2:00 P.M.
" CENTER HARBOR	9:45 "	2:45 "
" WOLFEBORO	11:10 "	4:10 "
" ALTON BAY	11:50 "	4:50 "
AR. WEIRS	1:15 P.M.	6:15 "

ROUND TRIPS FROM

WEIRS	9:00 A.M. AND 2:00 P.M.
CENTER HARBOR	9:45 A.M.
WOLFEBORO	11:10 "
ALTON BAY	11:50 "

SCHEDULE SUBJECT TO CHANGE WITHOUT NOTICE.

LUNCHEONETTE & SODA BAR ON BOARD

This 4 Hour Cruise on

LAKE WINNEPESAUKEE

offers the most wonderful combination of Lake, Island, Mountain and Shoreline Scenery to be found in America.

SIXTY-FIVE MILE ROUND TRIP

FARE — Round Trip, incl. tax - $2.00
Children under 12 - ½ Fare - under 5 - Free

Public Address System calls Attention to Points of Interest and Features of Lake Winnepesaukee.

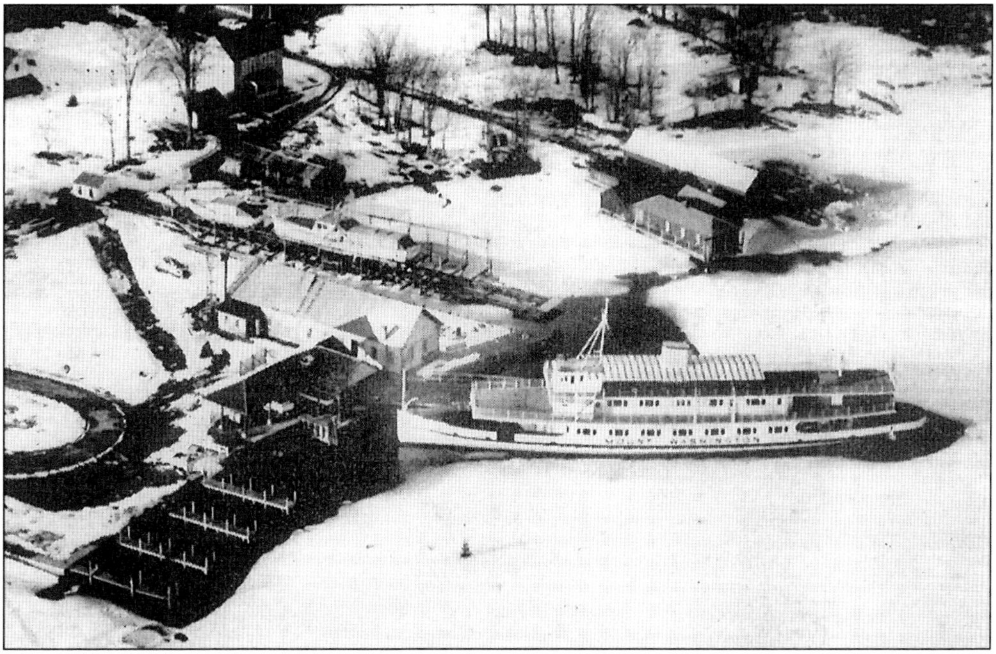

The M.V. *Mount Washington* docked at Center Harbor during the winter months, 1960–61. Notice the open water around the *Mount Washington* and town docks. During most winters the *Mount Washington* remains in the water with aquatherms placed around the vessel so as to keep the ice from forming around the hull.

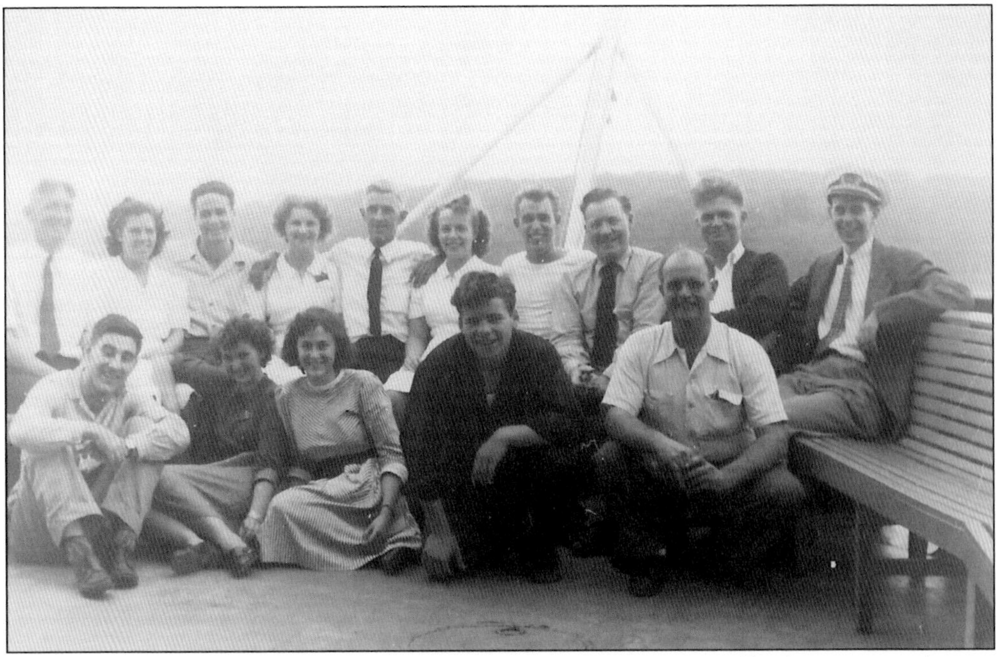

The crew of M.V. *Mount Washington*, 1948. Captain Bryan K. Avery (back row, center) poses with his crew on the fantail of the *Mount Washington*.

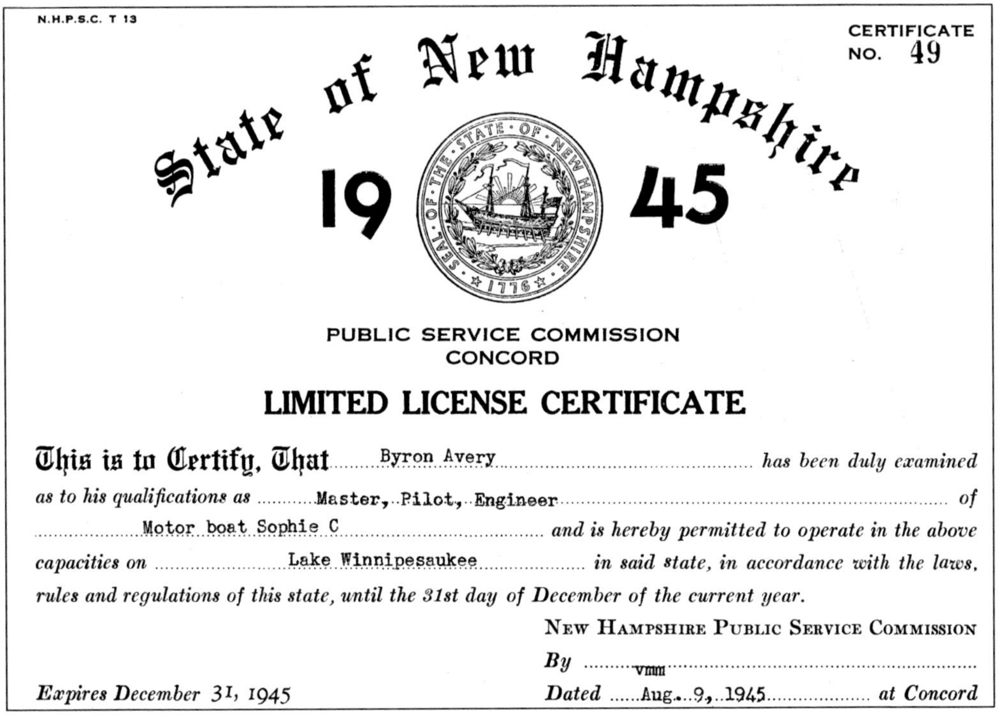

N.H.P.S.C. T 13

CERTIFICATE NO. 49

State of New Hampshire

19 45

PUBLIC SERVICE COMMISSION
CONCORD

LIMITED LICENSE CERTIFICATE

This is to Certify, That ...Byron Avery... *has been duly examined as to his qualifications as* ...Master, Pilot, Engineer... *of* ...Motor boat Sophie C... *and is hereby permitted to operate in the above capacities on* ...Lake Winnipesaukee... *in said state, in accordance with the laws, rules and regulations of this state, until the 31st day of December of the current year.*

NEW HAMPSHIRE PUBLIC SERVICE COMMISSION

By ...vmm...

Expires December 31, 1945

Dated ...Aug. 9, 1945... *at Concord*

Captain Bryan K. Avery's license to operate the *Mount Washington*, 1945. For nearly 50 years, Captain Avery was not only captain of the *Mount Washington*, but also a licensed "Master, Pilot, and Engineer."

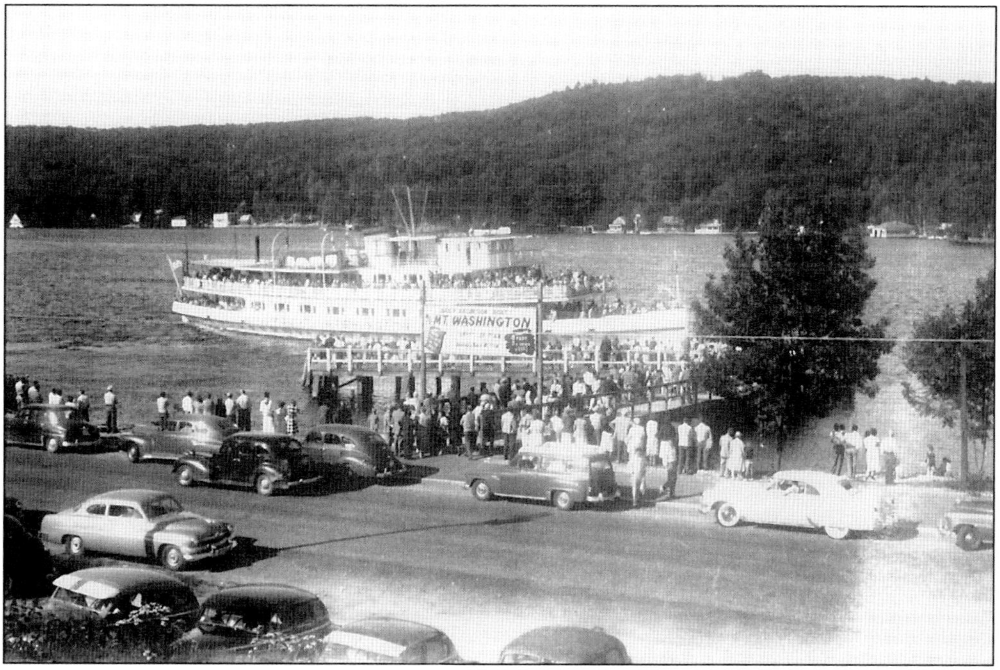

The M.V. *Mount Washington* docking at Alton Bay to take on more passengers for its four hour excursion around the lake. Notice the extension of the dock to the left piling, 1950s.

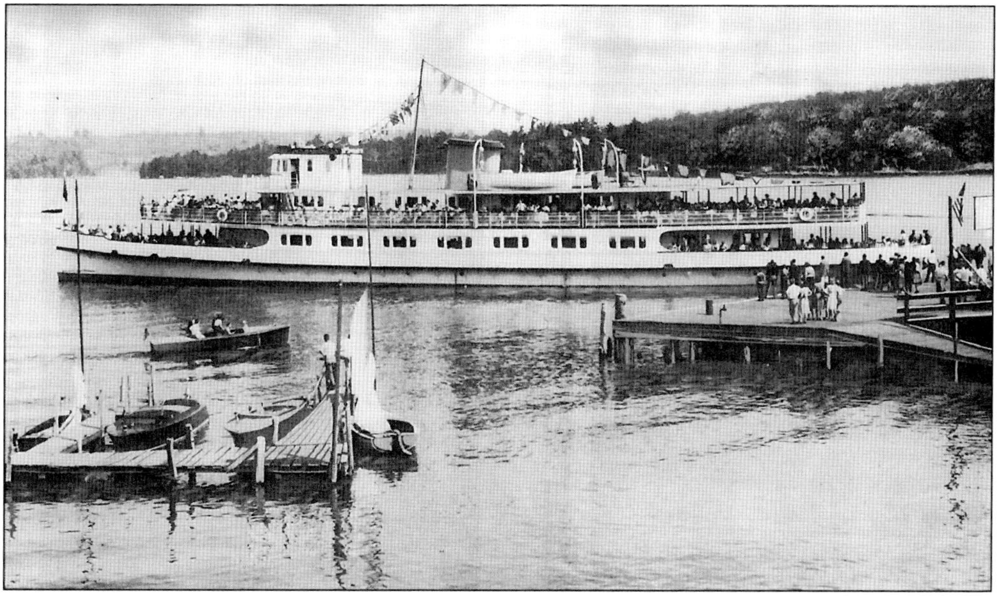

The M.V. *Mount Washington* leaving the dock at Weirs. In 1948 the *Mount Washington* was 205 feet long, weighed 600 tons, and was capable of carrying 1,200 passengers. This diesel-propelled steel vessel carried on the traditional voyages of past wooden-sided wheelers, fond in memories of those who loved them, sailing these waters for generations.

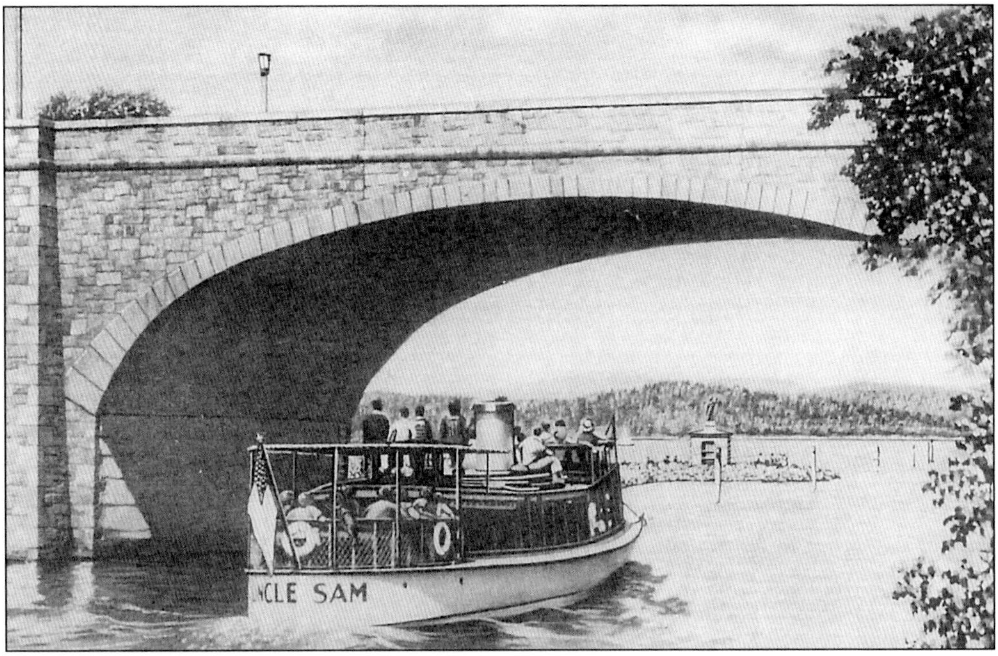

The U.S. mail boat *Uncle Sam* as she passes beneath the Aquedoctan Bridge at The Weirs. This bridge, which crosses the outlet of Lake Winnipesaukee into Paugus Bay, was once the site of the Aquedoctan Indian fishing place.

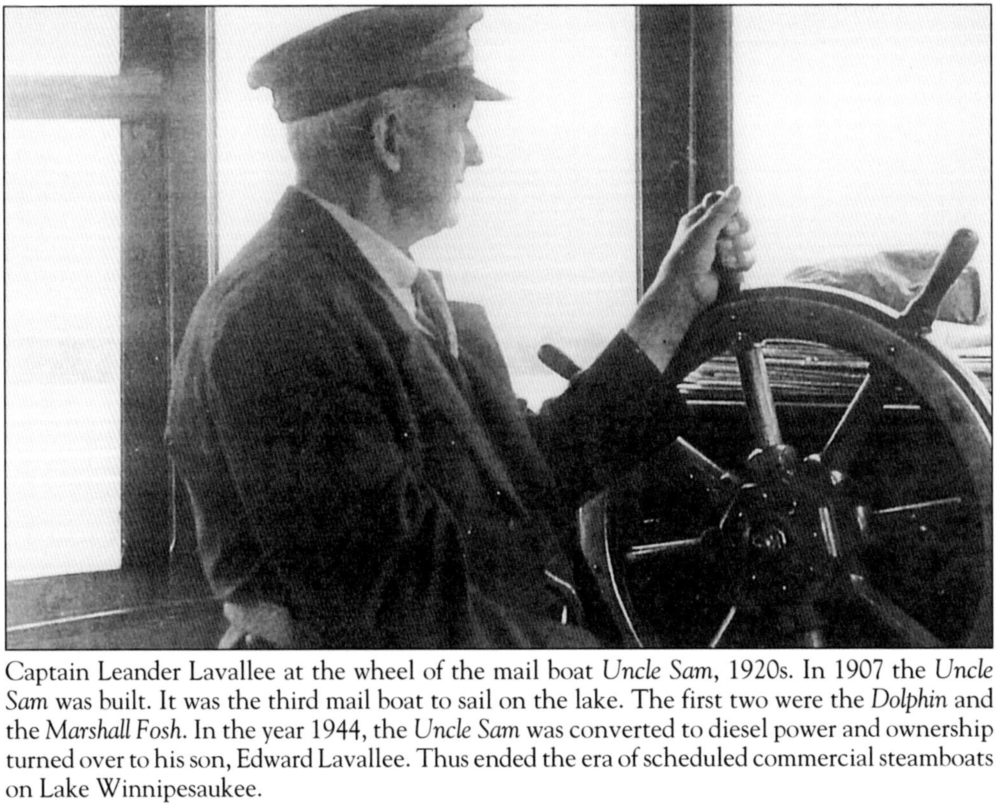

Captain Leander Lavallee at the wheel of the mail boat *Uncle Sam*, 1920s. In 1907 the *Uncle Sam* was built. It was the third mail boat to sail on the lake. The first two were the *Dolphin* and the *Marshall Fosh*. In the year 1944, the *Uncle Sam* was converted to diesel power and ownership turned over to his son, Edward Lavallee. Thus ended the era of scheduled commercial steamboats on Lake Winnipesaukee.

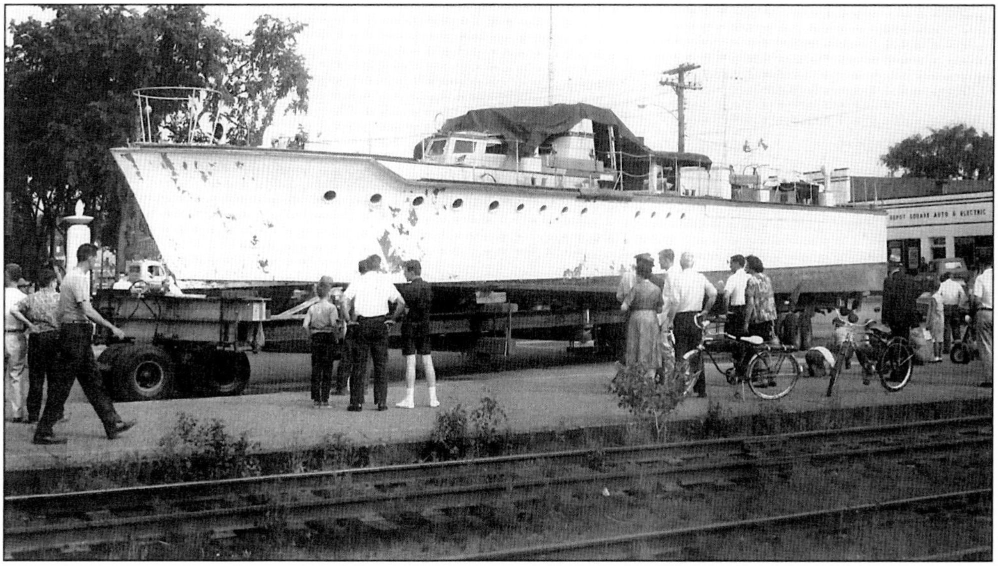

The *Uncle Sam II* at Depot Square in Laconia, New Hampshire, May 26, 1963. This converted PT boat, en-route to Lakeport from Portsmouth, was the largest boat ever to make the trip by highway. It was purchased by Vernon Cotton and Allan Perley, who formed a corporation known as the U.S. Mail Boat, Inc. The 72-foot, twin-screw vessel was to be named *Uncle Sam II*.

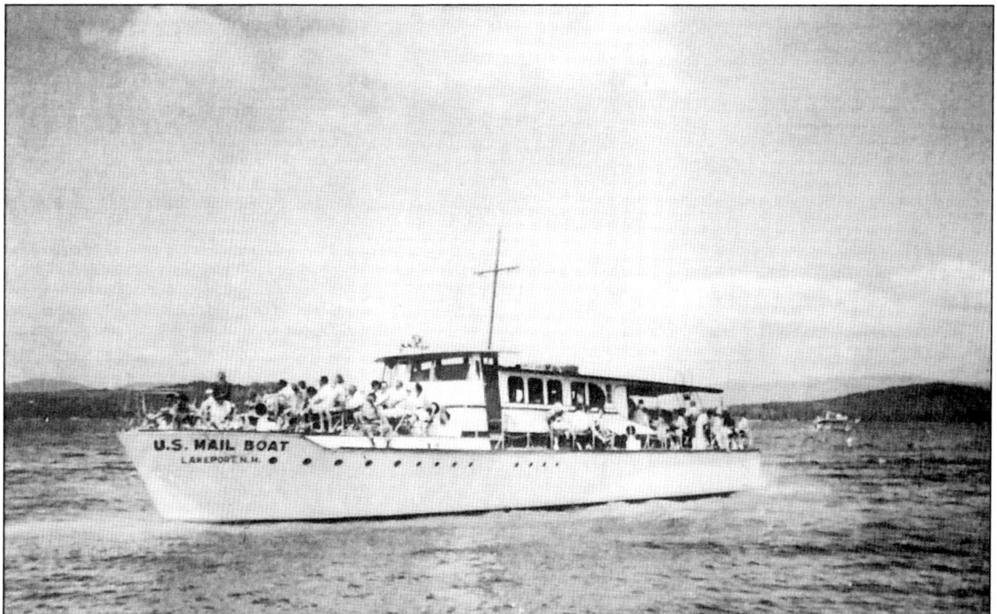

The U.S. mail boat *Uncle Sam II*. The craft was originally built as one of the famous PT boats (PT-719) for World War II, but never saw action. Here she is seen providing tourists with a pleasant cruise on the open waters while serving the many islands with mail service.

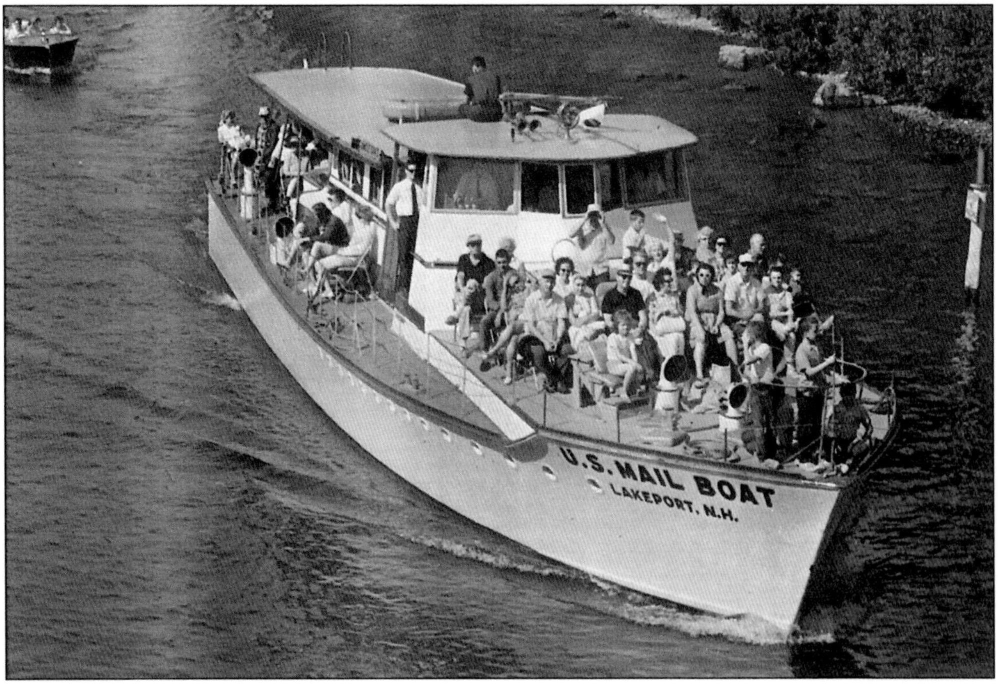

The *Uncle Sam II* in the channel at The Weirs. According to a 1969 article in the *Laconia Evening Citizen*, the *Uncle Sam II*, after six years on the freshwaters of Lake Winnipesaukee, was ". . . slated to return to the Atlantic Ocean. This craft was sold at auction to Frank Damrell of Andover, Massachusetts, and Southport, Maine for $5,500." Captain Edward Lavallee, postmaster of the mail boat since 1932, would continue his duties upon the *Sophie* C until his retirement. In the wheel house are owners Vernon Cotton and Allan Perley.

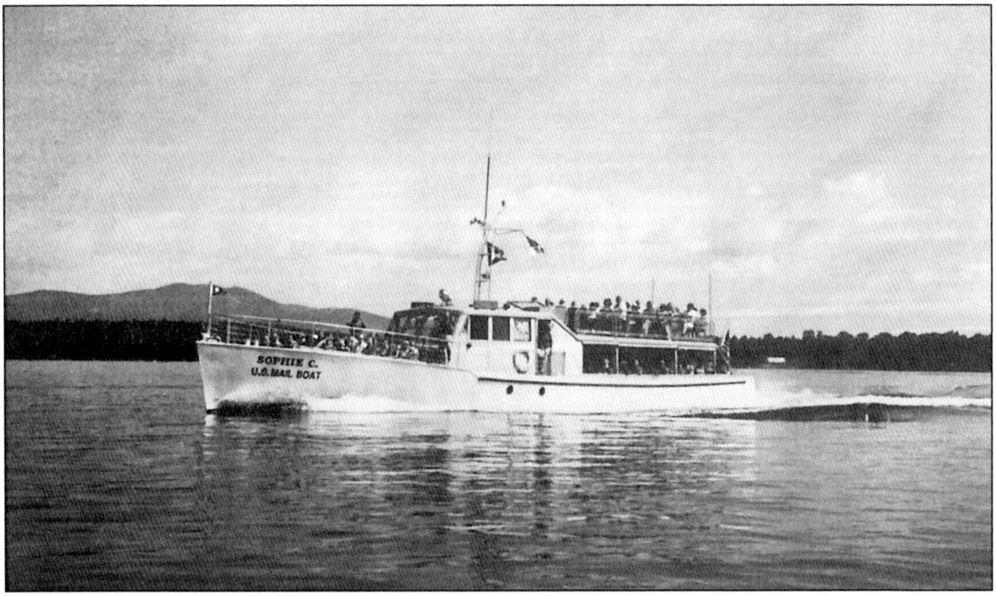

The U.S. mail boat *Sophie* C returning from her daily mail delivery among the islands. This 76-foot, diesel-powered steel boat has proven very popular with tourists desiring an intimate view of the lake's innumerable islands, 1970.

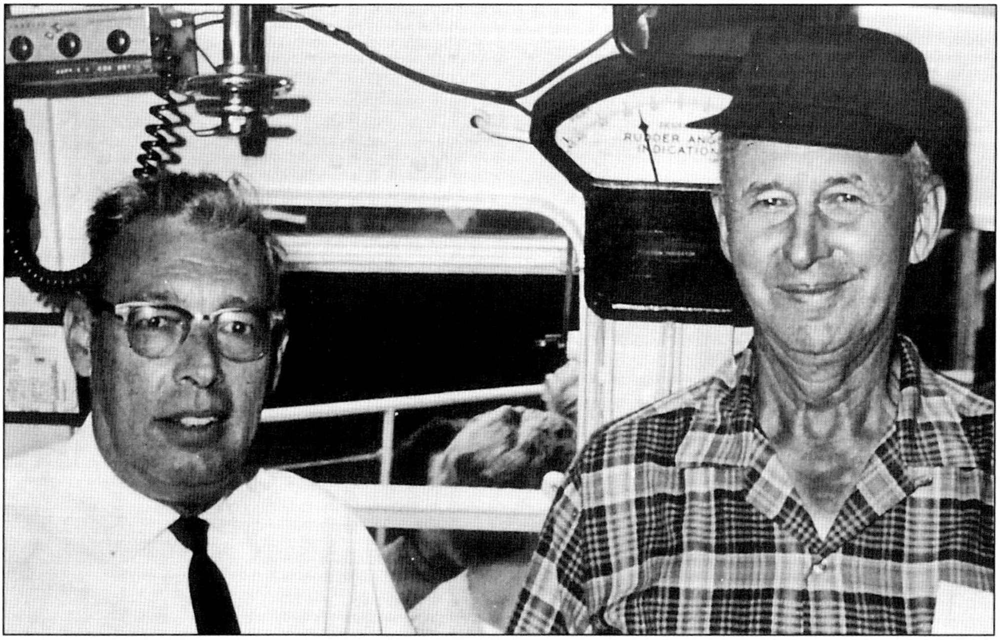

Captain Wilbur Bigelow and Postmaster Ed Lavallee of the mail boat *Sophie C*, 1971. Captain Edward Lavallee, son of Captain Leander Lavallee, took over the mail service on the vessel and continued as postmaster on Lake Winnipesaukee until his retirement in the early 1980s. Captain Bigelow served as captain of the *Sophie* C from 1965 until his retirement in the mid-80s.

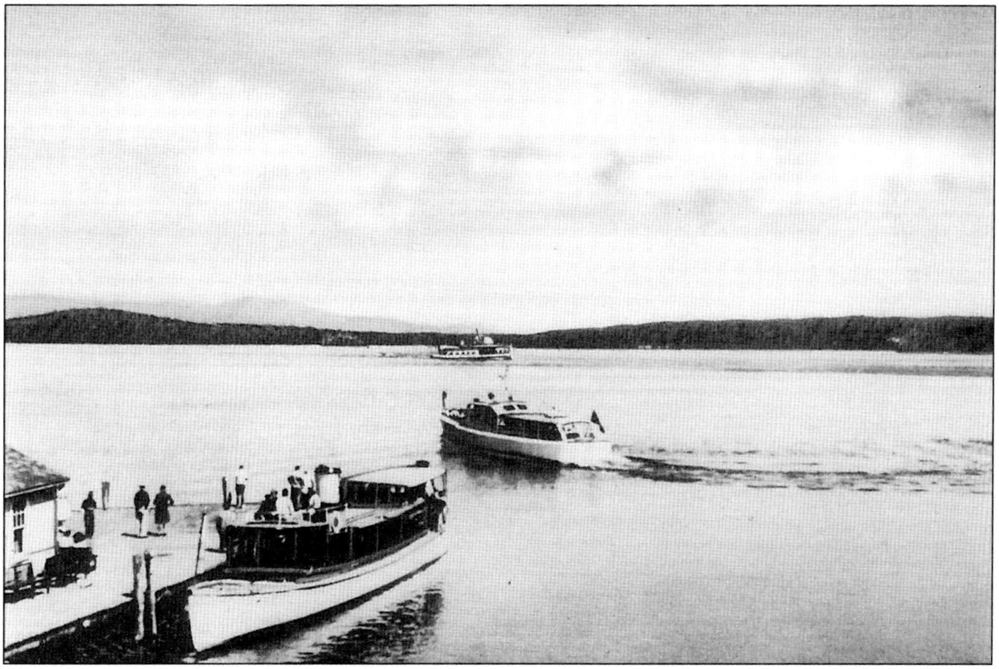

The U.S. mail boat *Uncle Sam*, the *Sophie* C, and the *Mount Washington* in Weirs Bay. These three boats, and many other craft, were responsible for the growing transportation of thousands of regular tourists among the islands and scenic grandeur of the lake.

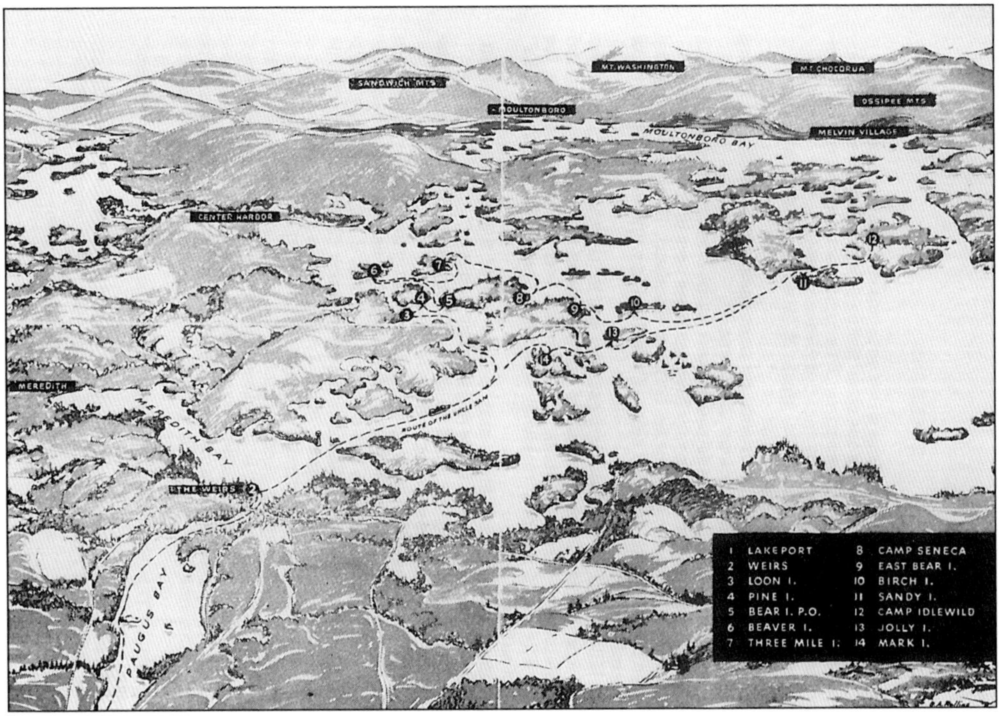

A map showing the route of a mail boat.

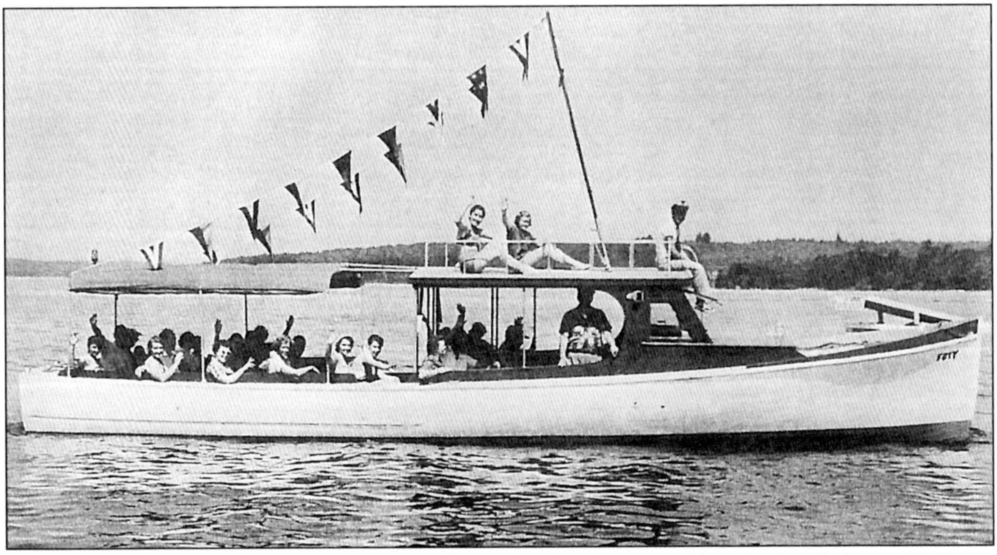

The *Foxy*, 1950. This 42-foot wooden craft, owned and operated by Carl and Amie Wallace, operated out of Paugus Bay (where Burger King is now located). The craft made daily excursions from Lakeport to The Weirs. From The Weirs it sailed among the Forty Islands, to Glendale, then under Governor's Island Bridge and back to The Weirs, and finally to its home port in Lakeport. During this time, the 2 1/2-hour cruise cost $1.10.

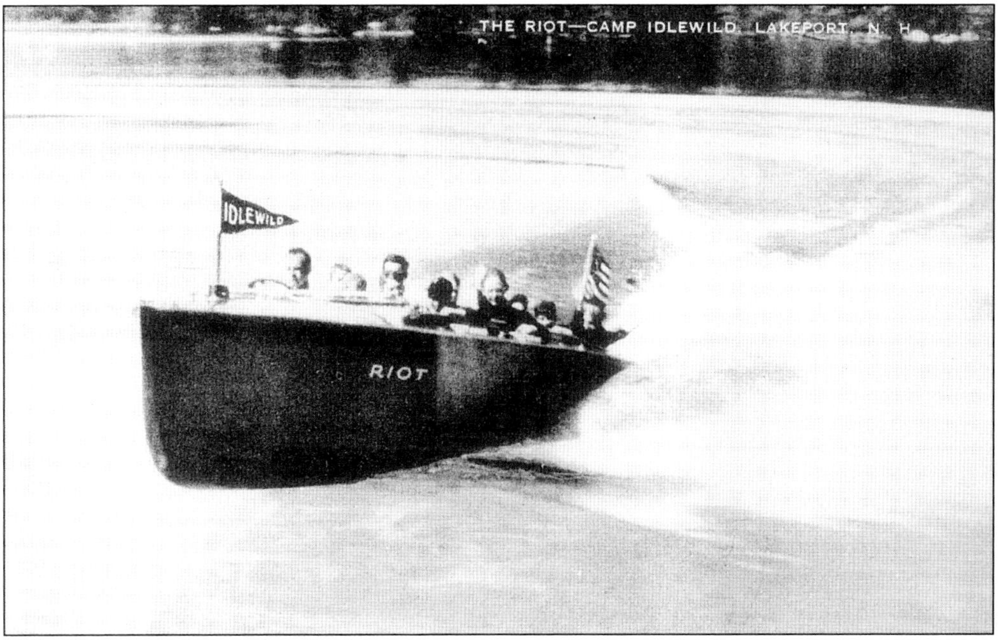

The *Riot* speed boat of Camp Idlewild on Cow Island, Tuftonboro, New Hampshire. This 28-foot speed boat is enjoying the open waters of Lake Winnipesaukee with campers aboard.

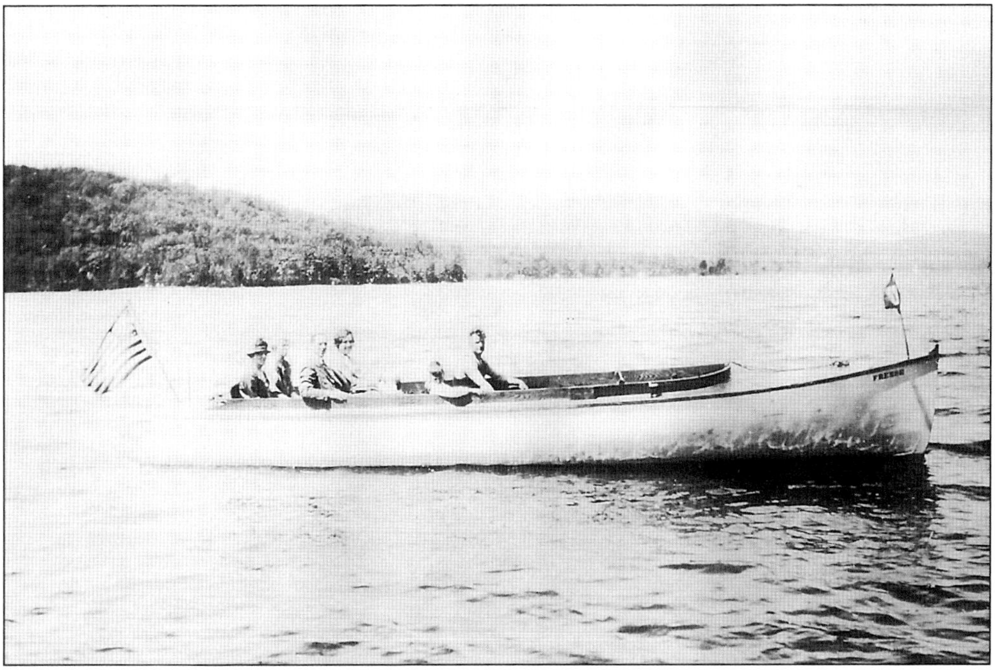

The *Freese*. The person driving the boat may be George E. Freese Sr. This picture was taken near Freese cottage in Alton Bay. This vessel is a 26-foot Johnson Laker.

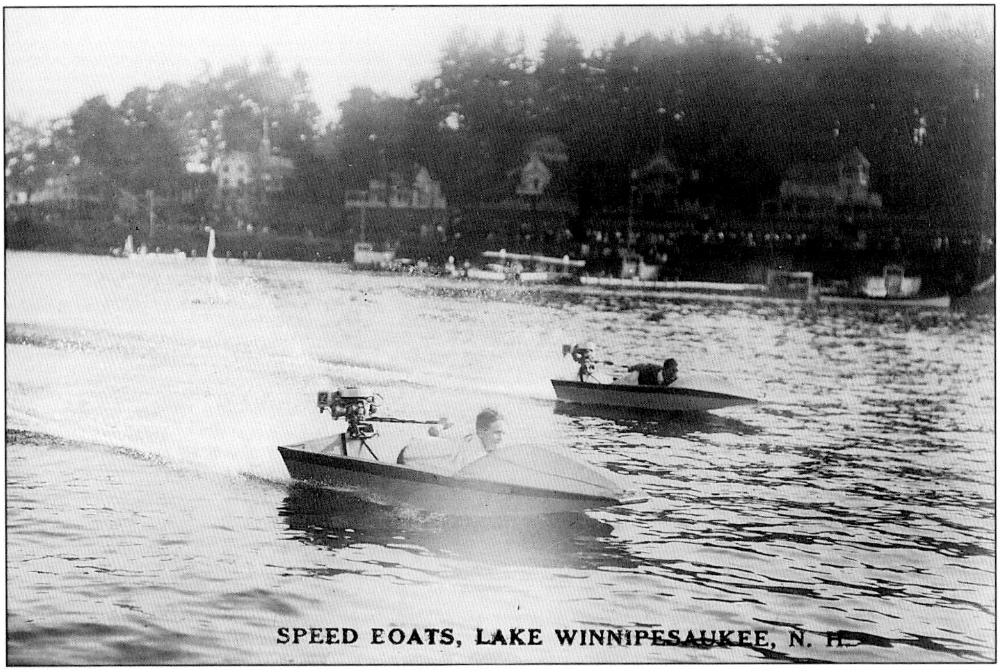

Speed boats at Weirs Beach, late 1920s. These races were sponsored by Jim Irwin and the Winnipesaukee Power Boat Association with the active assistance of Sam Dunsford of Concord, and Archie Gulliford of "724 Cigar" fame in Manchester. These gentlemen made special arrangements with the driver by offering them free gas to run their race boats, and with the Boston & Maine Railroad to commute people from Boston to Weirs Beach for the races. This event was very popular for many years.

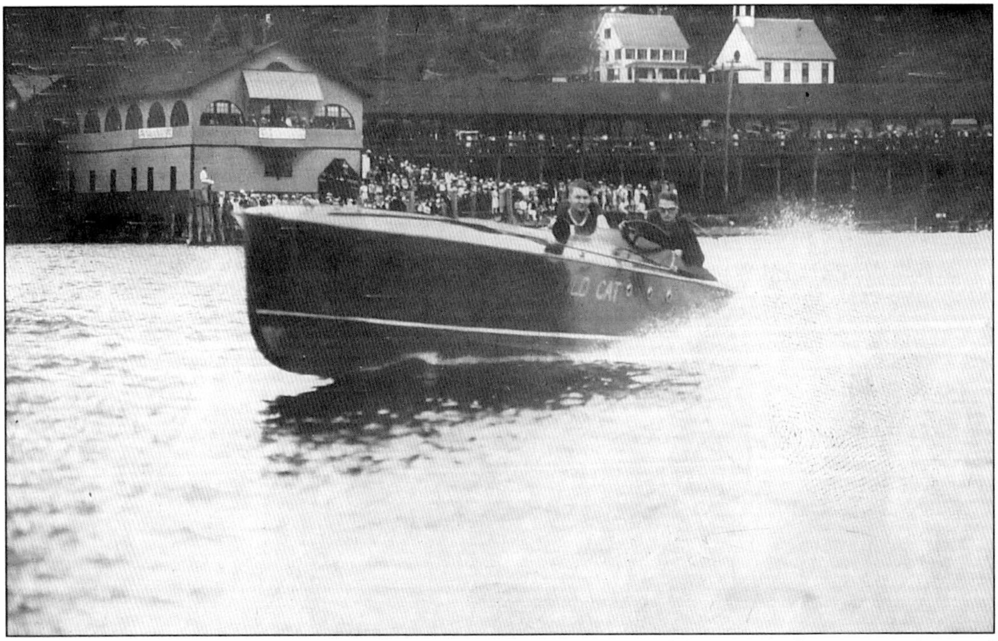

The *Wild Cat* at The Weirs race, late 1920s. This was a Ditchburn race boat manufactured during the 1920s with a Packard engine. It later became known as *Miss Alton Bay*.

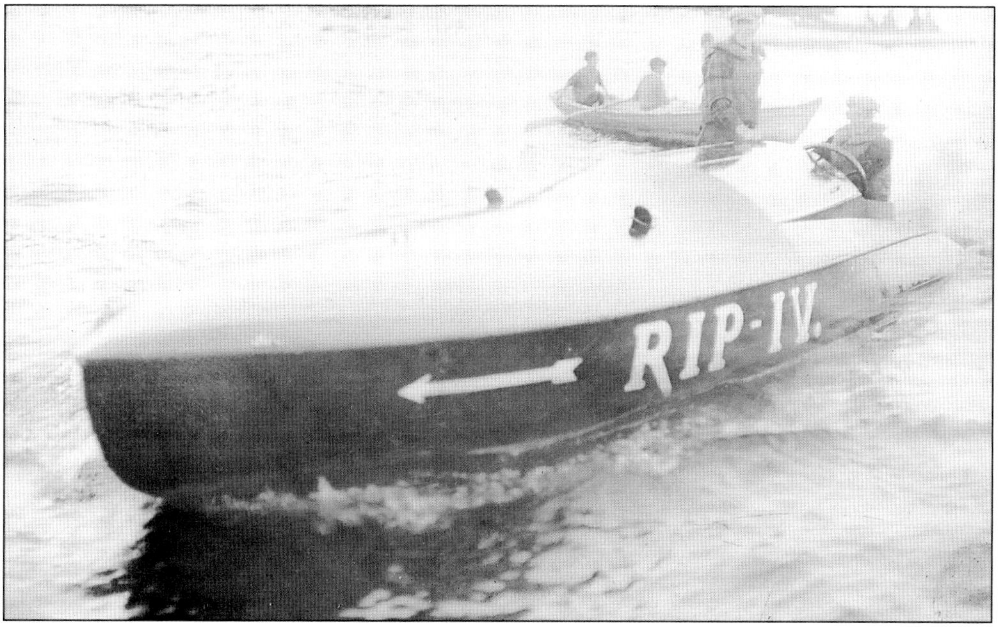

The *Rip-IV* at the Weirs race, late 1920s. This race boat was a Hacker craft owned and operated by Bob Peterson of Concord, New Hampshire.

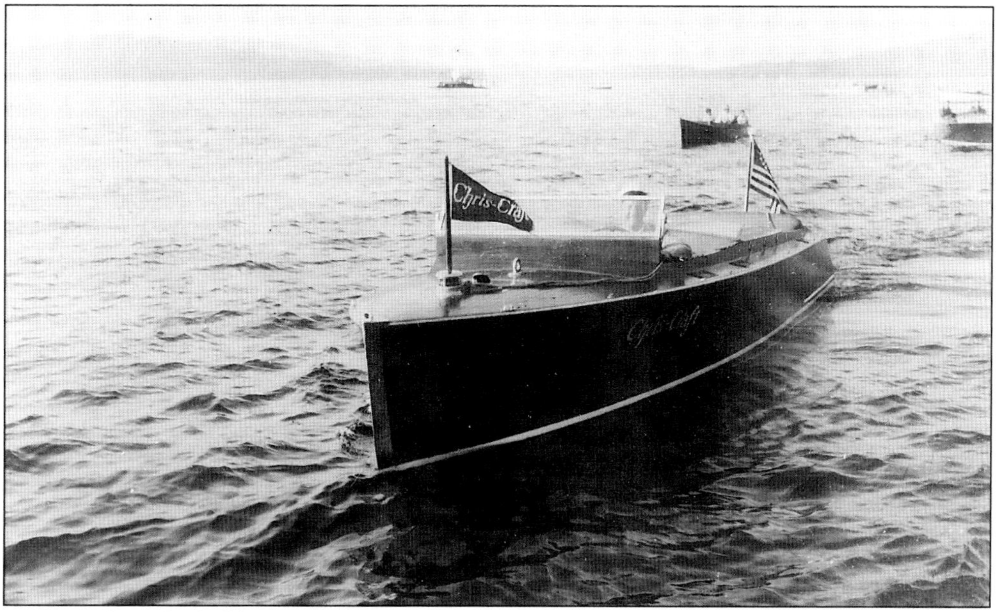

A 1927 Chris-Craft, 26-foot boat, being piloted by Jim Irwin.

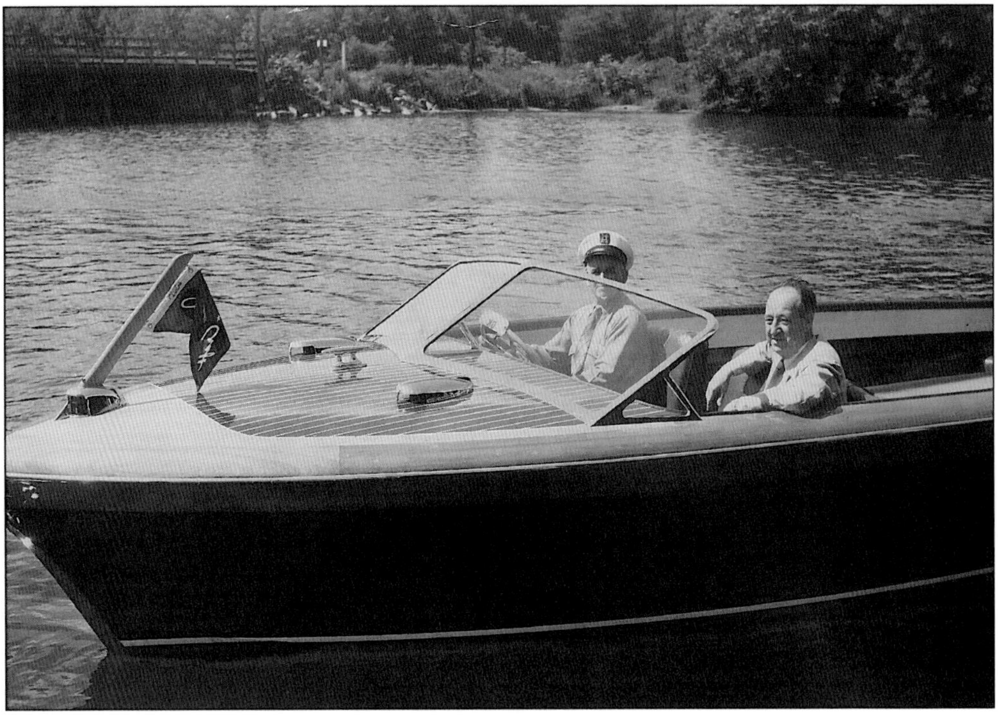

The Chris-Craft *Holiday*, 1952. Calvin Mallon and Jim Irwin Sr. are in the front seat. Presently this 24-foot, blond mahogany boat is owned by Don Minor. Jim Irwin only sold two of these boats.

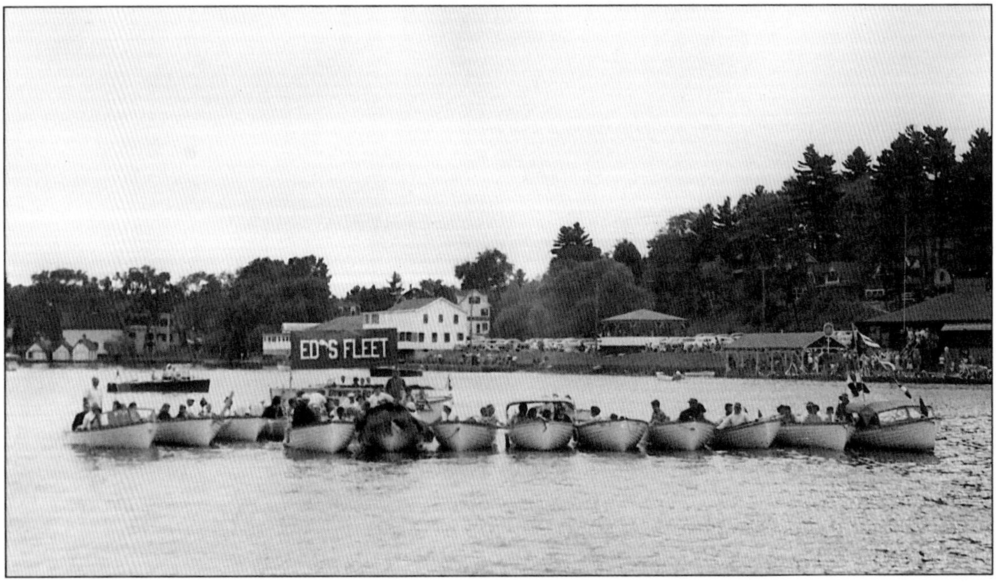

Ed's fleet in Alton Bay, New Hampshire, 1950s. Ed Downing was one of the early Lyman dealers in Alton Bay. This picture was taken to show off the boats Ed sold.

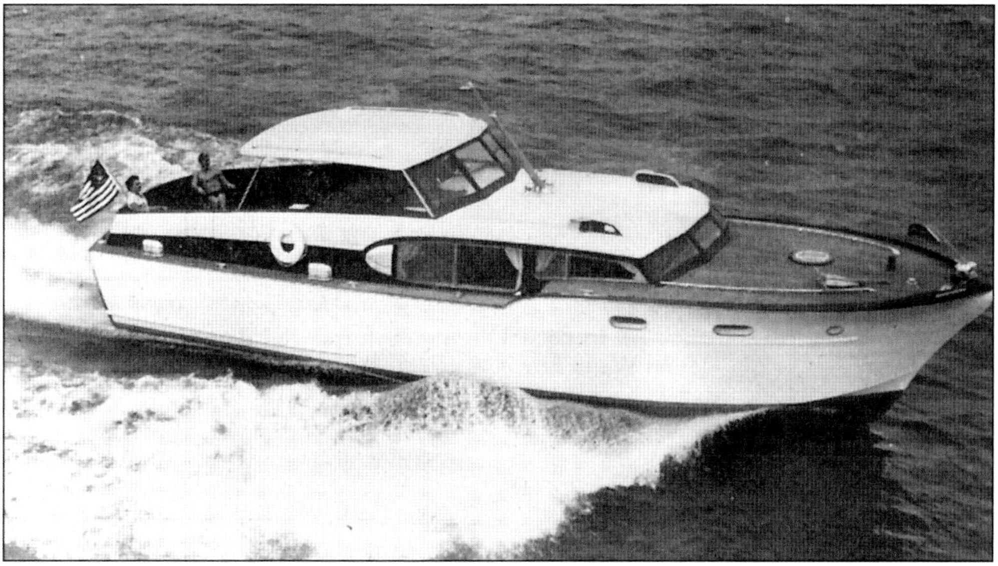

The *Mistress*. This 1953 sleek, 42-foot Chris-Craft Challenger, owned by William Chipman of So. Acton, Massachusetts, finds ample room to sail the open waters of the lake.

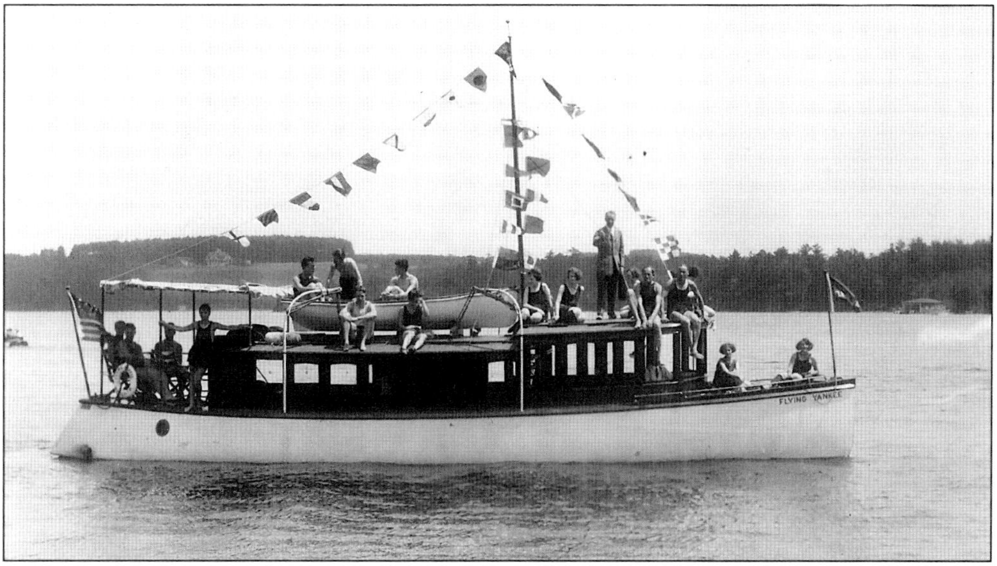

The *Flying Yankee*. This vessel was Jim Irwin's personal boat, a small four-cylinder engine, soon to be replaced with a Scripp. This was considered a 36-foot party boat. In the background we can see the governor's estate on Governor's Island. It is interesting to note that Jim's son Jack was a deckhand on this boat during 1944. At the age of 15, Jack earned his commercial pilot's license so that he could operate this and the *Miss Winnipesaukee* boats.

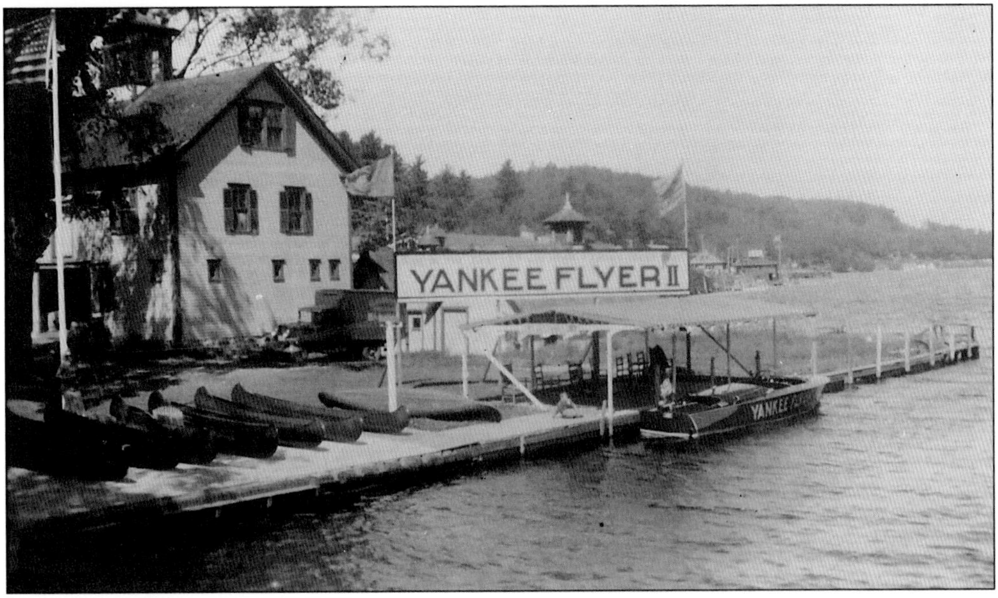

The *Yankee Flyer II* dock in Alton Bay, early 1930s. This vessel was originally owned by Carl Cramm. It was a 28-foot craft which had a 275-h.p., Dodge V-12 Lycomming engine. After World War II, the boat was owned and operated by the Johnson brothers from Lynn, Massachusetts.

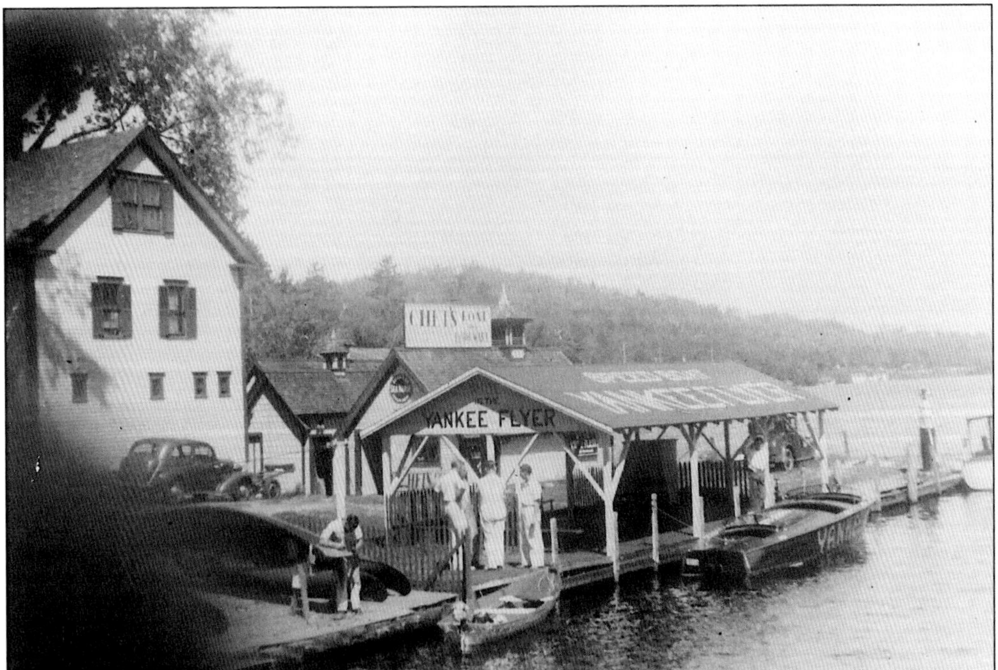

The *Yankee Flyer II*. During the late 1940s and early 1950s, the vessel was bought by Edward Wojcicki from Worcester, Massachusetts, who ran it as a commercial passenger boat. Al Horne was its driver at the time, and he remembers when the fare was 75¢ a ride.

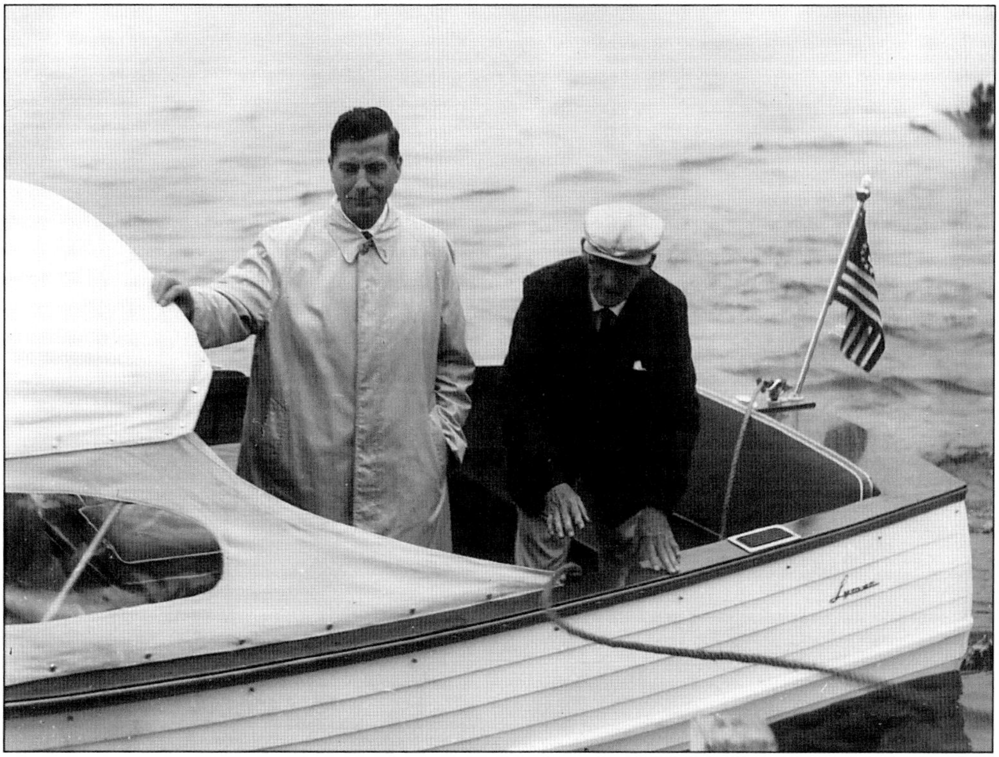

Governor Powell and Ed Downing, 1952. The governor came to view the boat races in Alton Bay. This particular boat is known as a Lyman Islander.

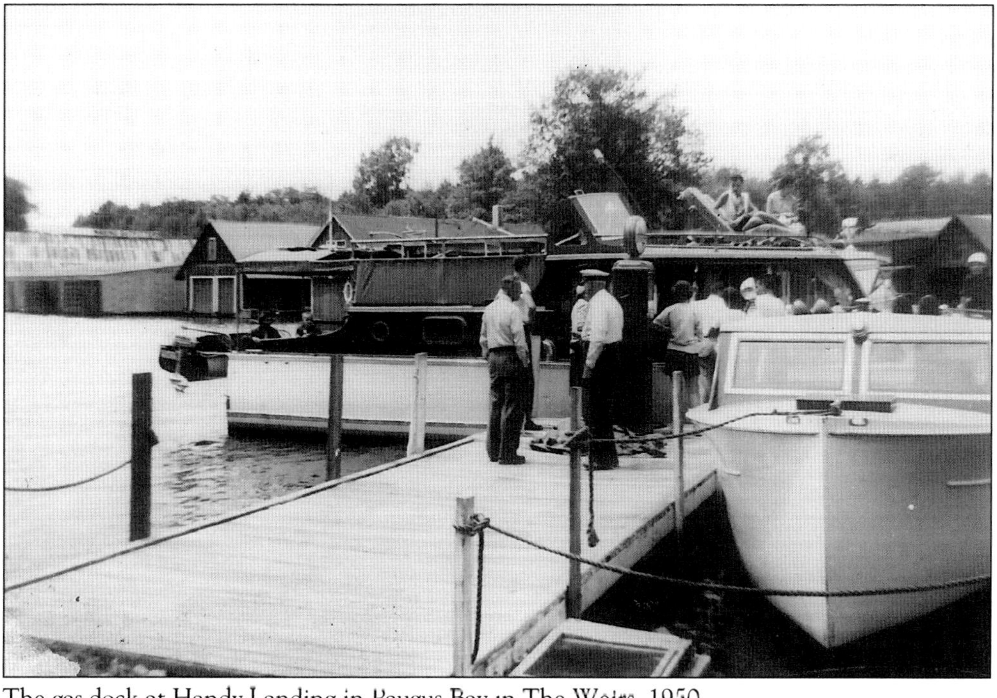

The gas dock at Handy Landing in Paugus Bay in The Weirs, 1950.

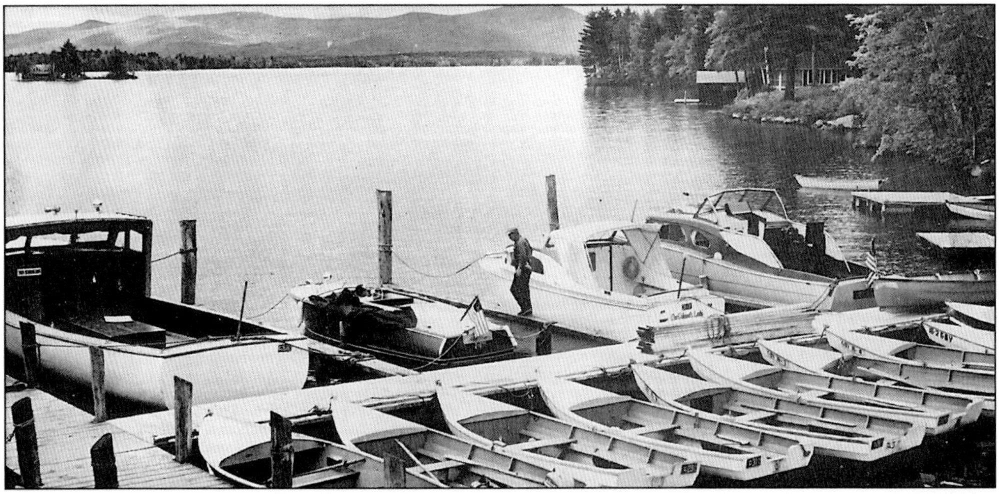

The Goodhue Boat Yard in Gilford on the shore of Lake Winnipesaukee. The mountains in the distance are the Ossipees and the small island on the left is Rock Island, located just south of Locke's Island, 1951.

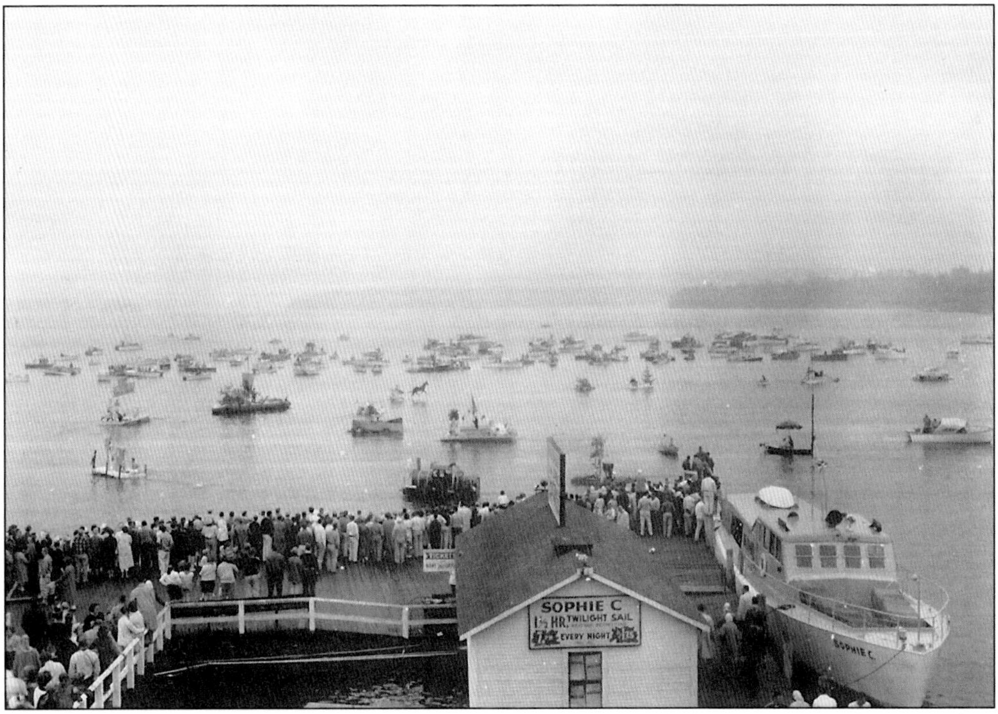

The Weirs Bay carnival of strange boats, 1950s. The small house in the foreground is where the Winnipesaukee Steamboat Co. sold their tickets for a ride on the *Mount Washington* and *Sophie C.*

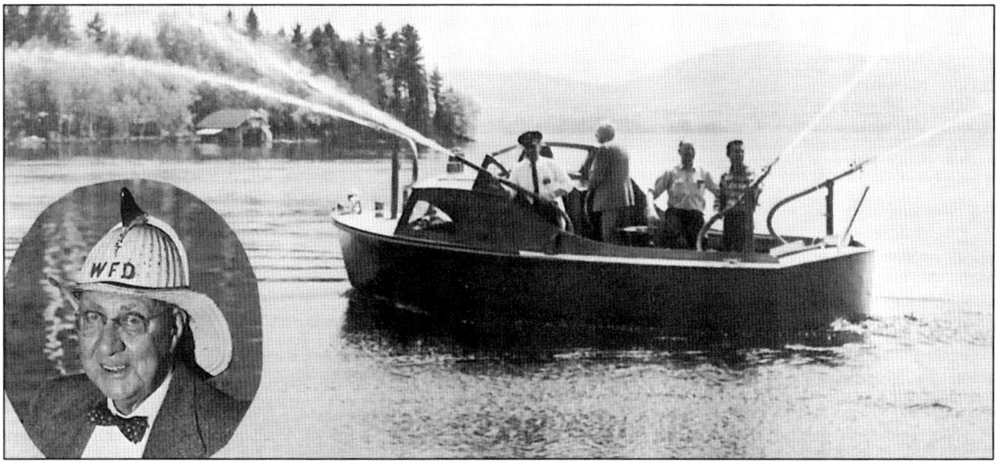

Dr. Herbert W. Drury's fire boat. In 1965, Captain Drury of Tuftonboro Neck is seen in this trim craft equipped with four custom-built nozzles which are powered by two nine-h.p. Gurham-Rupp pumps with an output of 310 gallons per minute. This craft can send a stream 150 feet in any direction. The apparatus is mounted on a 22-foot fiberglass hull, drawing 27 inches of water. Propelled by a 90 h.p. marine engine, the vessel can reach speeds of up to 25.6 knots.

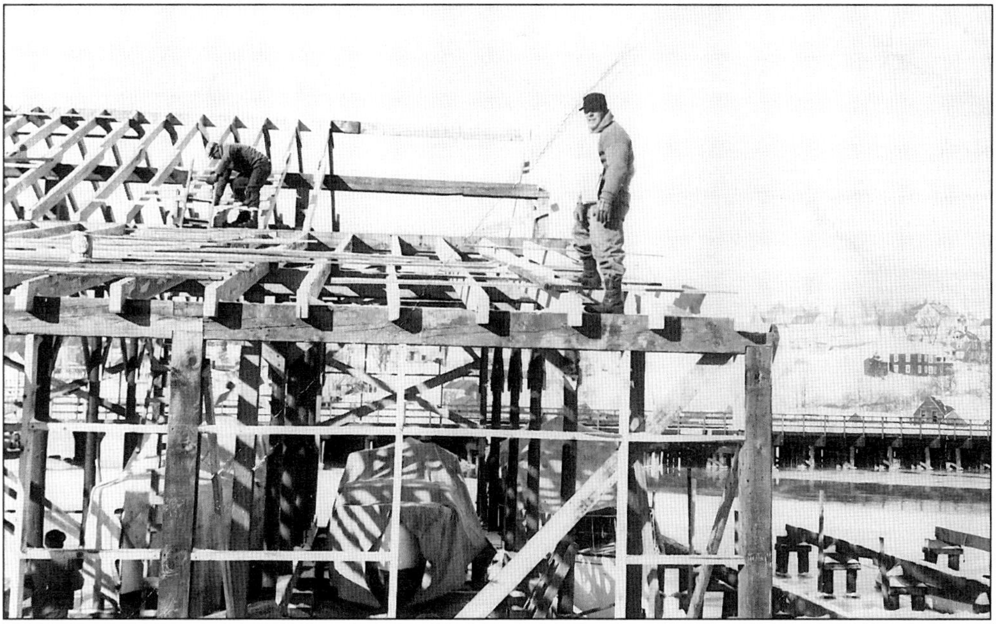

Irwin Marine under construction in Lakeport, New Hampshire, 1944–45. The temperature? Two degrees below zero. Pictured here are Floyd Dearborn and Bill Bastell. In order to build this structure, Jim Irwin had to buy an old railroad bridge in Winnisquam. They dismantled the bridge to get the old timbers. Due to the war effort, lumber was not readily available. This building was the original housing of what is now Irwin Marine on Union Avenue in Lakeport on Lake Paugus. The small boat on the right is the *Scamp*, a 77-foot boat.

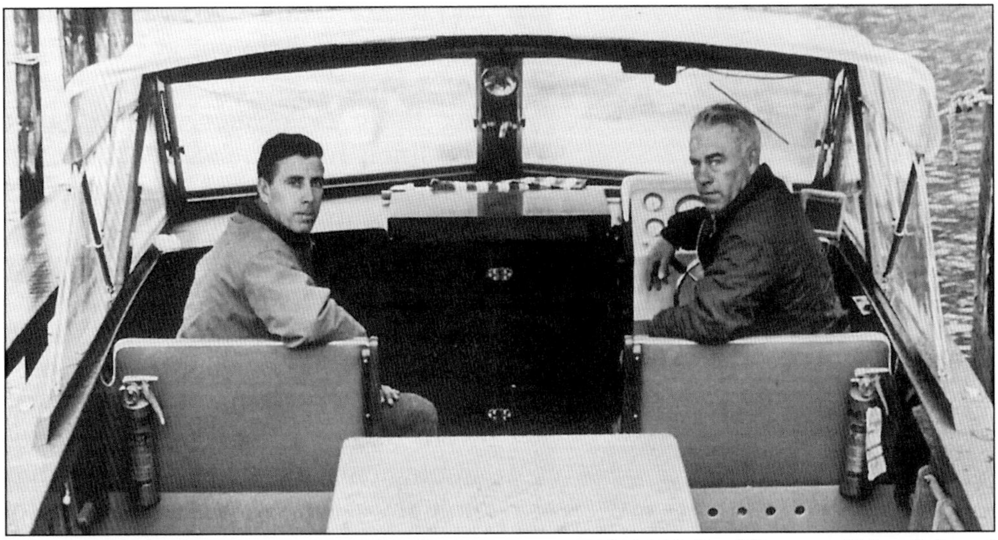

The New Hampshire Department of Safety's marine patrol, 1966. Brad Bryant of Meredith and Dick Dame of Laconia, lake supervisors for the department of safety, are seen in their patrol boat ready to set out on the "Big Lake" to ensure the safety of motorists and vacationers alike. Dick Dame, foreman of navigation, was charged with maintaining navigational aids on all New Hampshire's waters. Both men operated out of a Gilford marina, which the state had purchased in the fall of 1965.

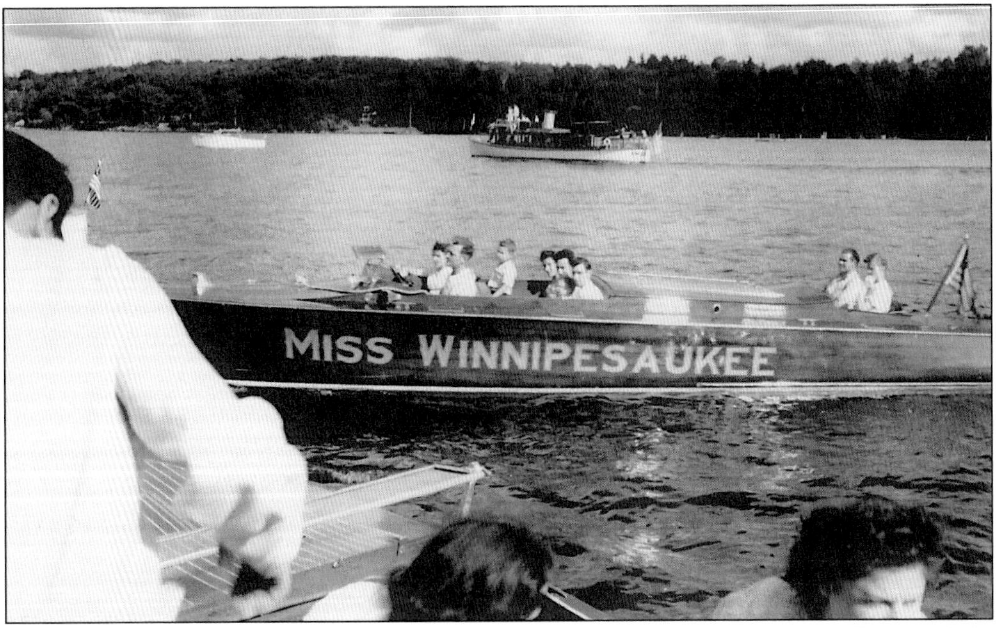

The *Miss Winnipesaukee* speed boat entertaining visitors on a boat ride in Weirs Bay, 1941. In 1931, Jim Irwin of Laconia started this boat service from The Weirs. Bob Belford is the pilot of the 28-foot craft. Notice the *Uncle Sam* in the back ground as she enters the bay on her trek to deliver mail to the many islands, and the small white boat in the far distance, which was a public utilities boat (a patrol boat) before the safety service came into operation. The small white spot on the right is the old Endicott raft before the beach was fully developed at The Weirs.

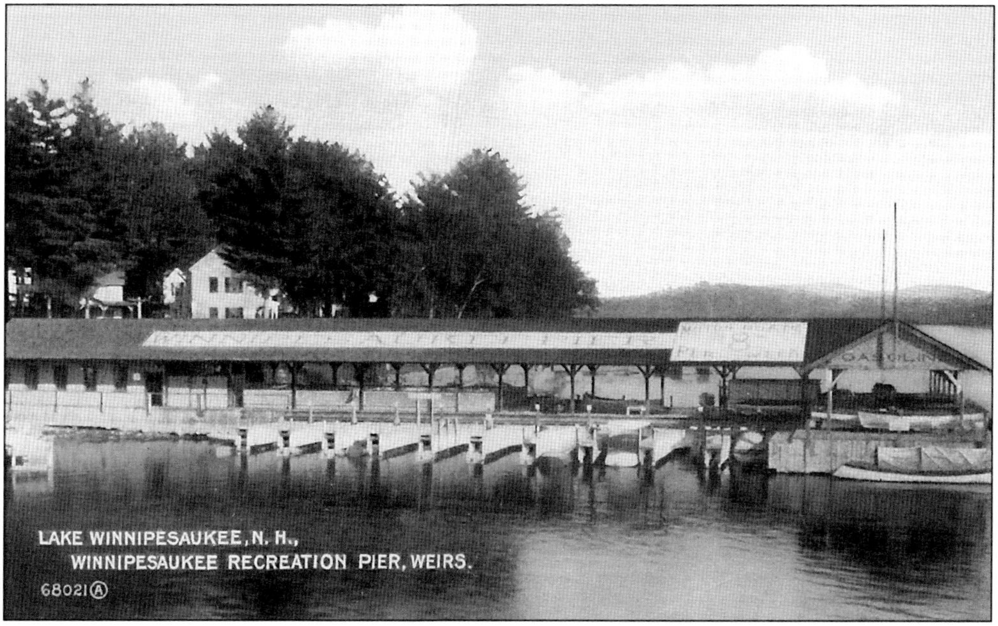

Winnipesaukee Pier, The Weirs, 1930s. "The largest motorboat 'Garage' in the world," says Jim Irwin. "Motorboat garage or livery may not be the right name to call my business of renting boats on Lake Winnipesaukee. Some have called it a marina garage, but we stick to our 'Winnipesaukee Pier Boats To-Let.' " Pictured are summer resorters about to start off in the standardized 20-footers.

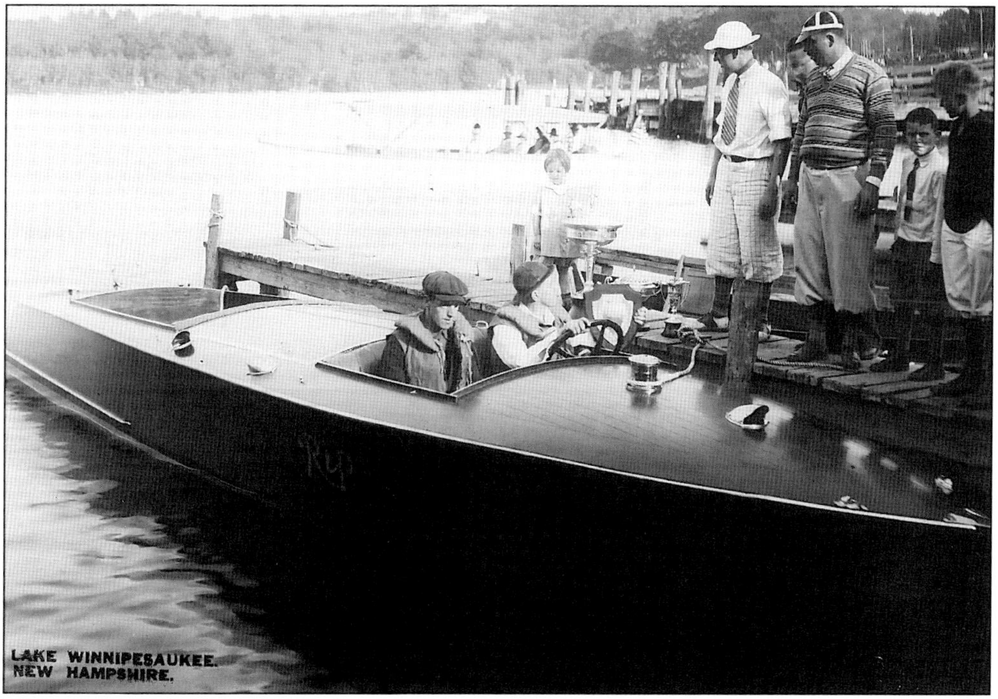

The *Rip III* and Glen Scott, pilot. Here Jim Irwin, wearing a white hat, is seen judging the annual boat show at The Weirs. The young girl looking on is Dotty Irwin, 1935.

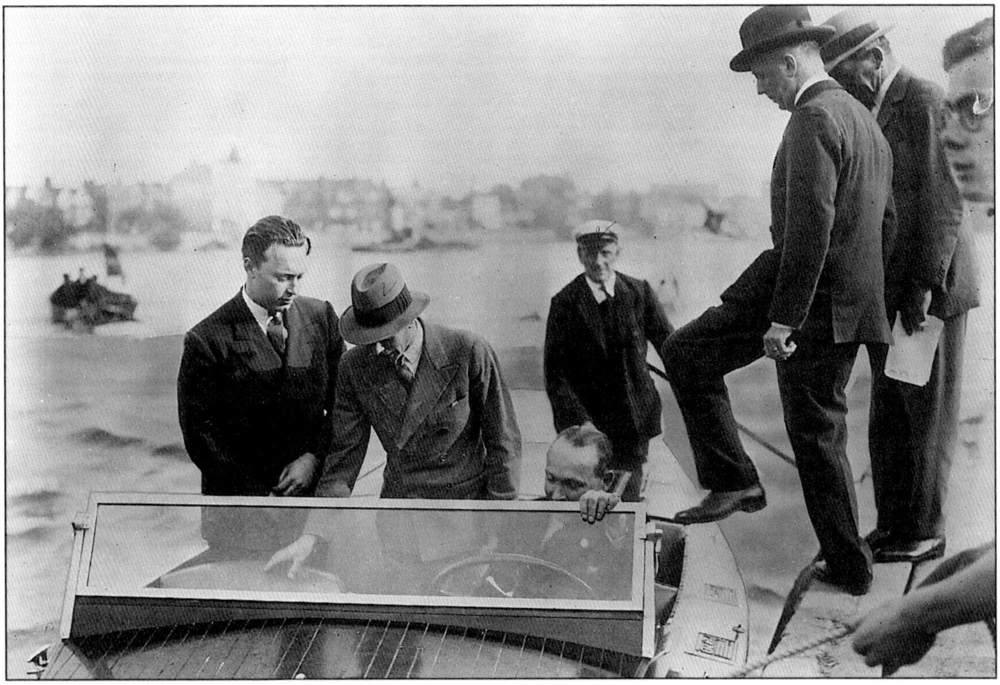

A rare photograph of Captain Lavallee, center with his white captain's hat, and John Goodhue at the helm, Paugus Bay, early 1930s.

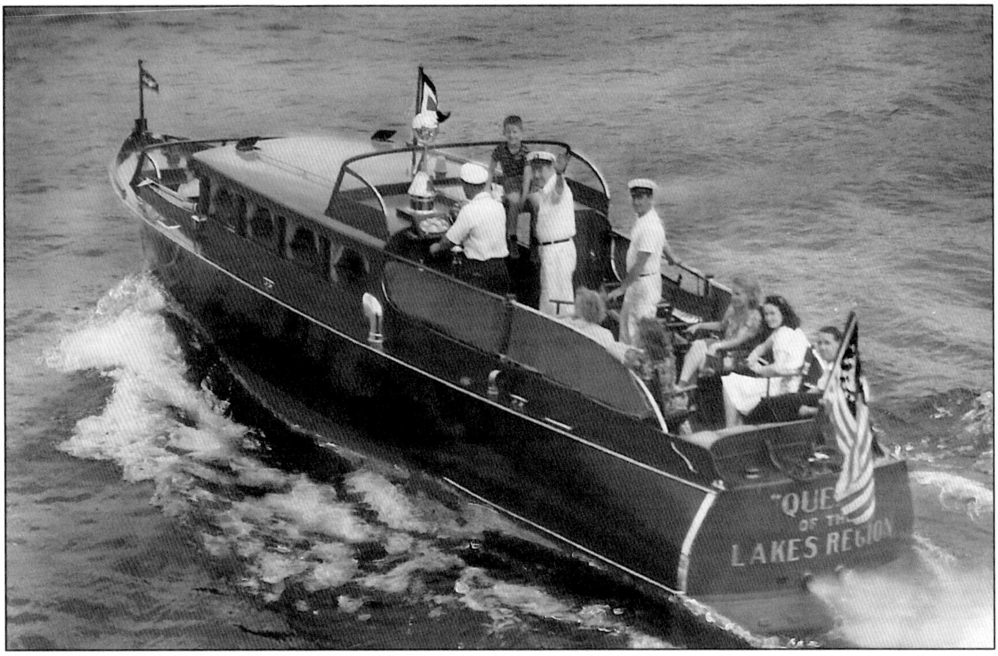

Queen of the Lakes Region. Piloted here by Floyd Dearborn, it was a Model A1-20—a 38-foot commuter with a single 275-h.p. V-8 Chris-Craft engine—owned by Jim Irwin. Jim is seen waving at the photographer with his son Jack sitting on the dash directly in front of him, early 1930s. In 1942, he donated the vessel to the Coast Guard for the war effort with the understanding that it would be returned after the war, but it never was.

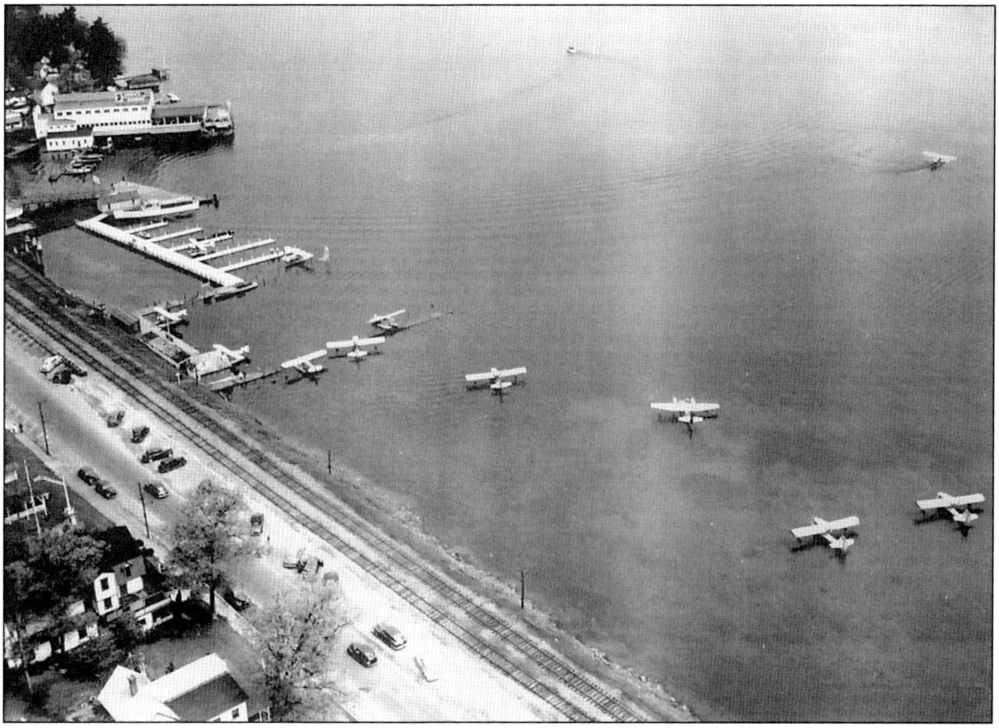

A gathering of sea planes at Weirs Beach, 1950s.

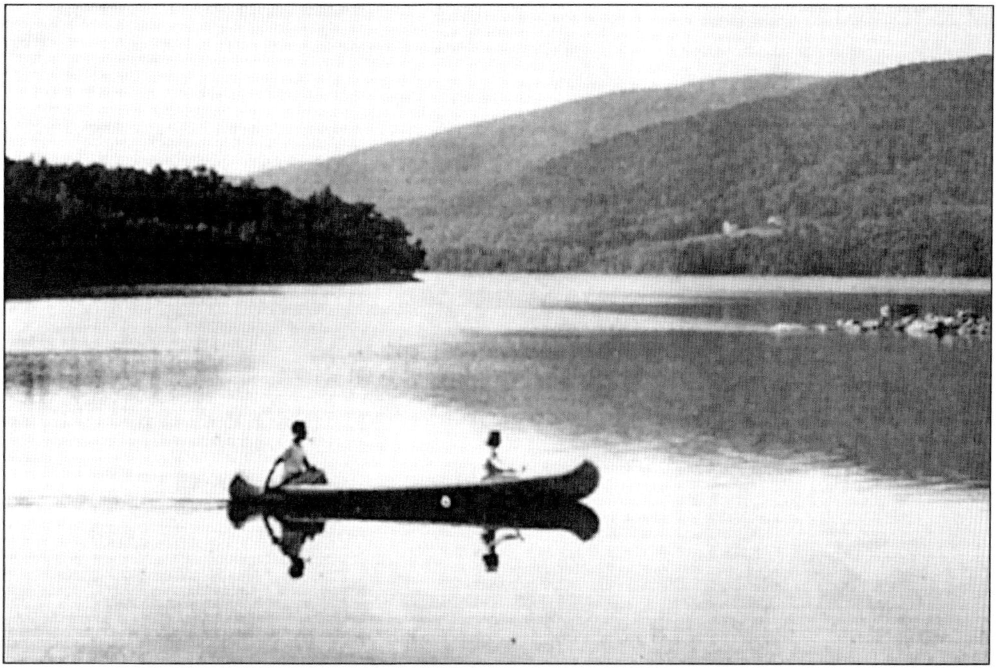

A quiet moment canoeing the calm water in Moultonboro. In the distance is Red Hill, majestically watching over Center Harbor and the northern bay of Winnipesaukee.

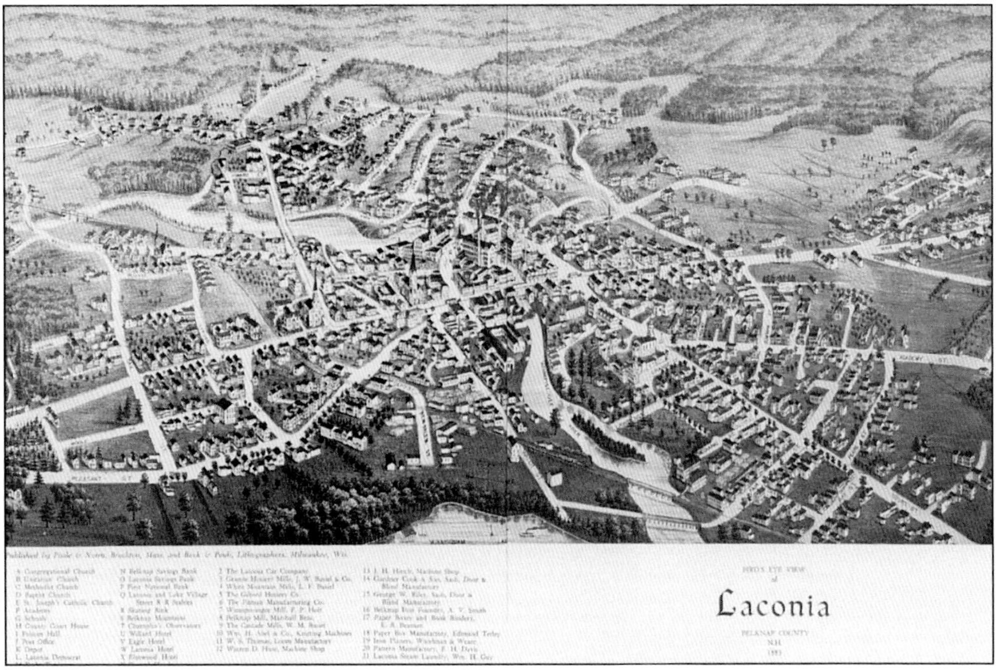

A bird's-eye view of Laconia, Belknap County, New Hampshire, 1883.

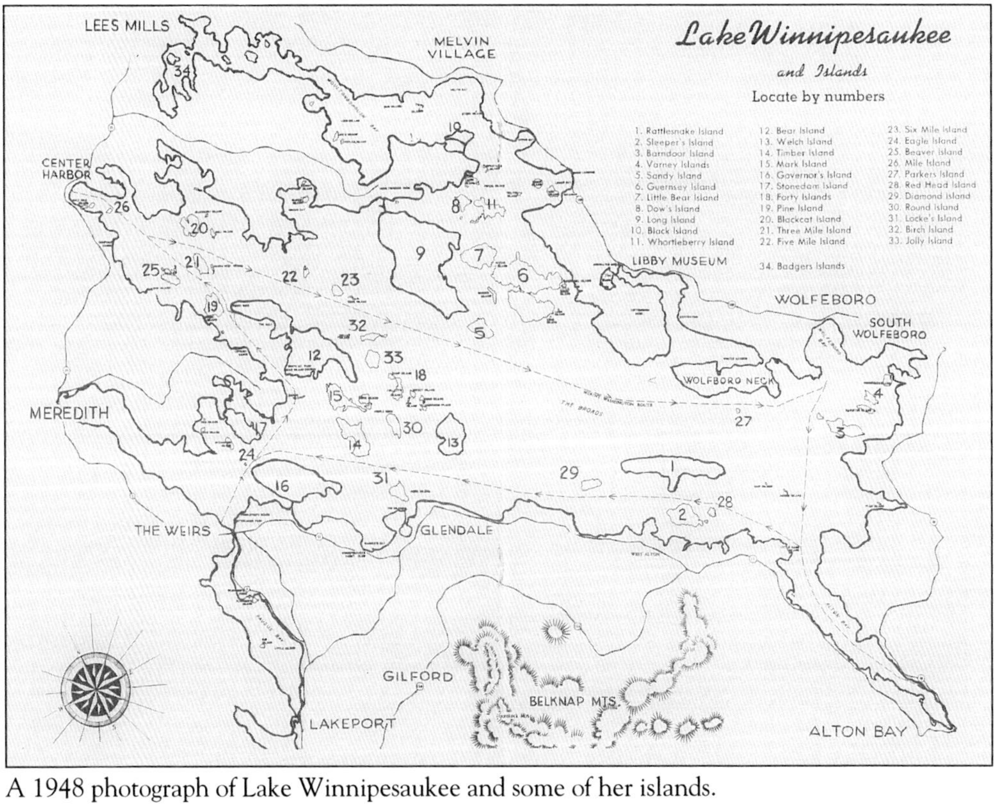

A 1948 photograph of Lake Winnipesaukee and some of her islands.

Four

Port Towns and Landmarks

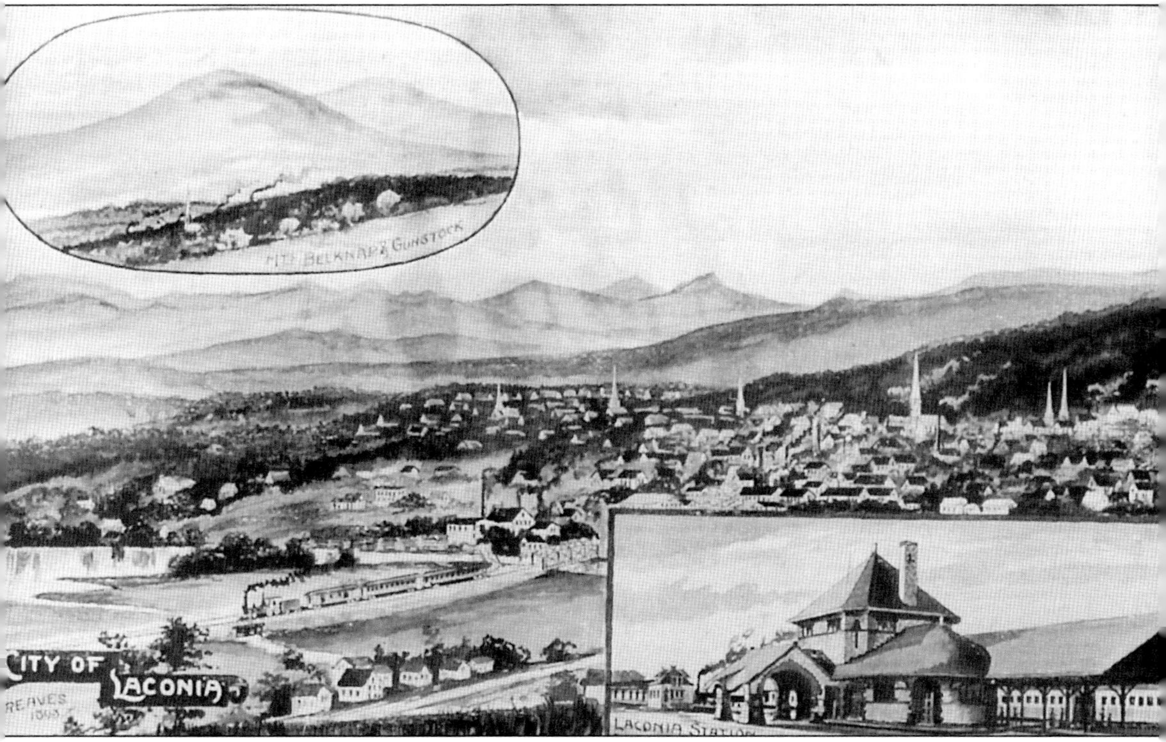

The city of Laconia, 1893. Along the eastern shore of Lake Winnisquam lies the city, its northern limits being only 1 or 2 miles removed from the mouth of Lake Winnipesaukee. On the east, its territory reaches into the Belknap section, and on the south joins the towns of Belmont, Tilton, and Winnisquam.

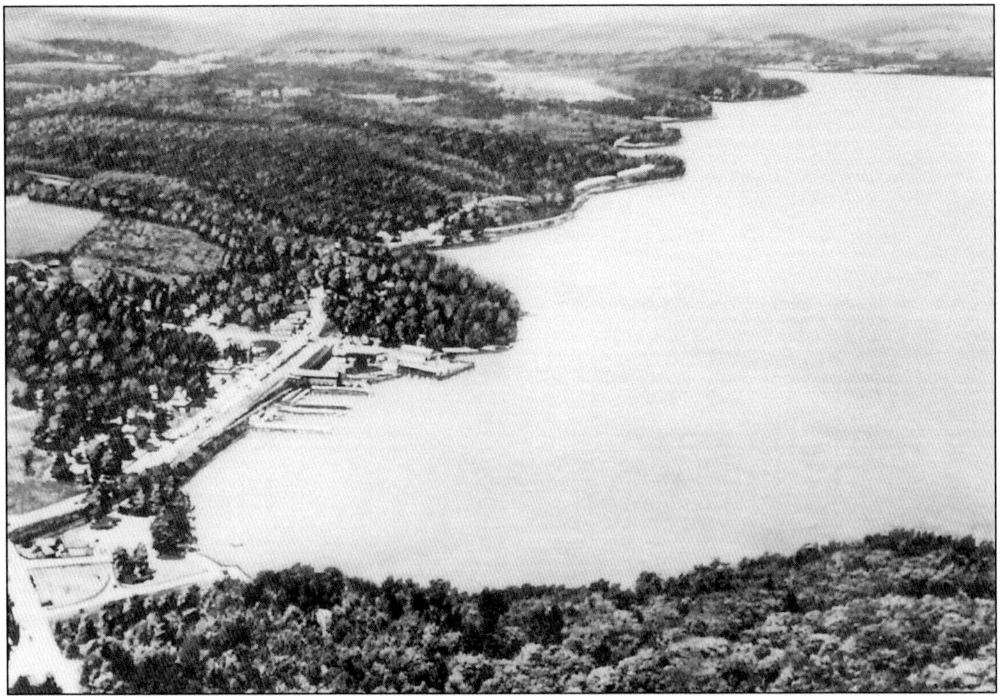

An aerial view of The Weirs and Meredith Bay. The Weirs derived its name from fish weirs, a trap constructed by Native Americans hundreds of years ago. Today, this community is a popular summer resort to keep both the old and young busy with amusements. In the distance (5 miles) is Meredith Village—the Latchkey to the White Mountains.

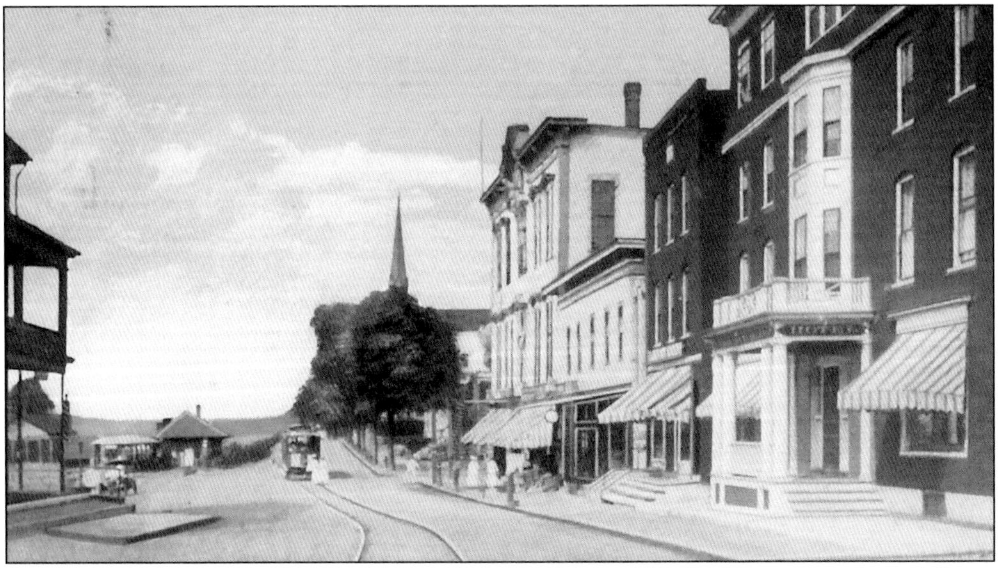

Lakeport, 1920. A railroad station is on the left with an early electric car running up Union Avenue. Over the years there have been many names applied to this section of Laconia. The area has been called Upper Village, Batchelder's Mills, Furnace Village, Slab City, Folsom's Falls, Petite Quebec, Lake Village, Lake City, and Lakeville. Today, however, it is popularly and officially known as Lakeport.

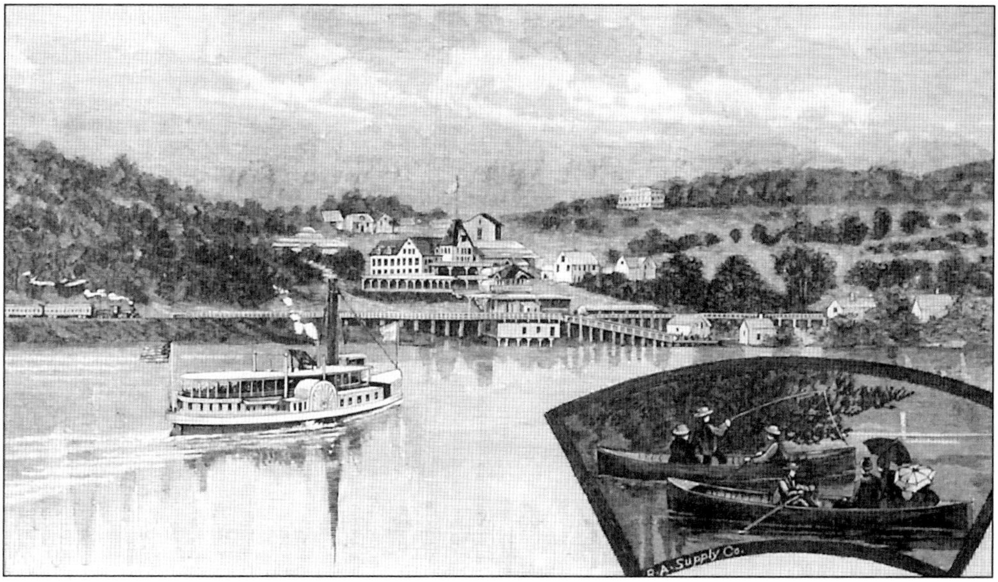

The Weirs during the mid-1800s with the Old Hotel Weirs on hillside. The Boston, Concord, & Montreal Railroad on the left is seen coming to the station to meet the steamer as it prepares to dock at the station.

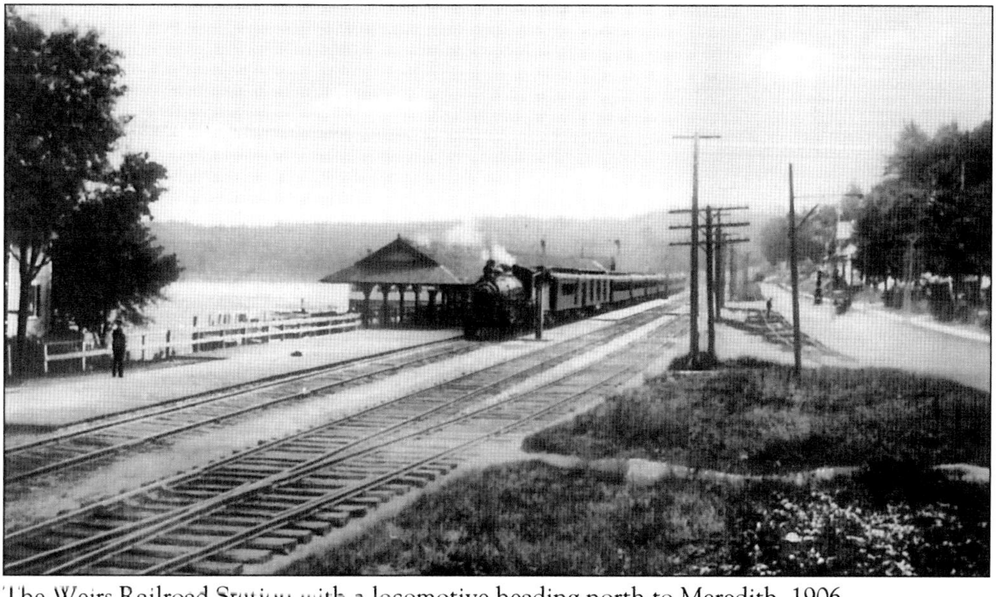

The Weirs Railroad Station with a locomotive heading north to Meredith, 1906.

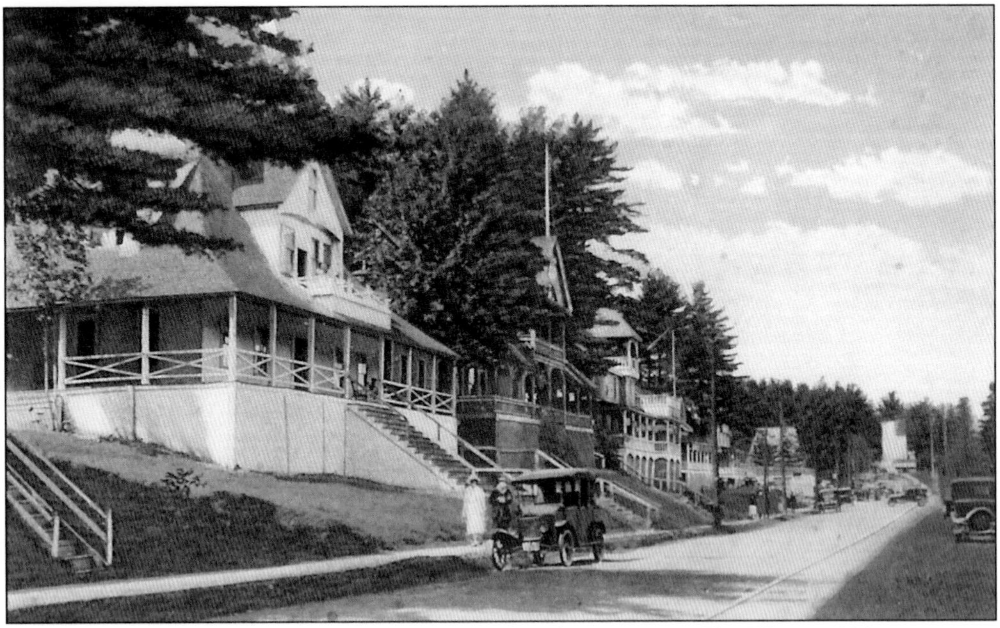

The New Hampshire Veterans' buildings and Lakeside Avenue at The Weirs, 1922.

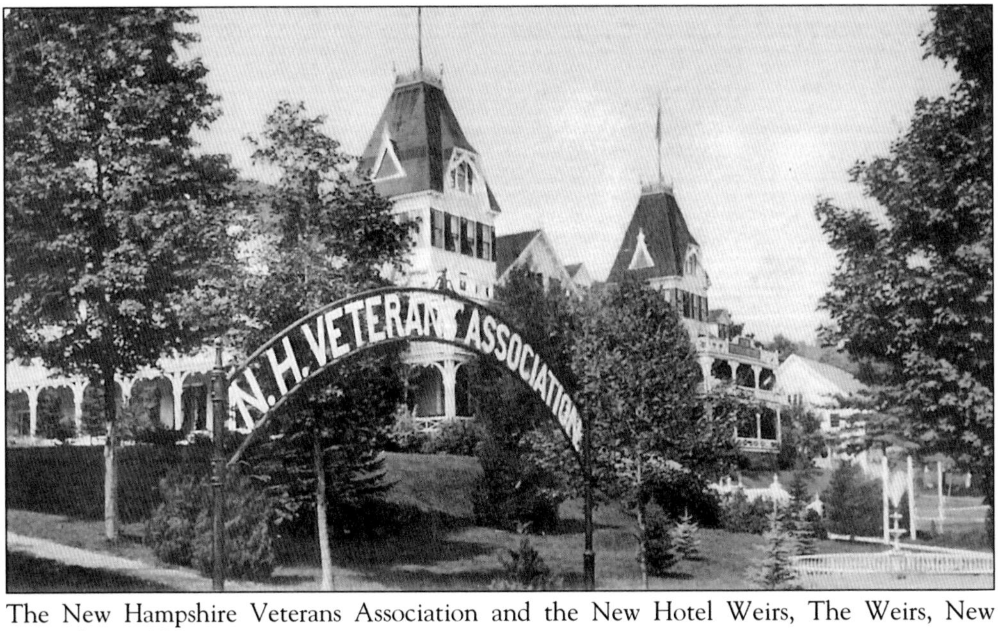

The New Hampshire Veterans Association and the New Hotel Weirs, The Weirs, New Hampshire, 1920s.

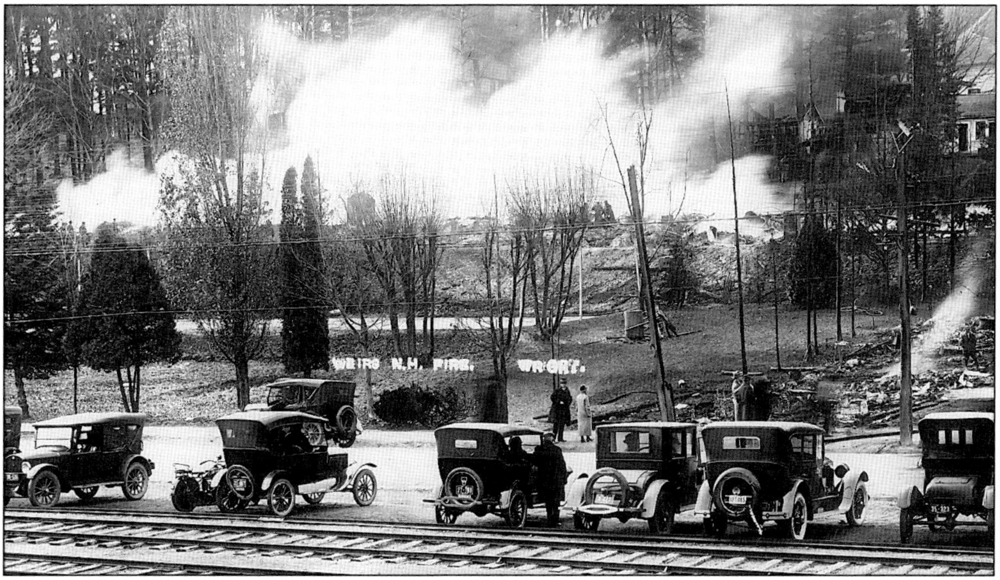

The New Hotel Weirs. The hotel, a popular summer resort in The Weirs for many years, burned to the ground on November 9, 1924. It burned along with 12 other landmarks on Lakeside Avenue and Tower Street, including the 1886 Methodist Church and the 1903 Music Hall. This photograph was taken from the Boardwalk and the Boston & Maine Railroad station.

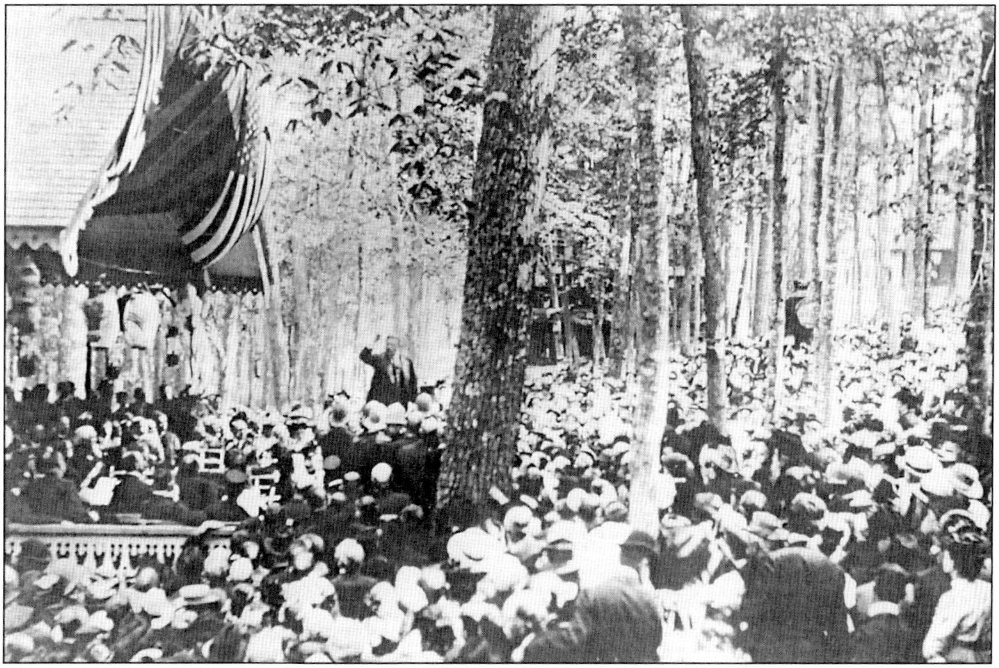

Teddy Roosevelt, seen here presenting a political speech during a brief stop at the Veterans Campgrounds while in route to the White Mountains.

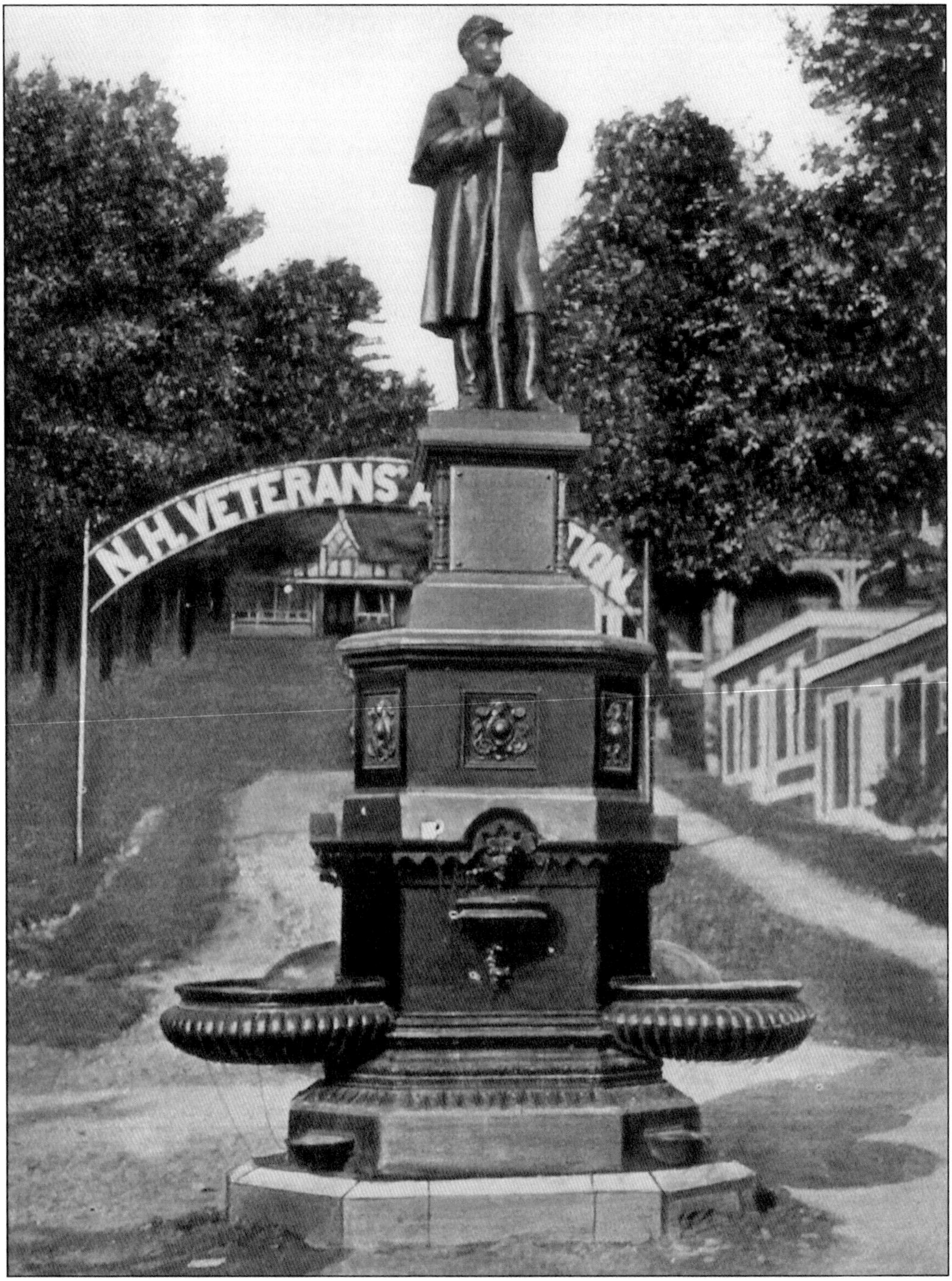

The Soldiers Monument at the Veterans' Headquarters on Lakeside Avenue at The Weirs. This monument is that of Loammi Bean, a member of the 8th New Hampshire Volunteer regiment, who was killed in the Battle of Georgia Landing, Louisiana, on October 27, 1862. Private Bean was one of the first men to fall, so in his honor "and to the memory of thousands of other gallant soldiers who laid down their lives that the Union might be preserved," his daughter erected this monument next to the headquarters of the New Hampshire Veterans' Association and Veterans' Avenue on August 29, 1894.

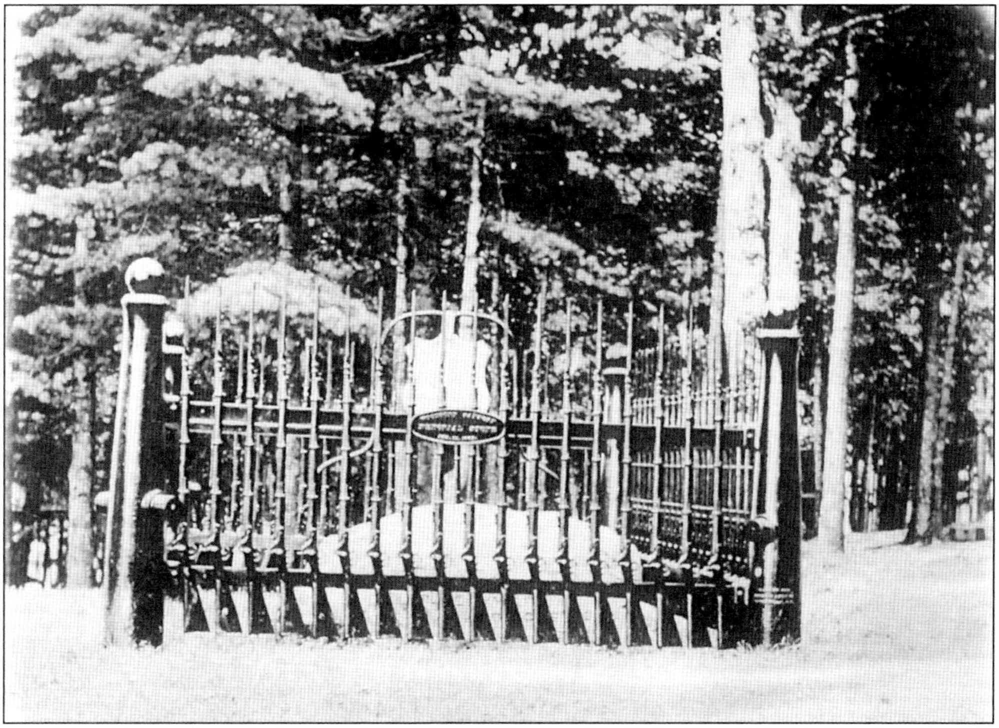

The Woodbury Sanborn Memorial at Veterans Grove at The Weirs. This stone was dedicated to the 12th New Hampshire Regiment in 1883, and was entirely enclosed by a cast-and-wrought-iron fence featuring pickets of cast-iron muskets with corner posts of vertical iron cannons, topped by cannonballs at Veterans Grove at The Weirs, 1880s.

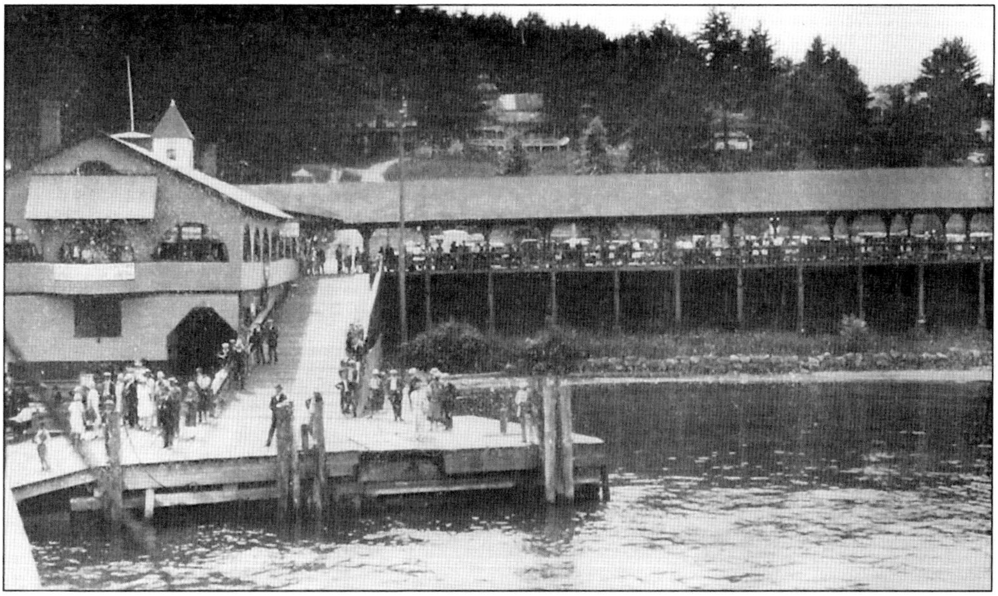

The Weirs Railroad Station and dock with the Veterans' campground in the distance as seen from the steamer *Mount Washington*, 1928.

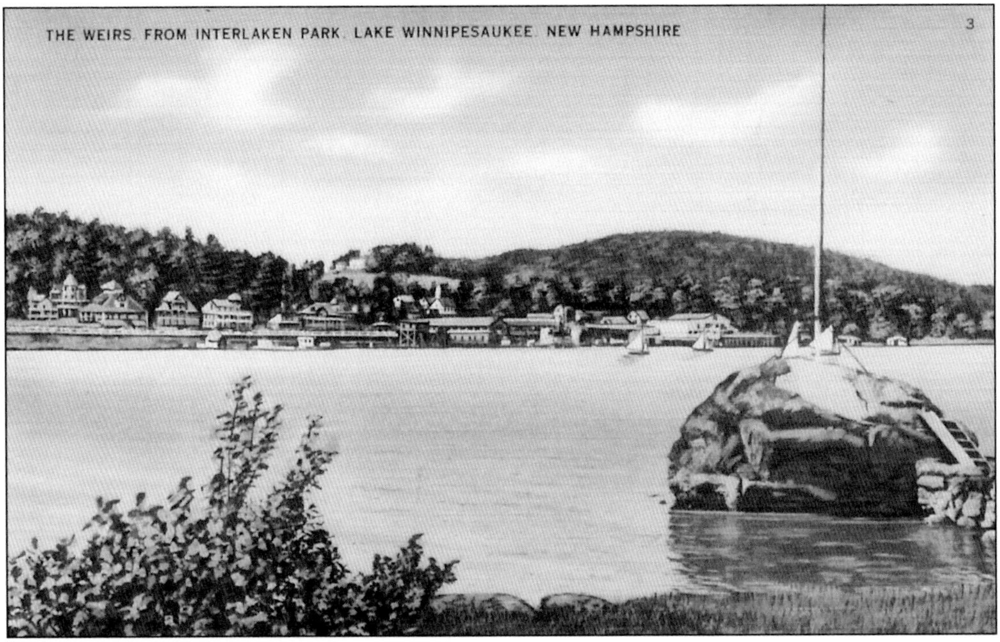

The Weirs as seen from Interlaken Park, 1940s.

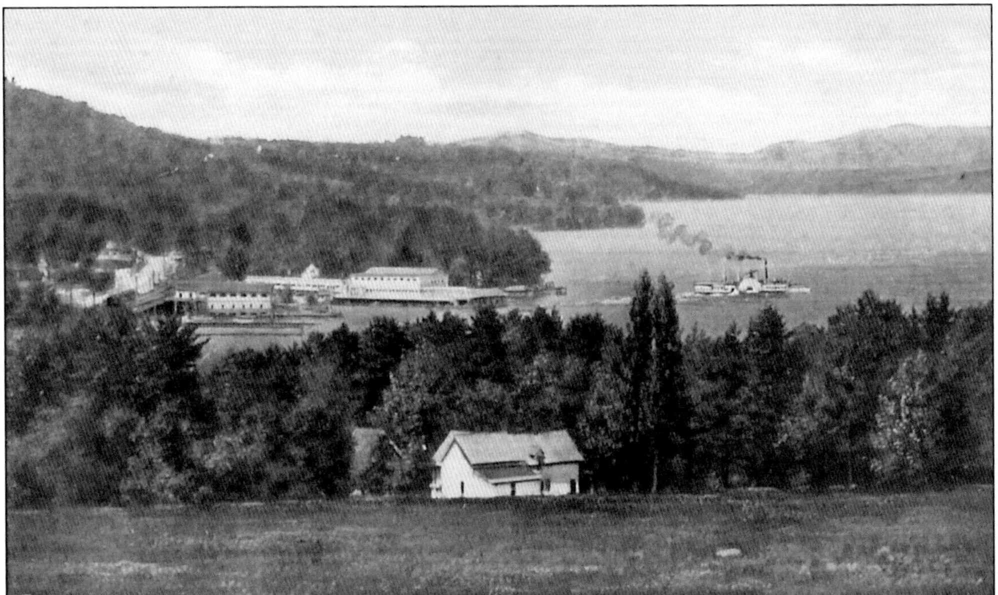

The Weirs and Meredith Bays as seen from White Oaks, 1930s. Note, the steamer *Mount Washington* has just left the dock on her daily trip around the lake.

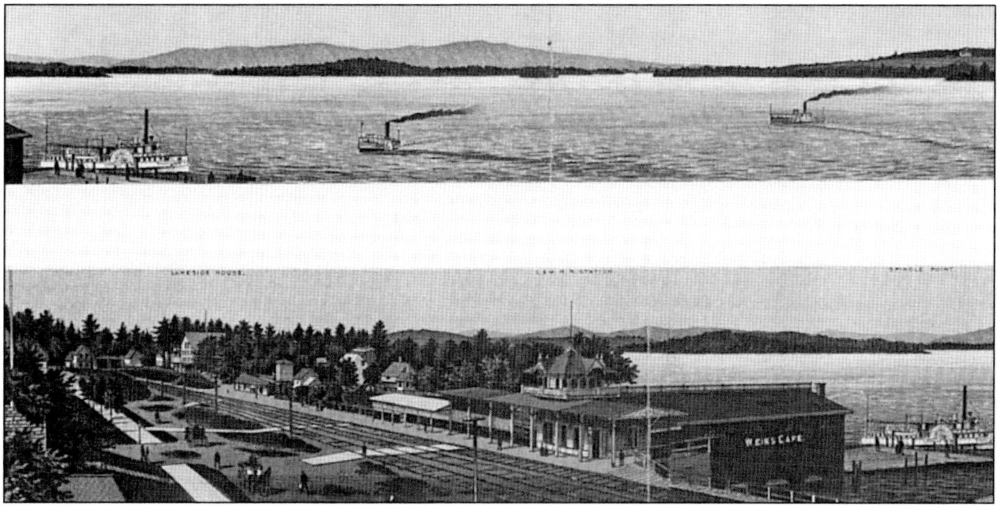

A panoramic view of the Weirs and Meredith Bays, with the *Lady of the Lake* at dockside, as seen from The Weirs during the 1880s.

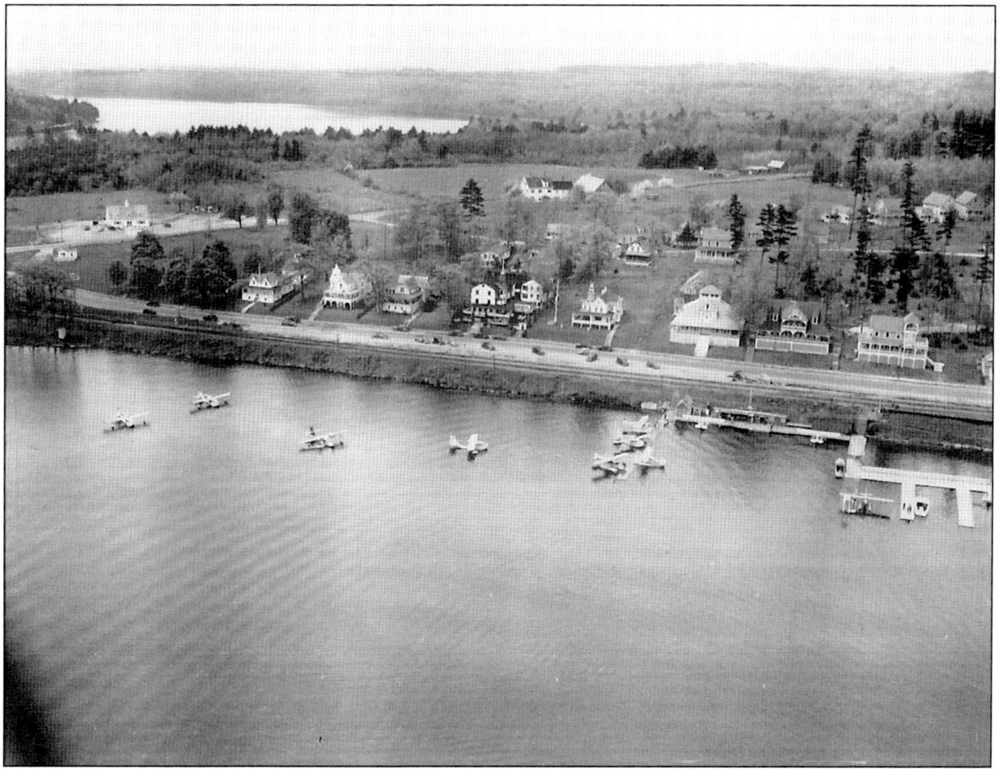

An aerial view of Weirs Beach and Paugus Bay as seen during the 1940s. Note the number of early sea planes stationed near the city docks. The body of water in the background, Paugus Bay, leads to Lakeport and Laconia, New Hampshire.

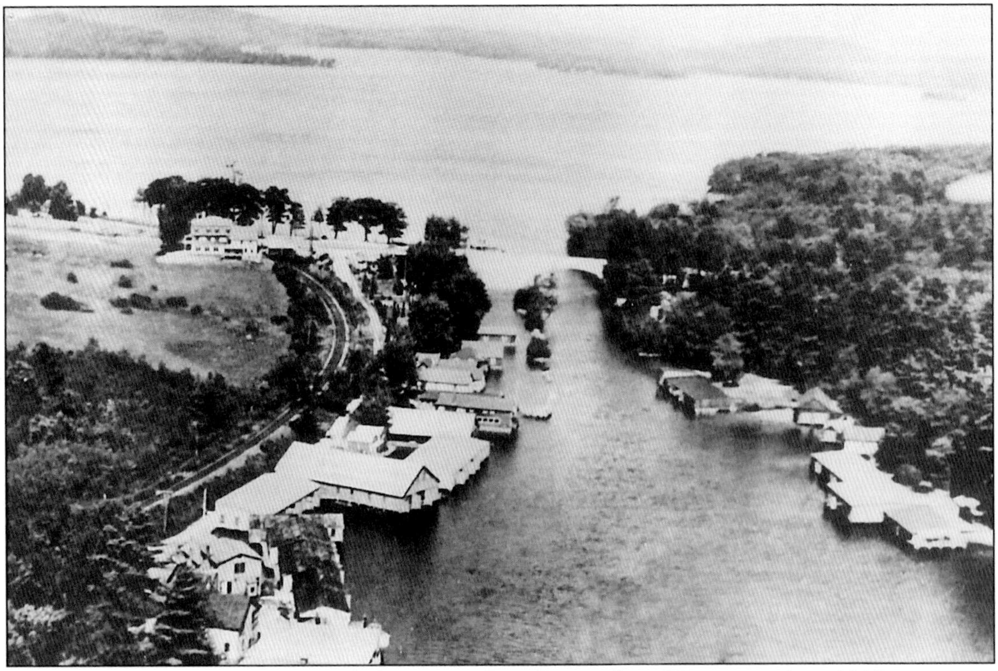

The Weirs Channel looking north from Long Bay (Paugus) to Winnipesaukee, 1910.

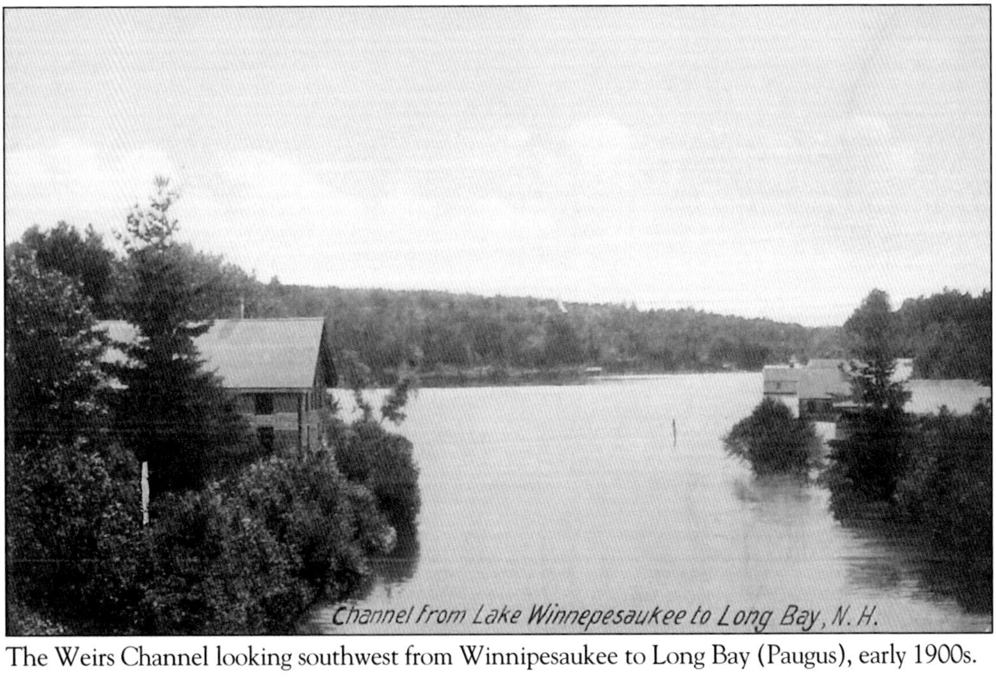

The Weirs Channel looking southwest from Winnipesaukee to Long Bay (Paugus), early 1900s.

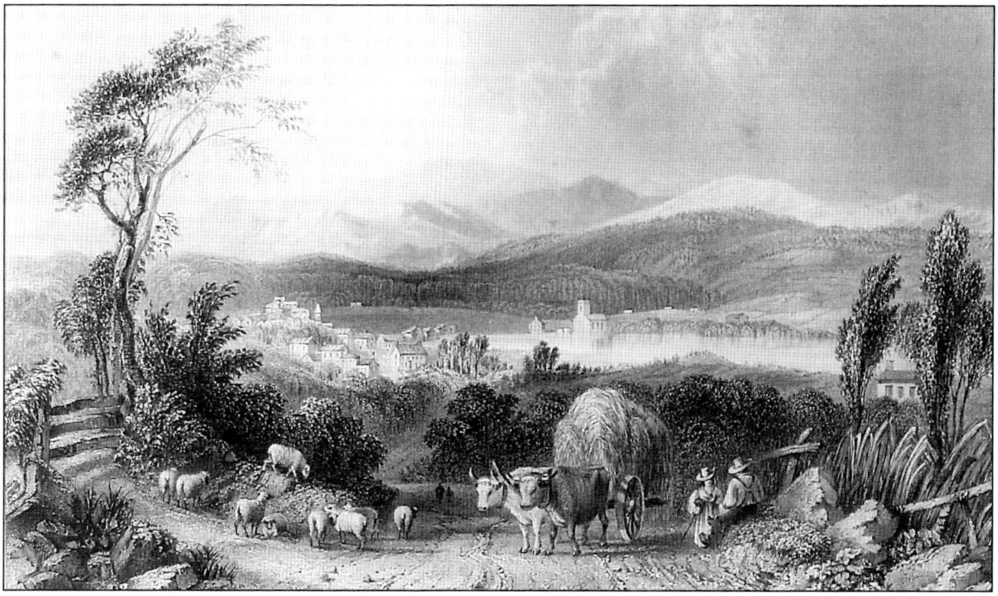

A view of Meredith and the White Mountains from Ladd Hill looking northwest, 1838. Meredith was first known as Palmer's Town, named so from Samuel Palmer of Hampton, New hampshire, an early settler who, as a teacher of surveying and navigation, laid out much of the land surrounding Lake Winnipesaukee. (Sketch by William H. Bartlett.)

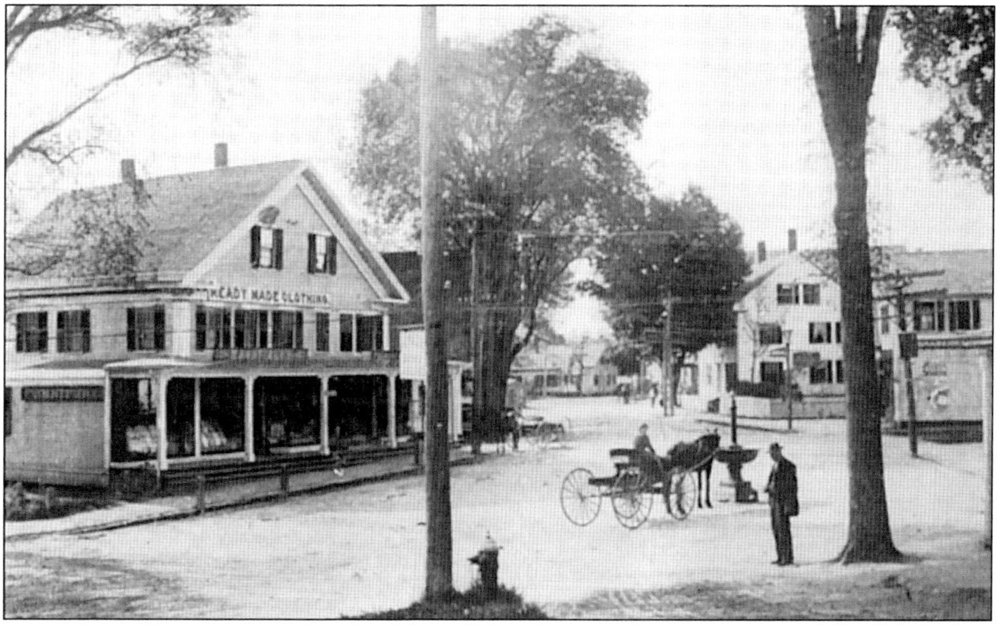

Post Office Square, Meredith, New Hampshire, 1880s. This community was one of the first towns to have a charter granted by the proprietors in 1748, and as most of the lots went to prospective colonizers from Salem, Massachusetts, it was next called New Salem. In 1768 it was regranted to those who had not settled and renamed Meredith, after Sir William Meredith, a prominent member of the English Parliament.

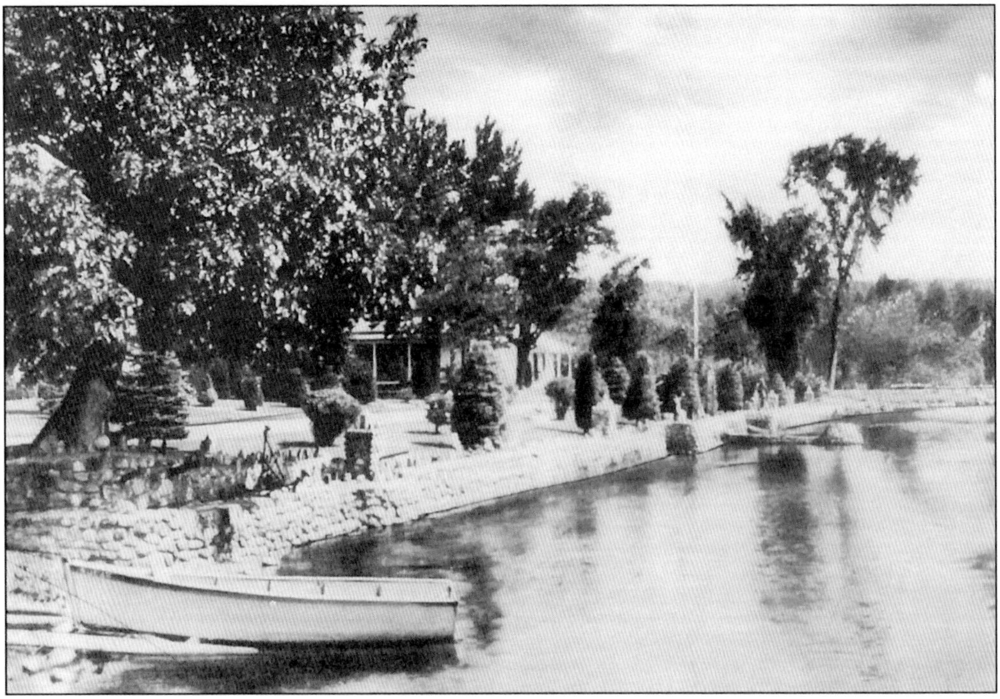

Clough Park on the northern shore of Lake Winnipesaukee, Meredith, New Hampshire. This town has the unique distinction of touching four beautiful lakes—Winnipesaukee, Winnisquam, Wicwas, and Waukewan.

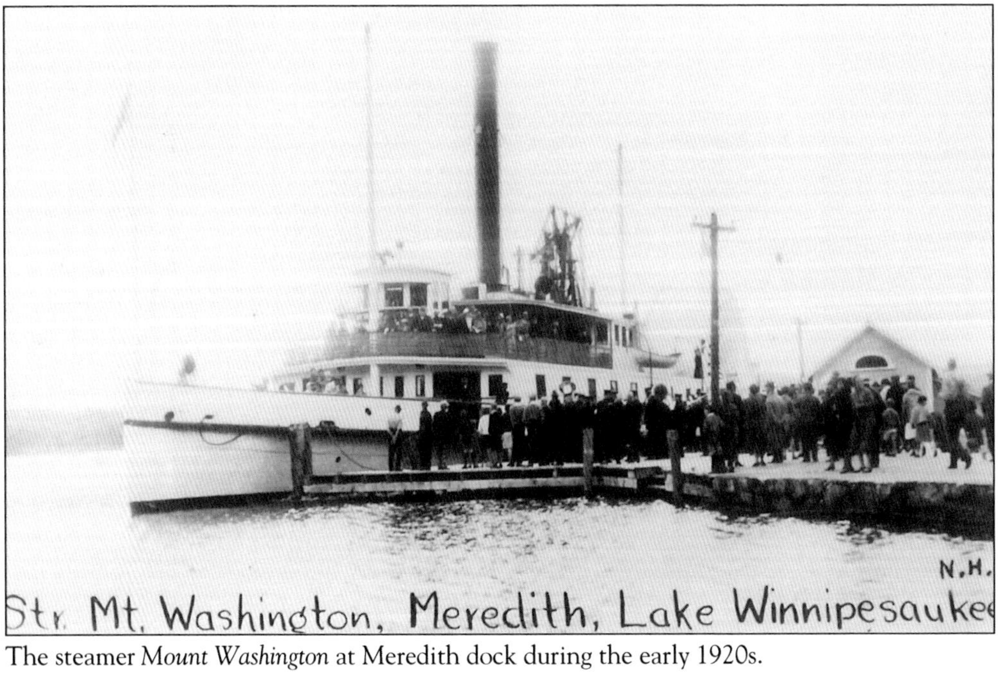

The steamer *Mount Washington* at Meredith dock during the early 1920s.

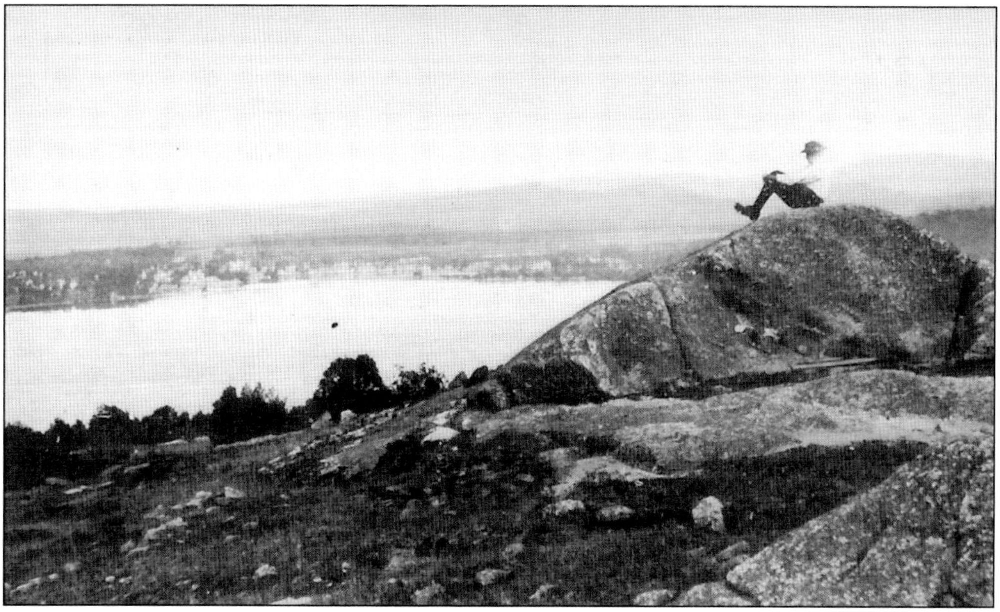

Meredith Village from the Pinnacle and Pinnacle Rock, Meredith, New Hampshire, 1900s.

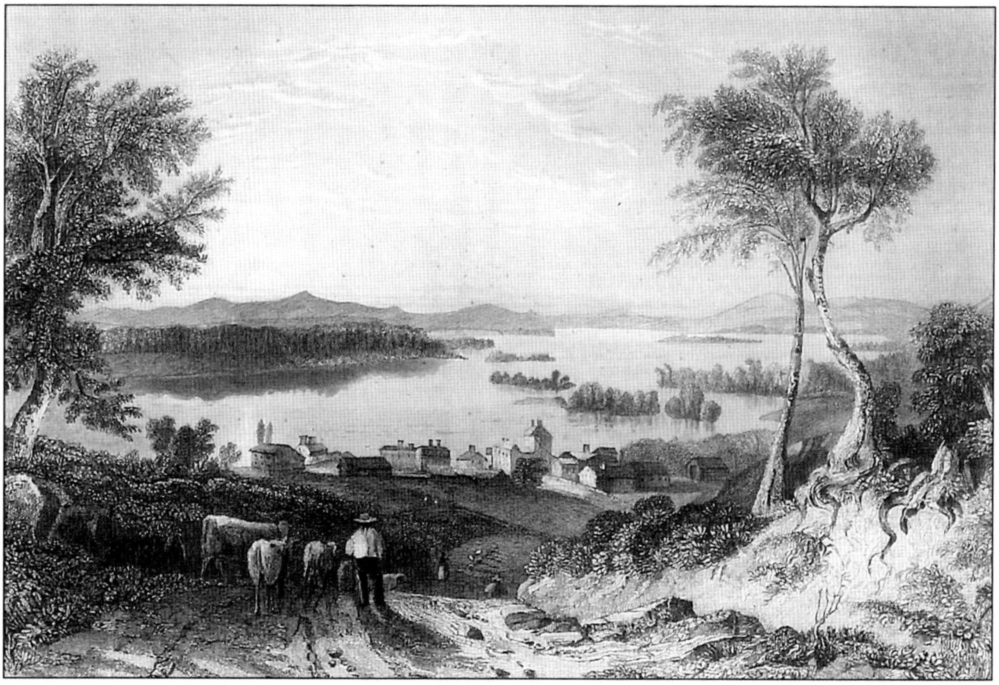

Center Harbor, New Hampshire, 1836. This village is beautifully situated at the northern tip of the lake among mountainous landmasses cloaked with stately evergreens. Towering elms along the shoreline are reminiscent of the days when John Greenleaf Whittier sat beneath them and was inspired to write poetic passages on the grandeur of the land and lake. (A 1836 William H. Bartlett print.)

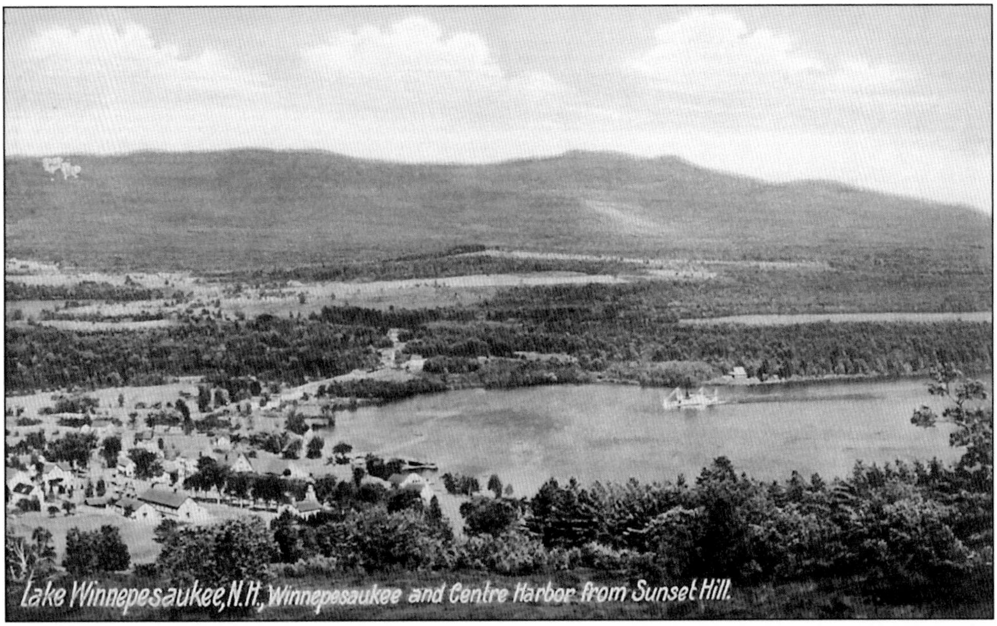

Lake Winnipesaukee and Center Harbor from Sunset Hill during the early 1900s. In the background is the Ossipee Mountain Range, which frames the eastern slope of the valley. Note the steamer *Mount Washington* in the center of the bay as it makes its final approach to the town dock.

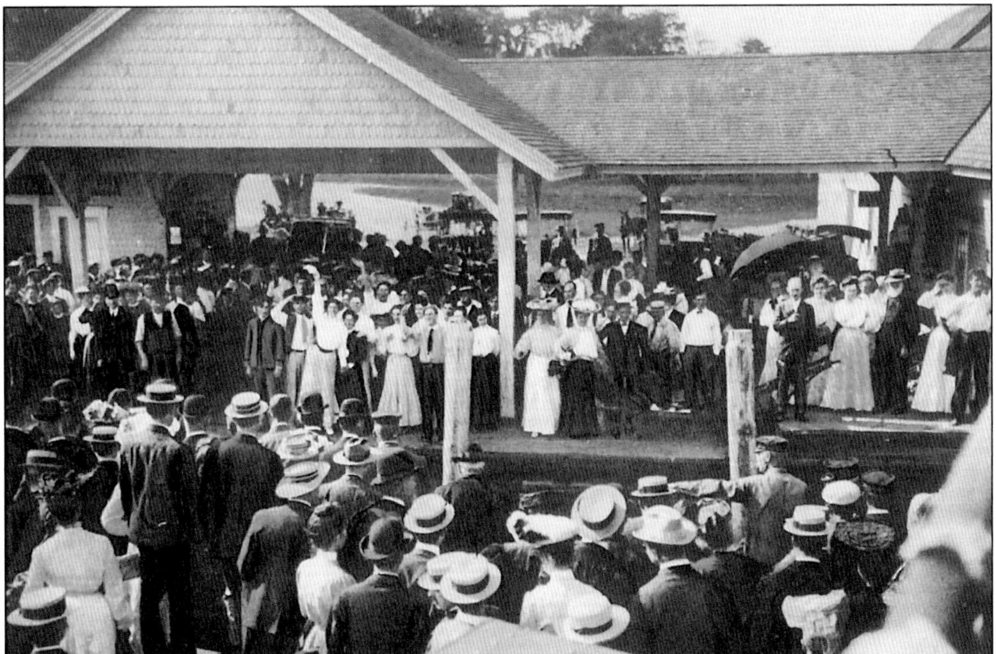

The Landing at Center Harbor. The side-wheeler *Mount Washington* prepares to dock at the landing in Center Harbor so as to take on passengers and unload baggage, early 1900s. The town has become one of New Hampshire's important summer resorts, being a landing place for the many lake steamers and a stagecoach terminus for tourists.

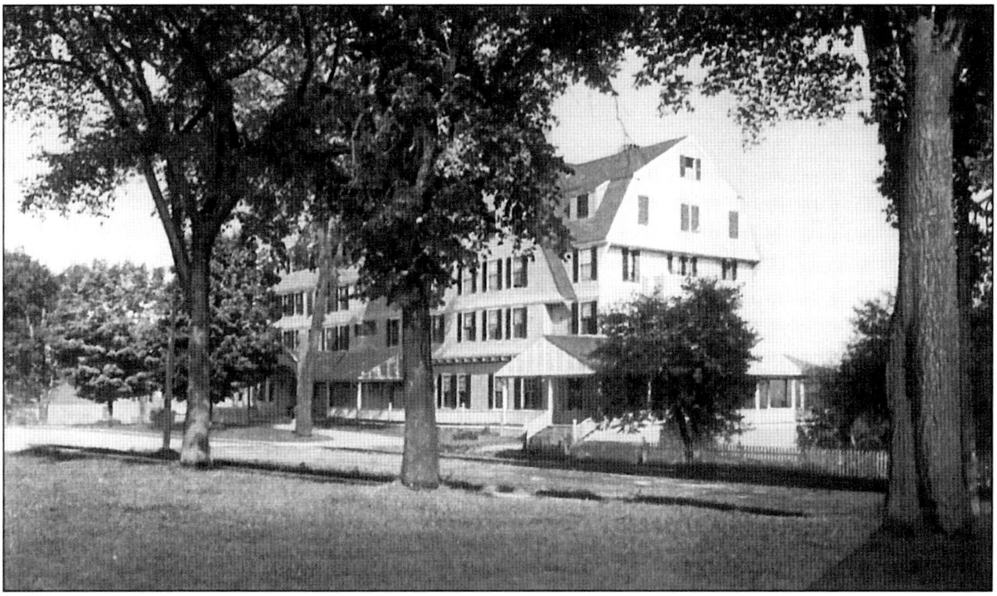

The Colonial Hotel in Center Harbor, New Hampshire, overlooking Winnipesaukee and the Ossipee Mountains, 1906. This hotel was originally known as the Senter Hotel. According to their promotional brochure, the hotel boasted 15 double fireplaces and 91 sleeping quarters. The name of the hotel was later changed to The Colonial. On June 20, 1919, the grand old hotel was destroyed by a fire.

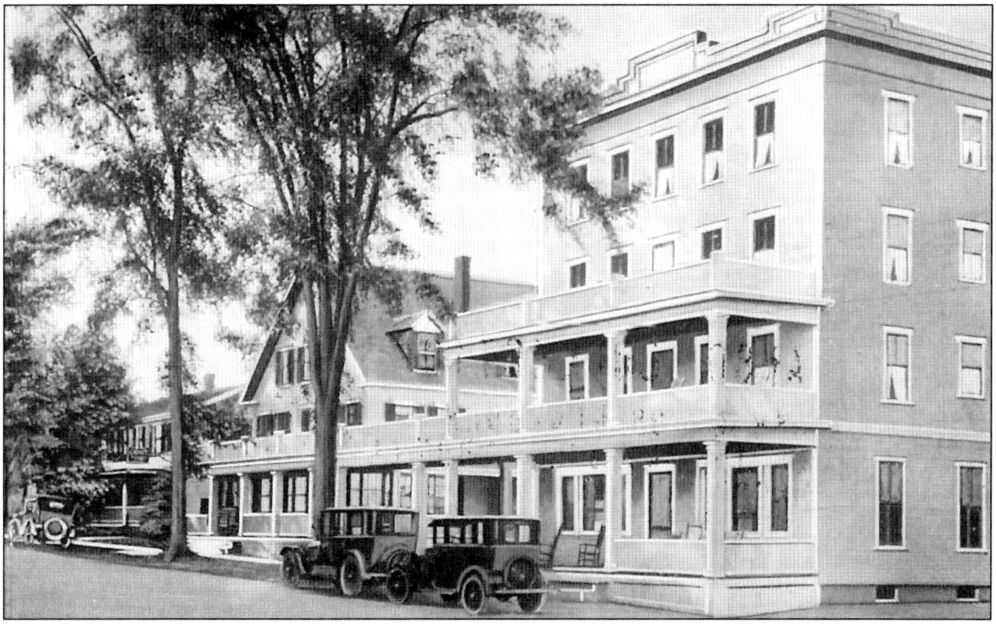

The Garnet Inn, Center Harbor, New Hampshire, 1920s. This quaint inn was extremely successful during the early 1900s, and among its visitors were the Roosevelts and the Duponts. Next to the Garnet Inn was a large building known as Independence Hall, later known as the Lamprey Hall. For a short time the inn was the home of the New Hampshire Summer Symphony. Due to disrepair and neglect, the inn has recently been taken down and now open land fills its void.

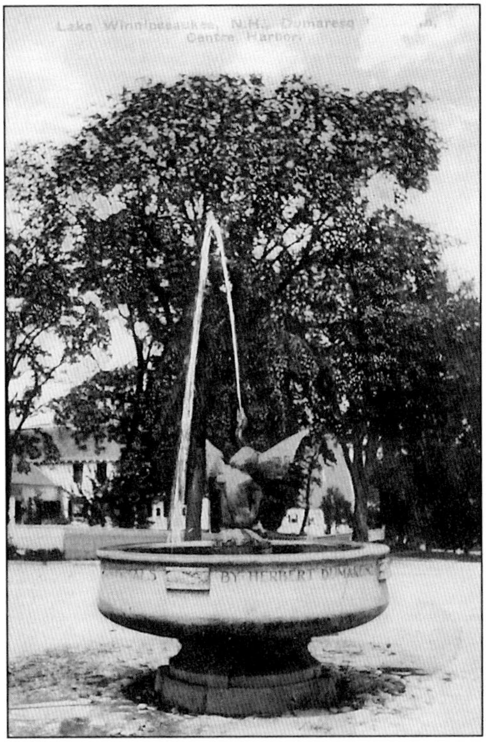

The Kona (Dumaresq) Fountain in Center Harbor. On September 23, 1907, Mr. Herbert Dumaresq gave a beautiful drinking fountain to the village of Center Harbor. This fountain has been a source of pride for the community ever since its inception.

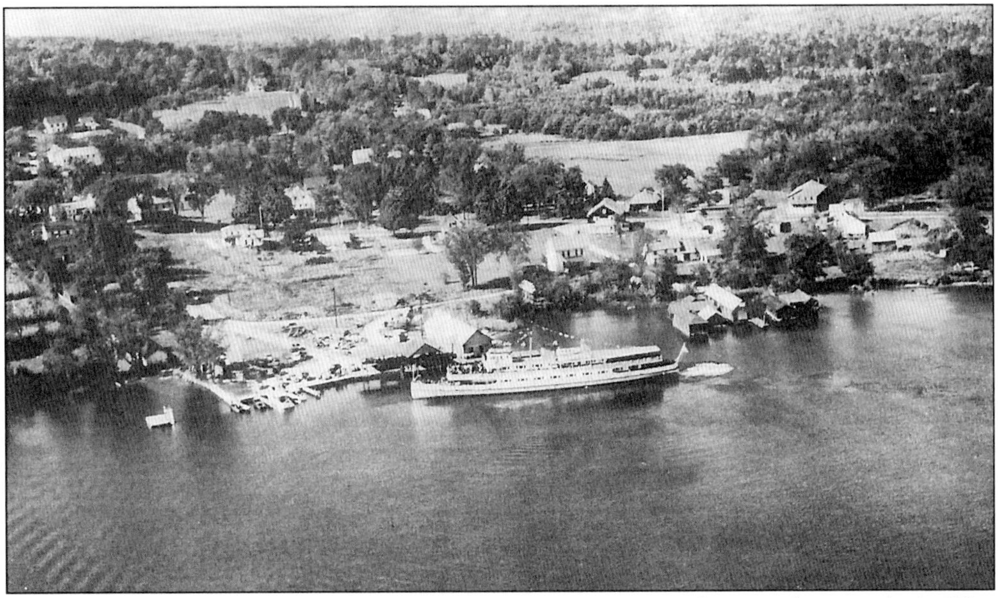

An aerial view of Center Harbor showing the M.V. *Mount Washington* about to dock. This quiet little hamlet lies within the mountain fold at the end of the long northern bay of Lake Winnipesaukee. Originally this town was known as "Centre Harbour," Mountonboro Harbor being east, and Meredith Harbor west, making this the center of the three harbors (thus the name).

Center Harbor also borders on Lake Squam, Waukewan, Kanasatka, and Winona, and commands a magnificent view of both lakes and mountains.

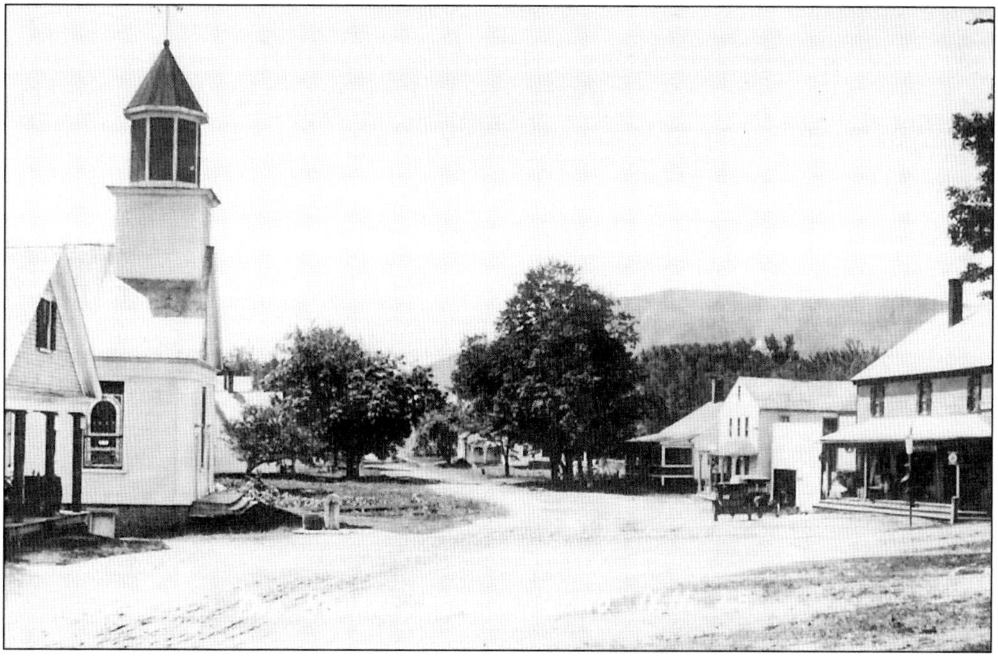

Main Street in Mountonboro, 1925. This photograph was taken looking west on Route 25 toward Red Hill. Note the Olde Country Store on the right. Originally this store was known as Freeze's Tavern, and has been in continuous operation since 1793 as a country store. This fine old establishment is presently listed on the National Register of Historic Places.

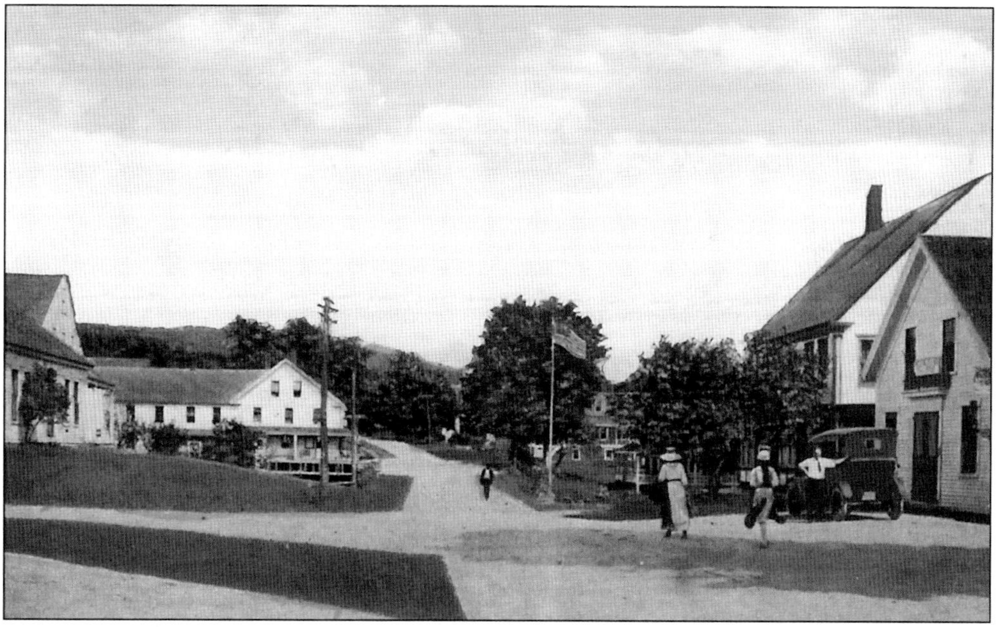

Main Street, the post office, and the general store in Melvin Village, New Hampshire, 1931. Tuftonboro includes the village of Melvin Corner, Melvin Village, and Mirror Lake. The name Melvin was given in honor of David and Eleazer Melvin, who fought in the French and Indian War. Tuftonboro has the distinction of being the only town once having been owned entirely by one man, John Tufton Mason, after whom it was named in 1750.

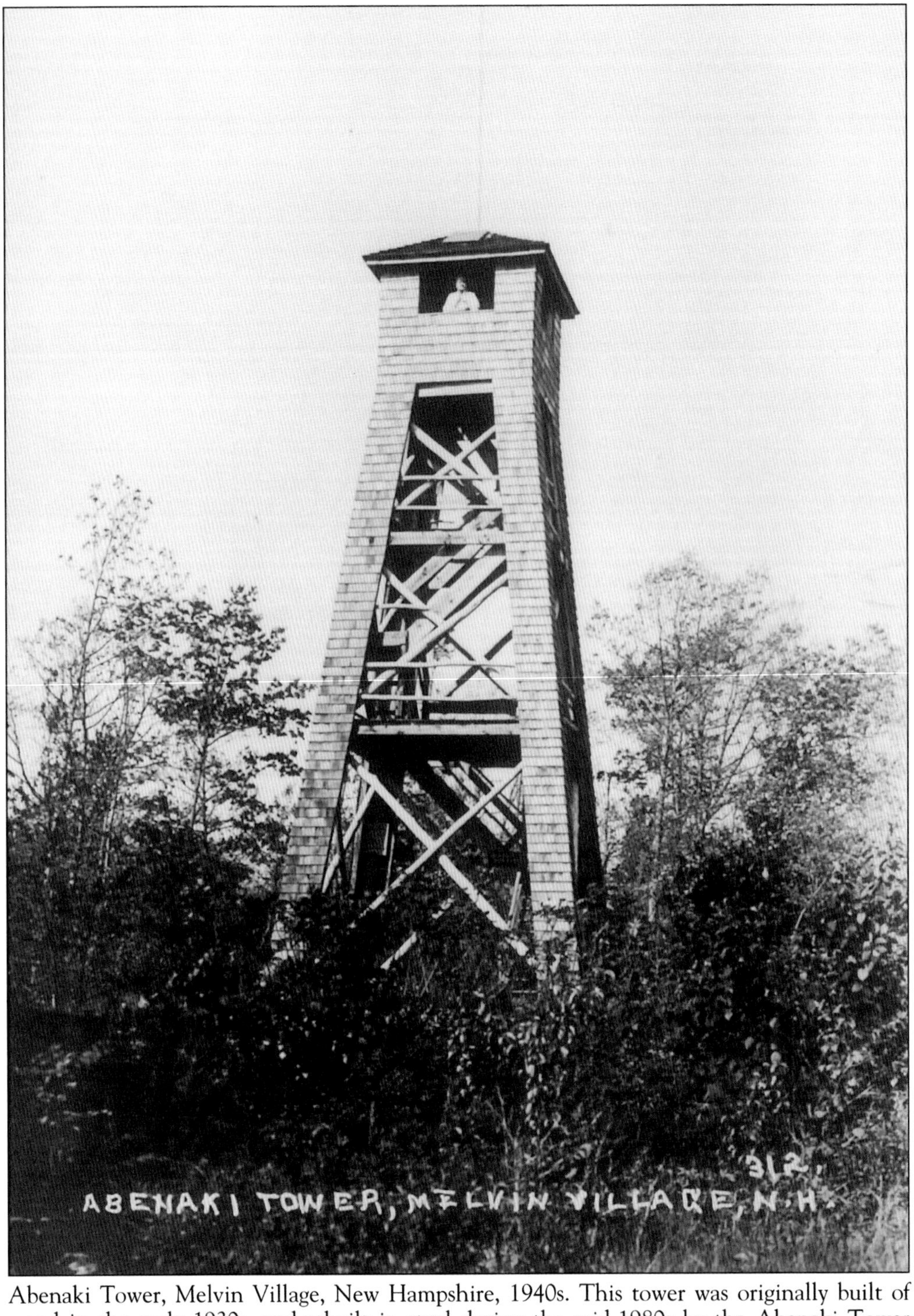

Abenaki Tower, Melvin Village, New Hampshire, 1940s. This tower was originally built of wood in the early 1930s, and rebuilt in steel during the mid-1980s by the Abenaki Tower Association, residents of the 19 and 20 Mile Bays in Tuftonboro, New Hampshire.

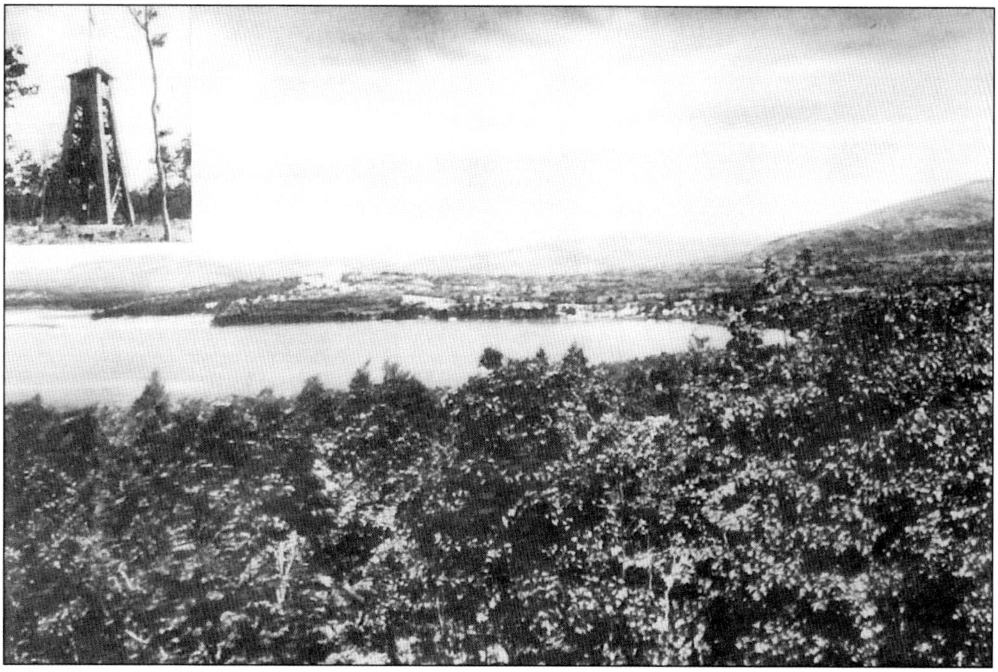

Lake Winnipesaukee and Melvin Bay from Abenaki Tower. From this vantage point we have a fine view of Melvin Village at the end of the bay, and of the Bald Peak Colony Club.

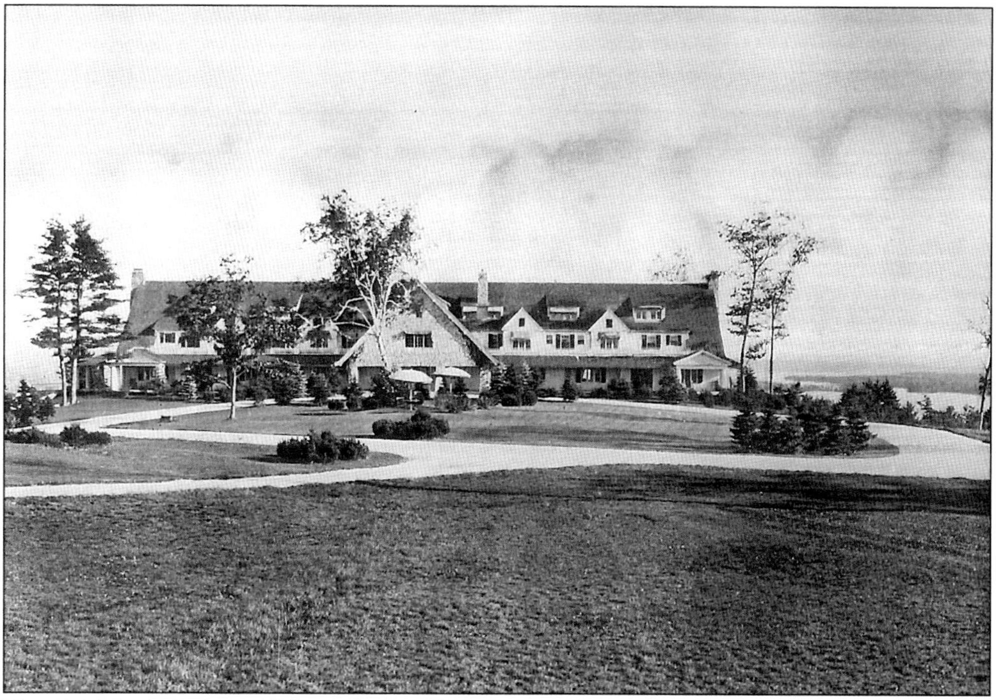

The Bald Peak Colony Club, Melvin Village, New Hampshire, 1930s. This country club has one of the most picturesque and exclusive golf courses in New Hampshire, situated on the high ground overlooking Lake Winnipesaukee. In the background may be seen Long Island in Lake Winnipesaukee.

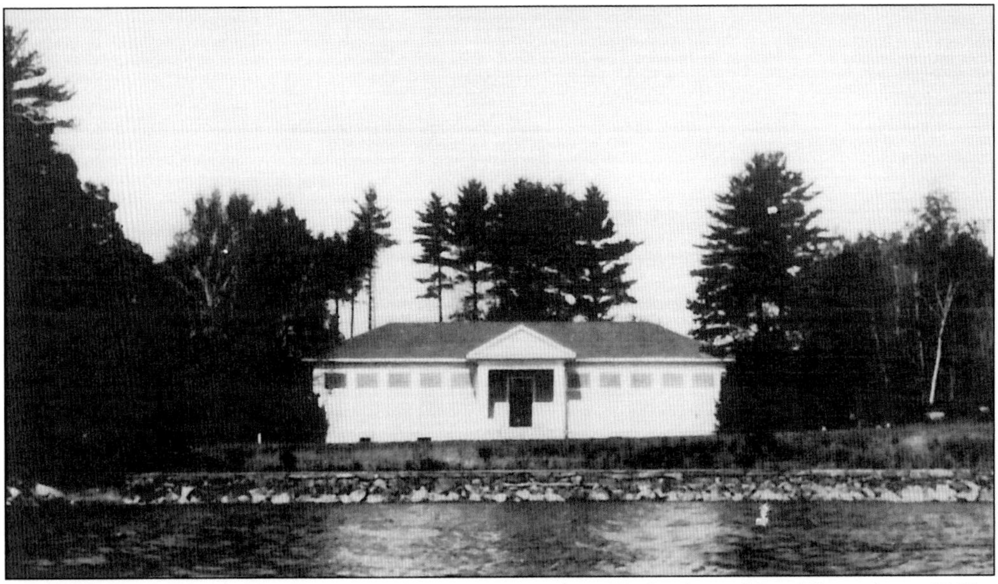

The Libby Museum on the shore of Lake Winnipesaukee, Tuftonboro, New Hampshire, 1929.

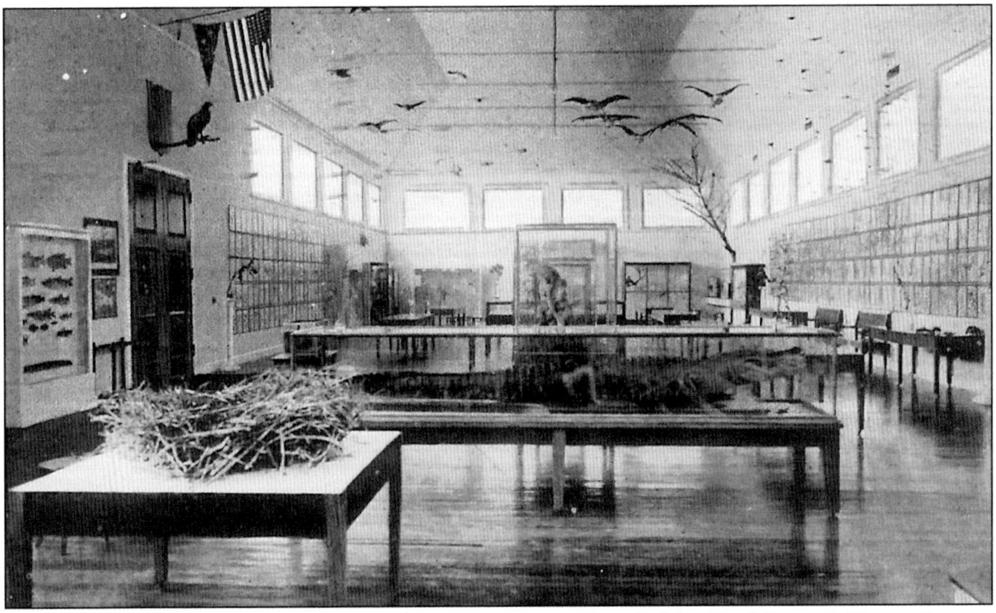

The interior of the Libby Museum. This museum was founded by Dr. Henry Libby, a Boston dentist, and contains a fine collection of birds, fish, and snakes, skillfully mounted in cases showing their natural habitats. Across from the museum is a charming view of Winnipesaukee and the Belknap Mountain Range, 1929.

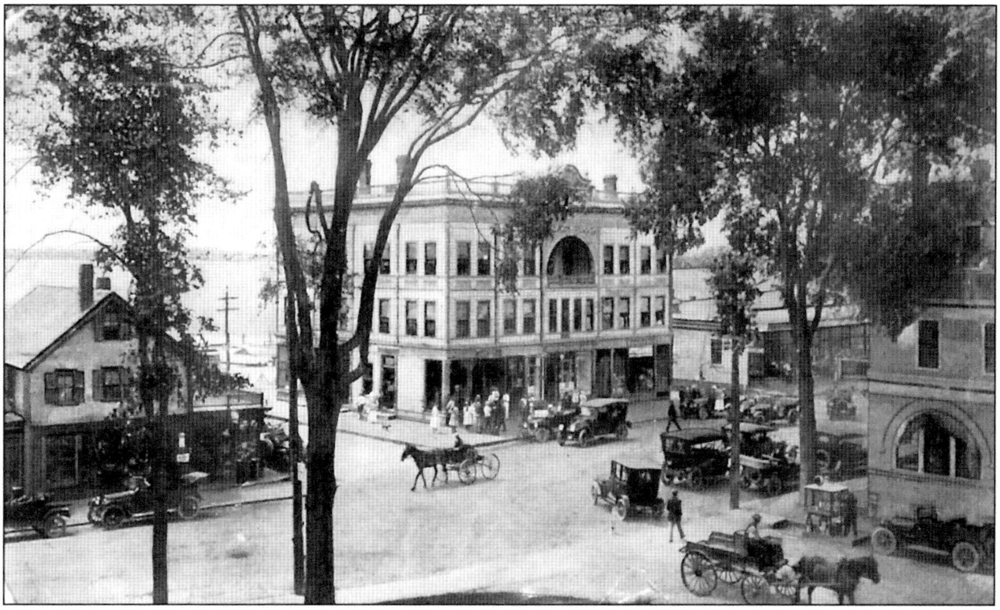

Post Office Square in Wolfeboro, New Hampshire, during the late 1800s. The main section of Wolfeboro was granted on October 5, 1759. Five weeks later the grantees gave it the name of Wolfe-borough, honoring General James Wolfe, who had recently fallen at the Plains of Abraham, Quebec. The original grant was added to over the years. The Wolfeboro addition was made in 1800, parts of Alton were added in 1849, Tuftonboro in 1858, and in 1895, four islands in Lake Winnipesaukee, formerly belonging to Alton, became part of Wolfeboro.

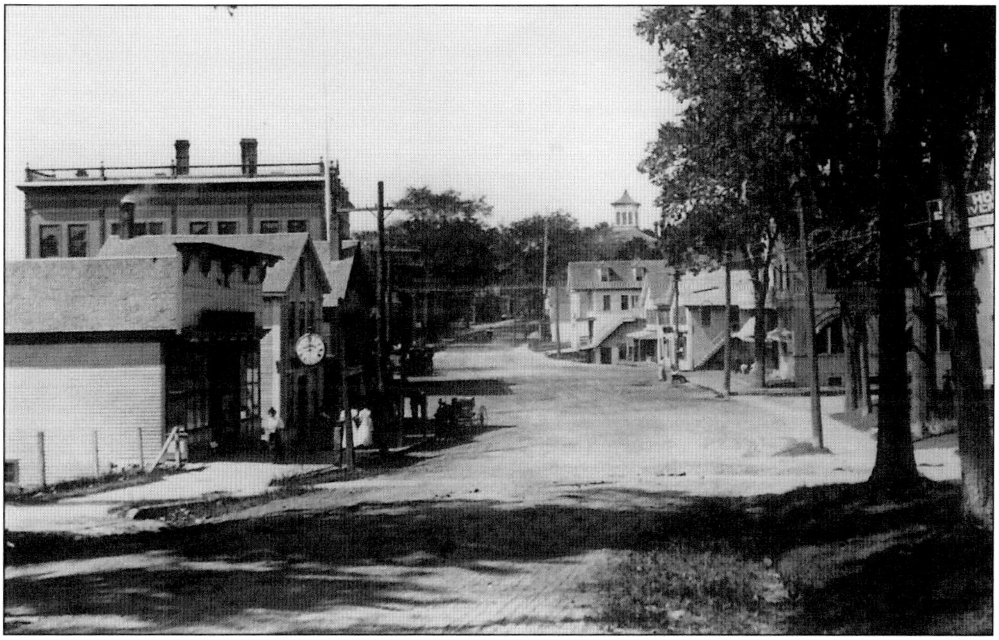

Main Street in Wolfeboro, New Hampshire, looking north, early 1900s. This restful lake resort is situated at the foot of a quiet bay on the eastern shore, along the slopes of two hills which decline toward the fine village shops near the outlet of Lake Wentworth. An early pastime was taking peaceful excursions on the steamers leaving the town docks.

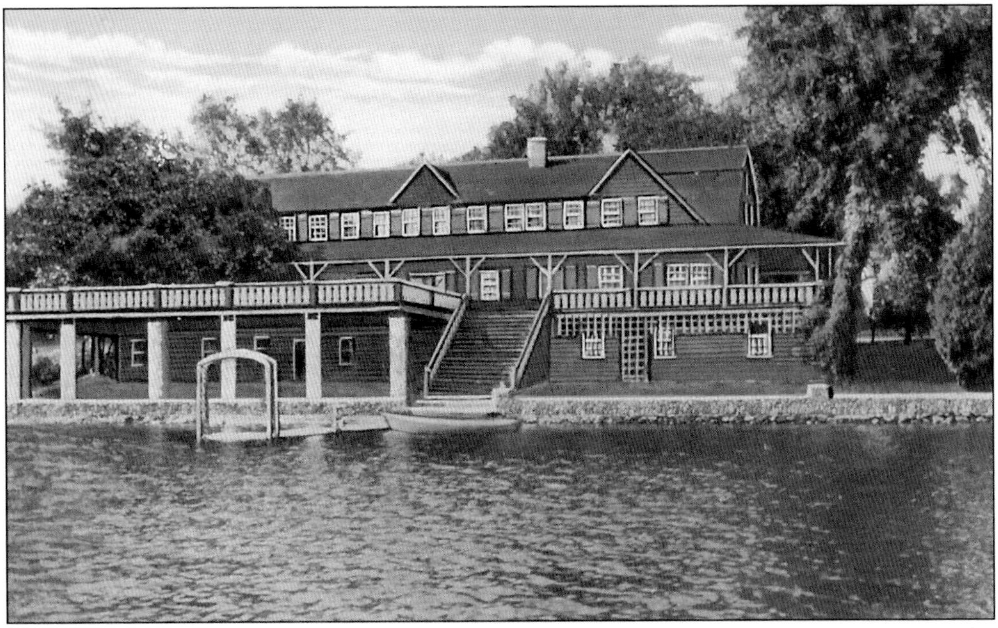

The Casino in Wolfeboro, New Hampshire, 1931. This was a popular attraction during the 1920s and 1930s.

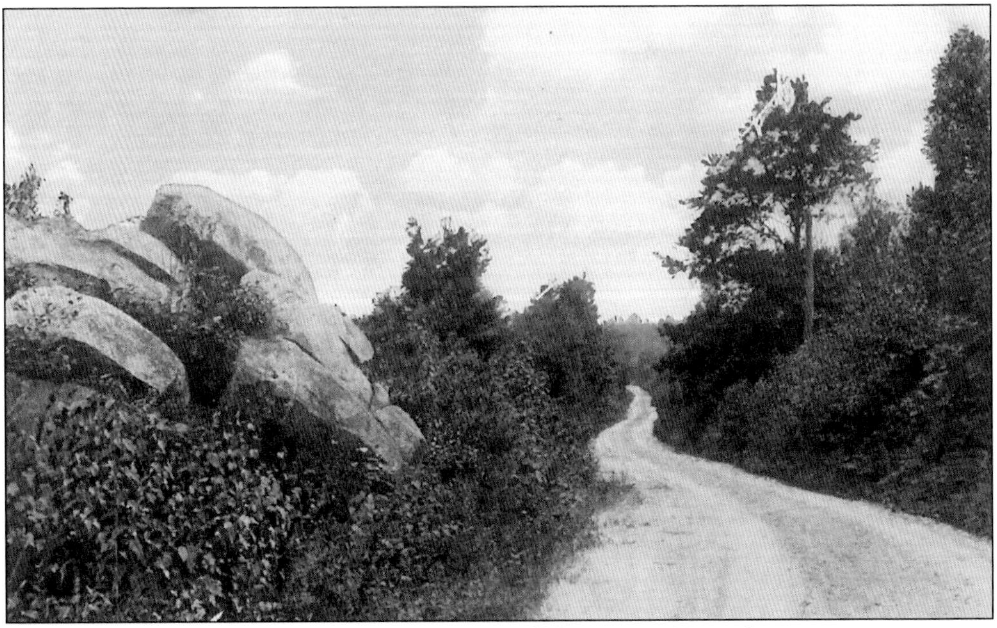

The Old Man's Face near Pine Hill Cemetery, Wolfeboro, New Hampshire.

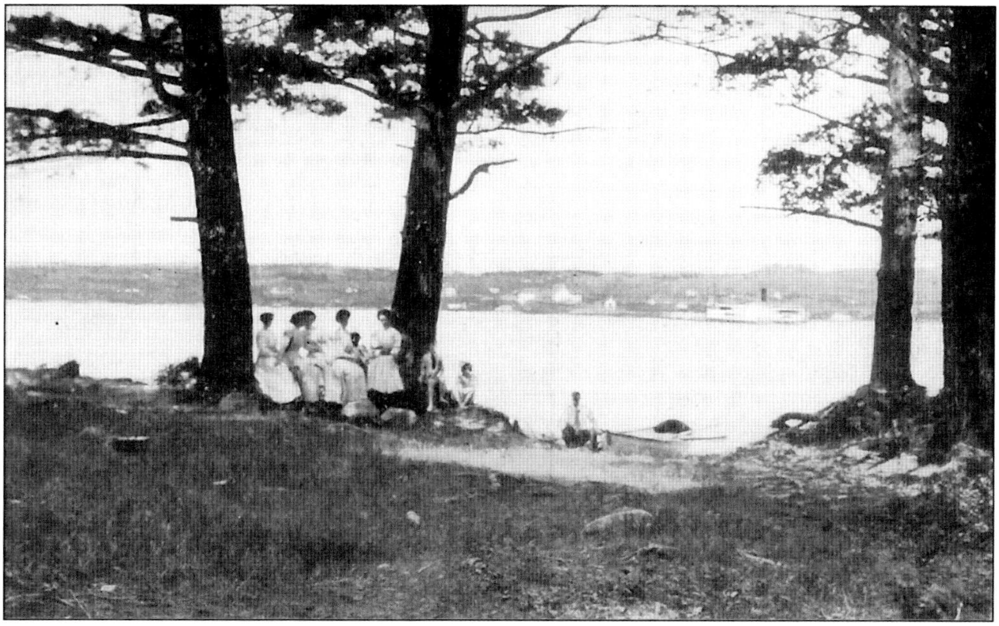

Clarks Point, Wolfeboro, New Hampshire. The steamer *Mount Washington* is seen at the public docks, early 1900s.

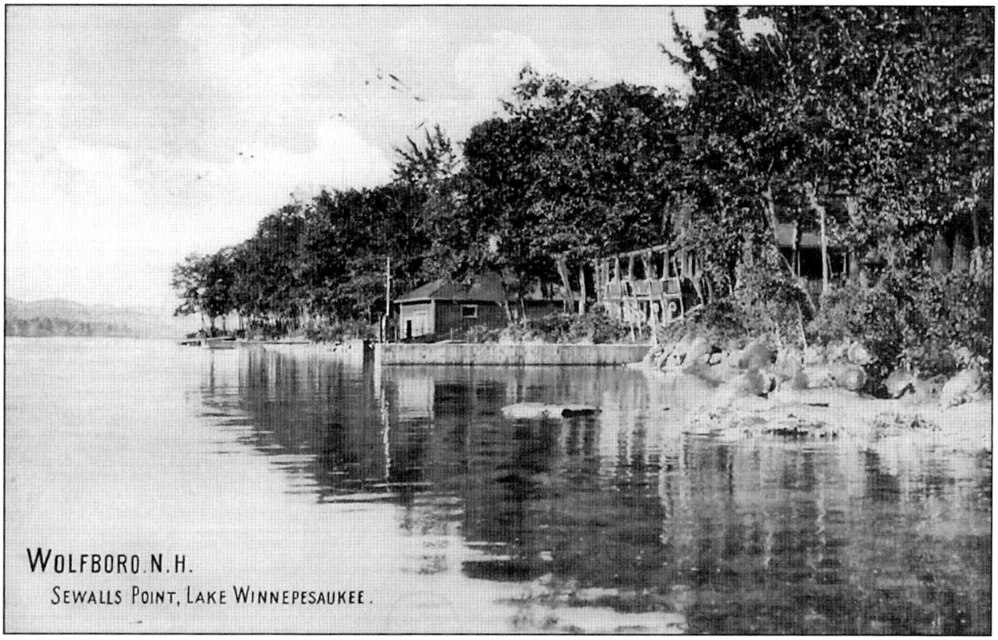

Sewall's Point, Wolfeboro, New Hampshire, 1908. This point was named after Judge David Sewell, an attorney-at-law from Portsmouth, New Hampshire. According to public records, this property was owned by Judge Sewell at the time of its settlement.

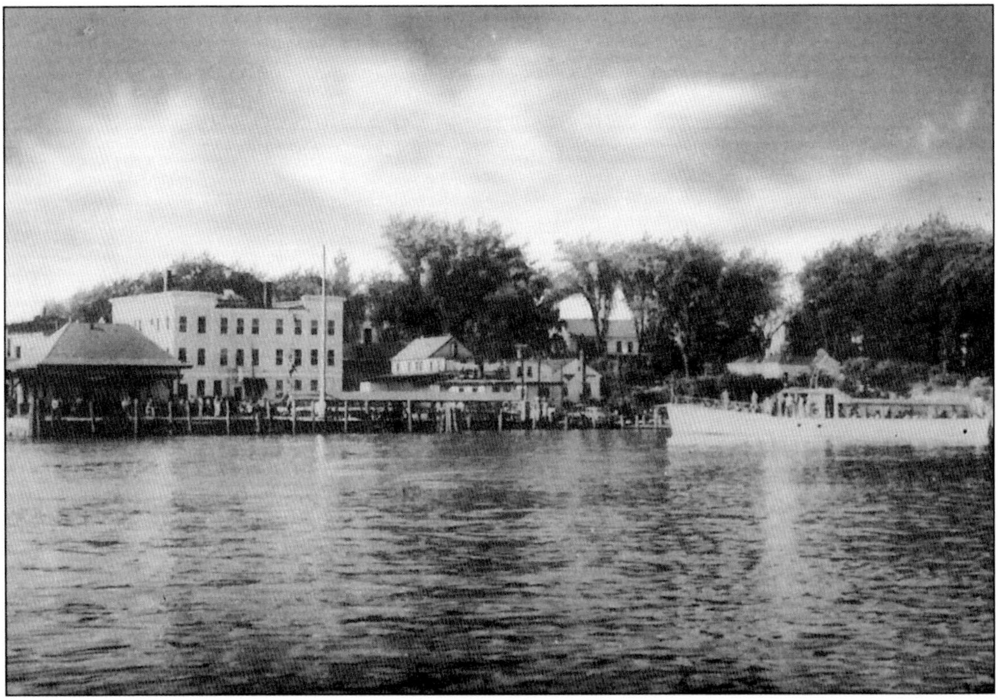

The *Sophie C* approaching the Wolfeboro public docks. Many summer tourists travel to Wolfeboro on this all-steel boat to shop in Wolfeboro's attractive village, 1946.

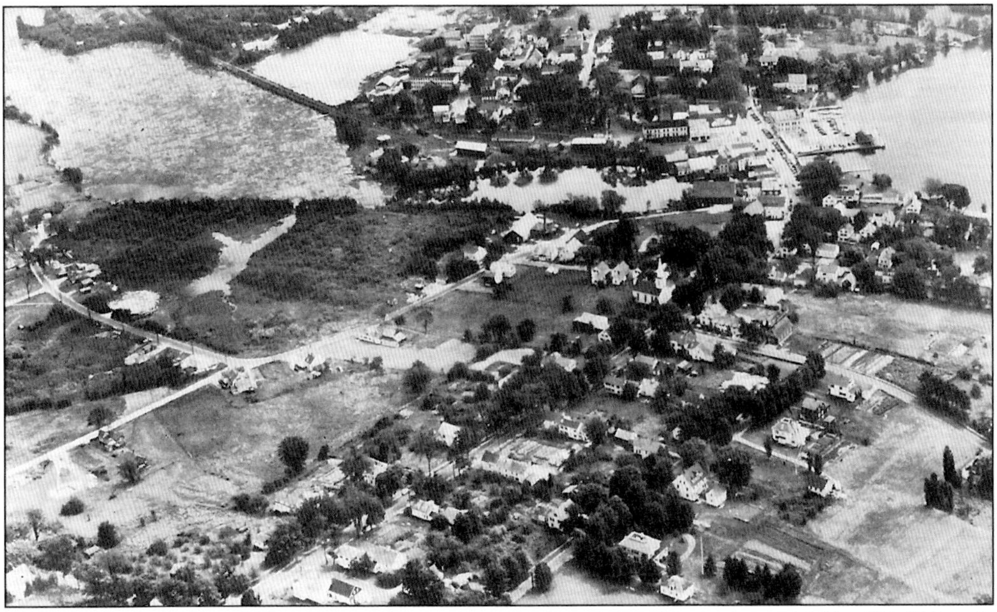

An aerial view of Wolfeboro on Lake Winnipesaukee, New Hampshire, 1950s. Wolfeboro's claim to being "the oldest summer resort in America" is well founded, as Governor John Wentworth built the first extensive summer home on this continent in 1764. Many fine summer residences have since dotted this still-growing community. The town was first called "King's Wood" because its original grant required that its tallest mast trees be saved for the King's Navy.

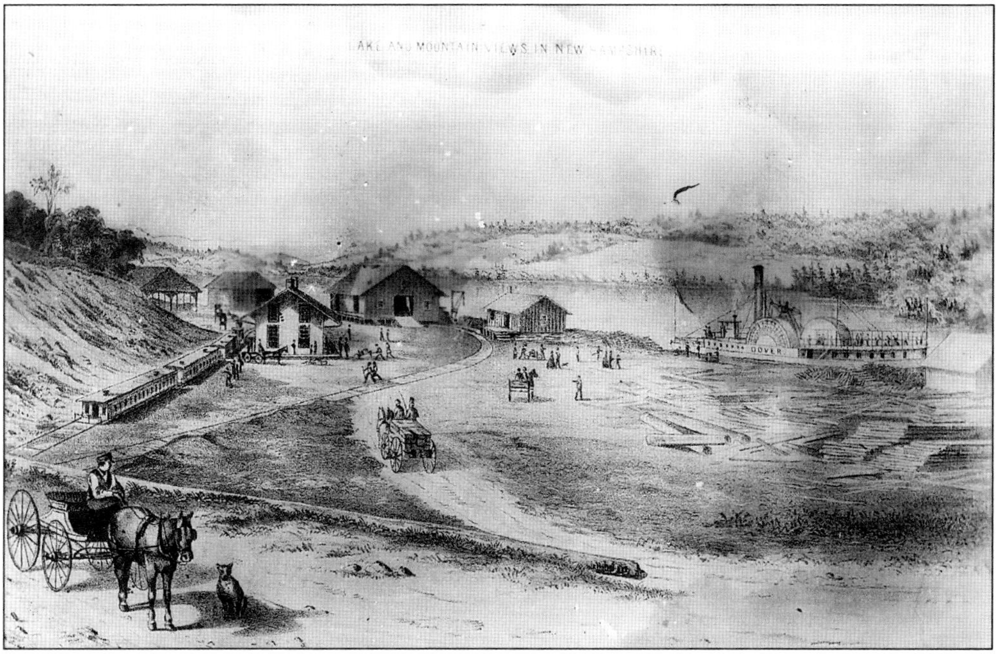

The Alton Bay Railroad and Steamboat Station, Alton Bay, New Hampshire, from the Winnipiseogee House, 1868. The steamer *Dover* is located at dockside at the station. Alton Bay is the southern extremity of Lake Winnipesaukee, and is considered the oldest port for shipping and trade on the lake since 1832.

Alton Bay, New Hampshire, looking north with a sea plane about to take off from the beach, 1940s. Alton Bay is located 1 mile north of the town of Alton and is one of the most picturesque and widely known summer vacation spots in New England.

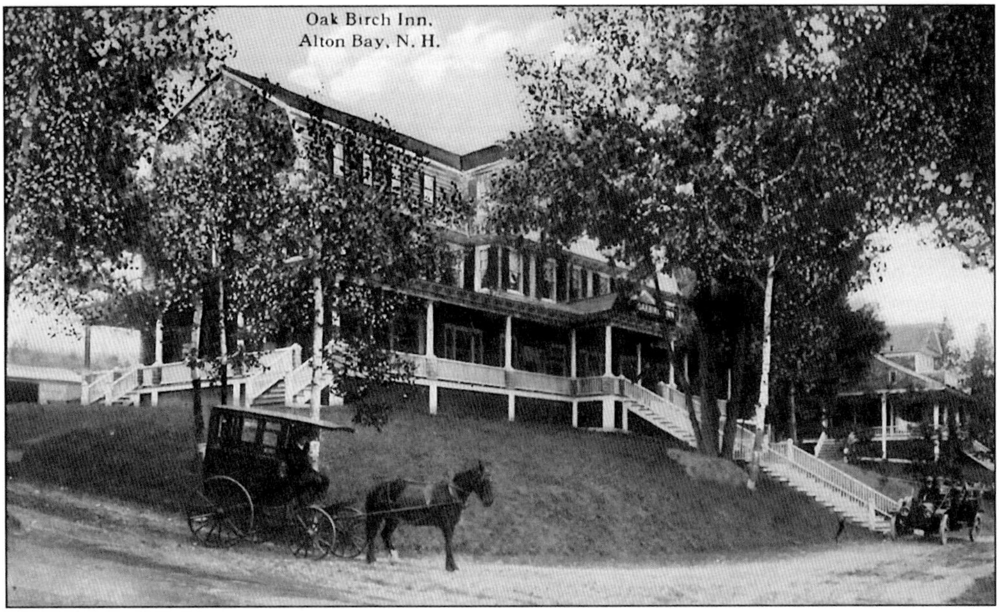

The Oak Birch Inn near the shore of Lake Winnipesaukee, 1917.

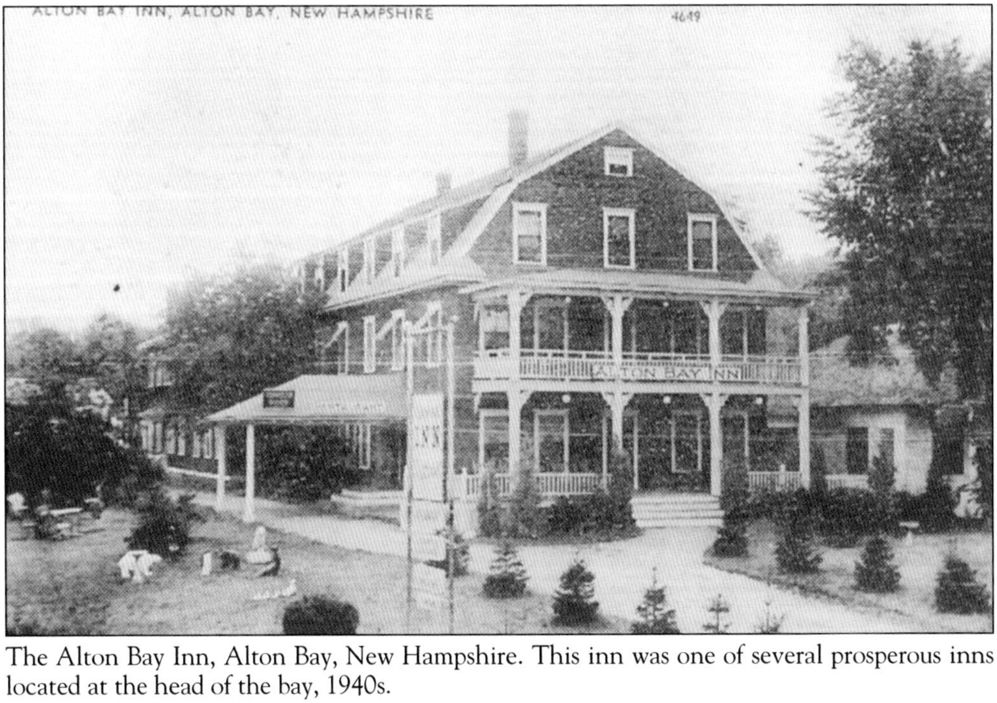

The Alton Bay Inn, Alton Bay, New Hampshire. This inn was one of several prosperous inns located at the head of the bay, 1940s.

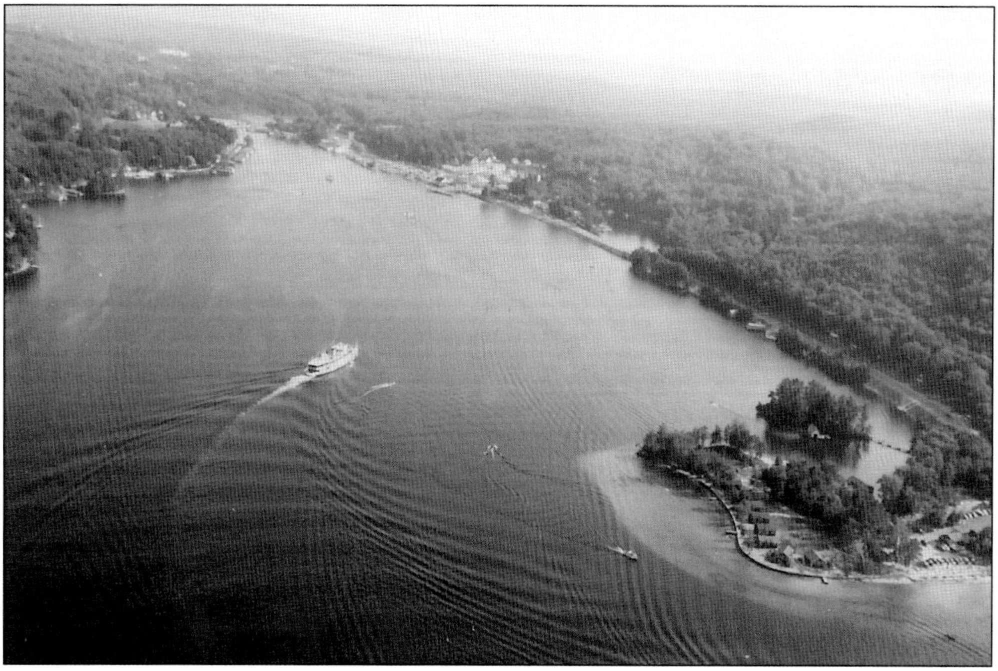

An aerial view of the *Mount Washington* passing Sandy Point in Alton Bay as she prepares to dock near Victoria Pier, 1950s.

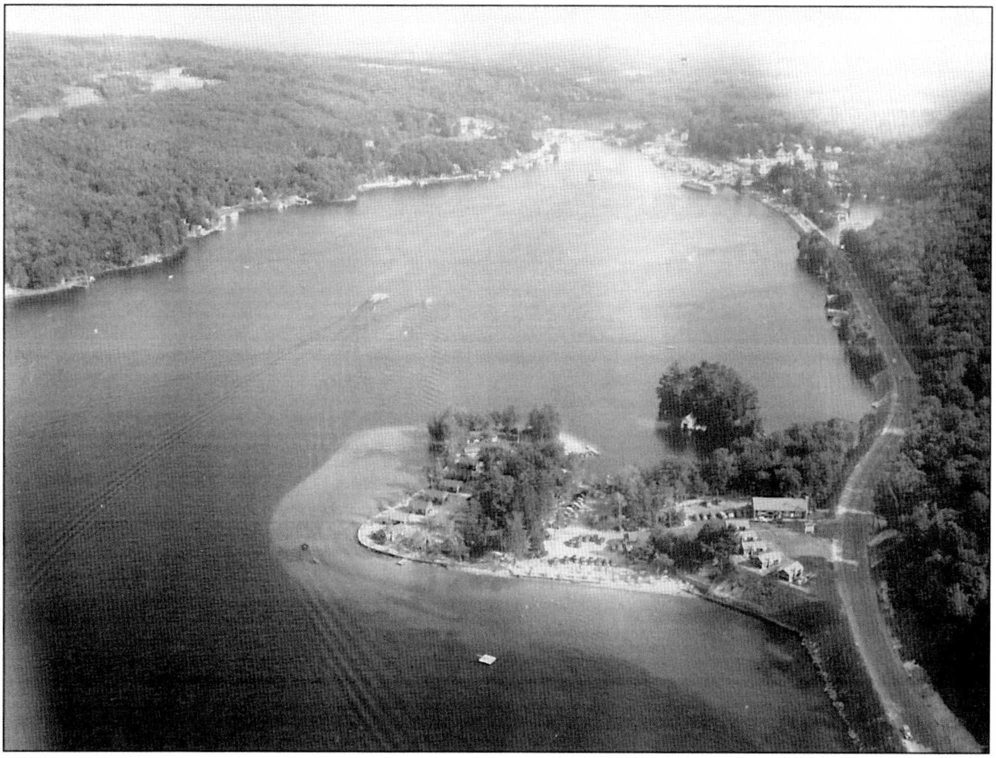

An aerial view of Sandy Point, Alton Bay, with the *Mount Washington* docked at her pier, 1940s.

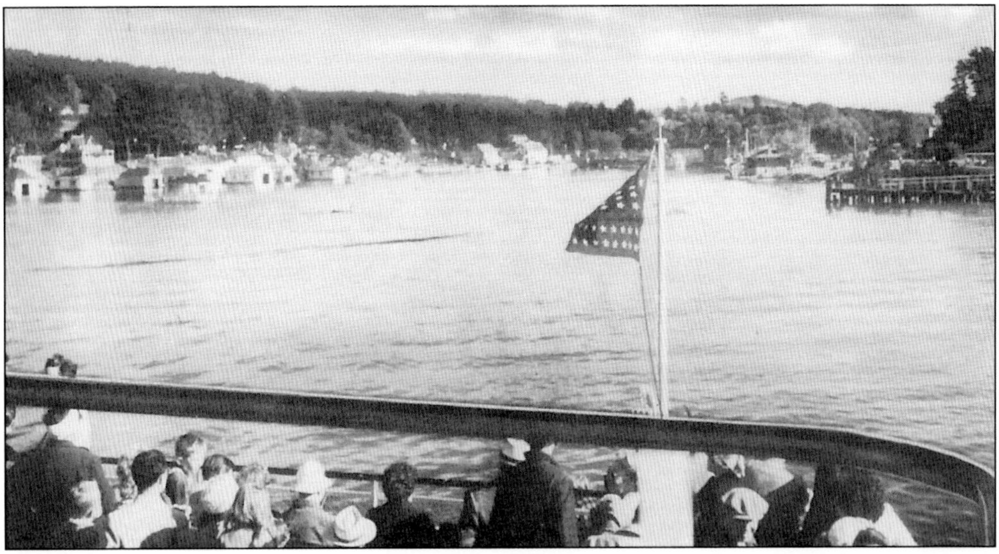

Alton Bay as seen from the bridge of the *Mount Washington*. This 5-mile-long bay commands attention as the majestic *Mount Washington* glides to her pier at this active resort port, 1950s.

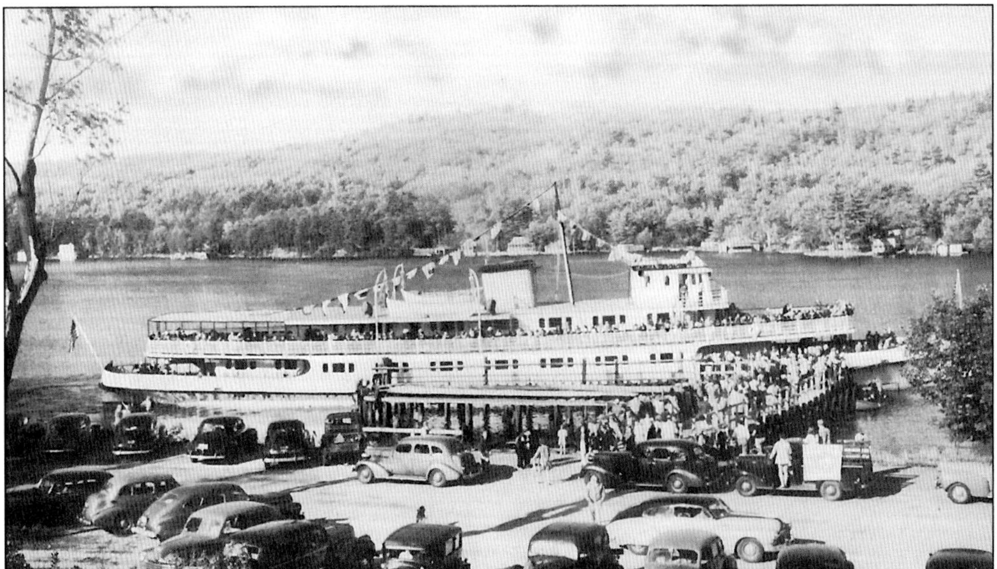

The *Mount Washington* at Alton Bay taking on additional passengers during her daily cruise around the lake. Twice each day the *Mount Washington* calls to all and a scurry of excitement runs through the bay as the majestic boat docks, 1940s.

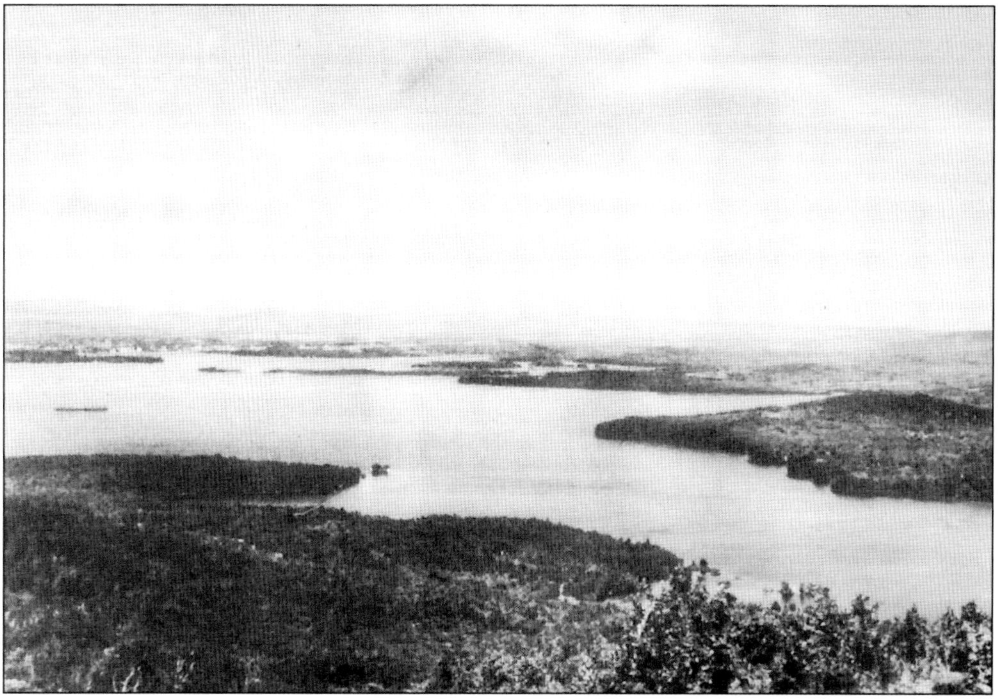

The entrance to Alton Bay as seen from Mount Major looking toward Wolfeboro at the distant end of the lake. This entrance leads to the town of Alton, a distance of 5 miles south, and is the longest bay of Lake Winnipesaukee.

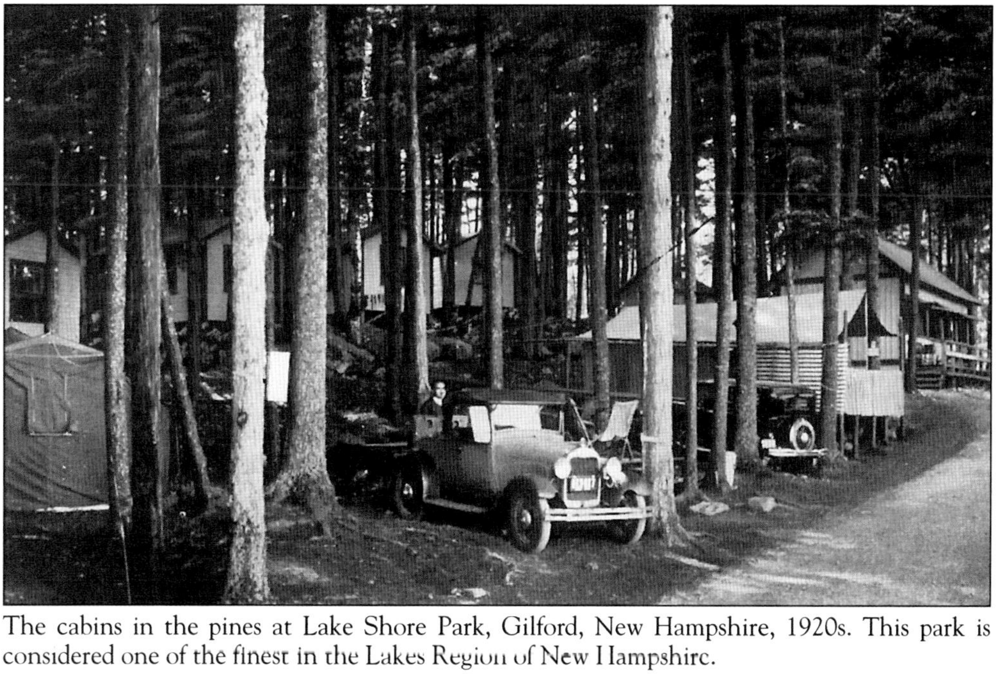

The cabins in the pines at Lake Shore Park, Gilford, New Hampshire, 1920s. This park is considered one of the finest in the Lakes Region of New Hampshire.

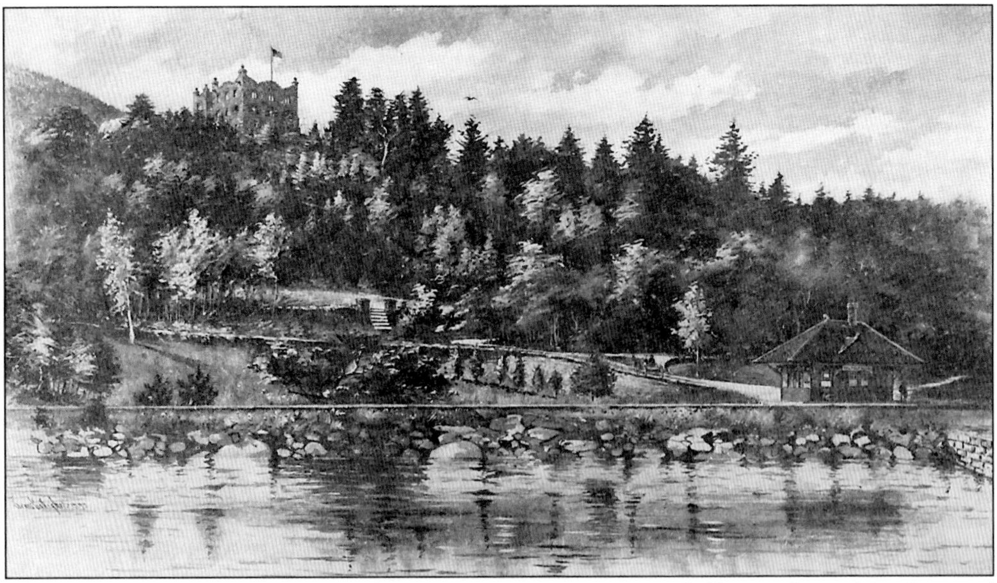

The Broads. The summer home of the Hon. Benjamin Ames Kimball, president of the Concord and Montreal Railroads, Concord, New Hampshire, as seen from the lake and the Lakeshore Railroad Station in Glendale.

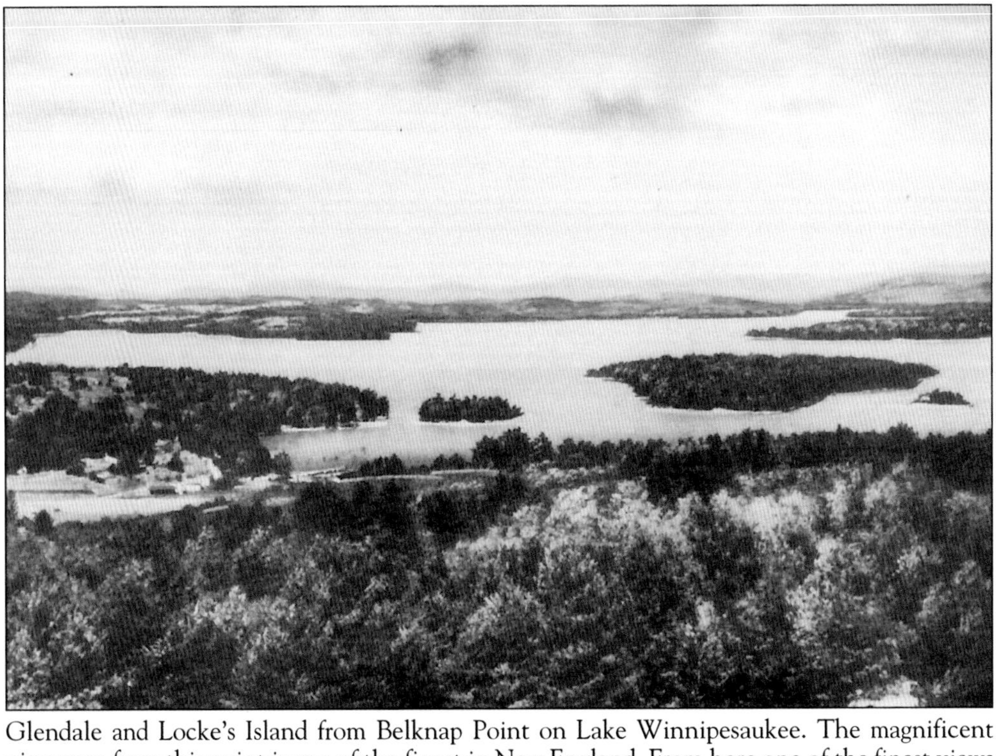

Glendale and Locke's Island from Belknap Point on Lake Winnipesaukee. The magnificent view seen from this point is one of the finest in New England. From here one of the finest views can be seen of the Presidential Range and Mount Washington anywhere in the region. Locke's Island is said to be the first island inhabited by the early settlers during the colonial times.

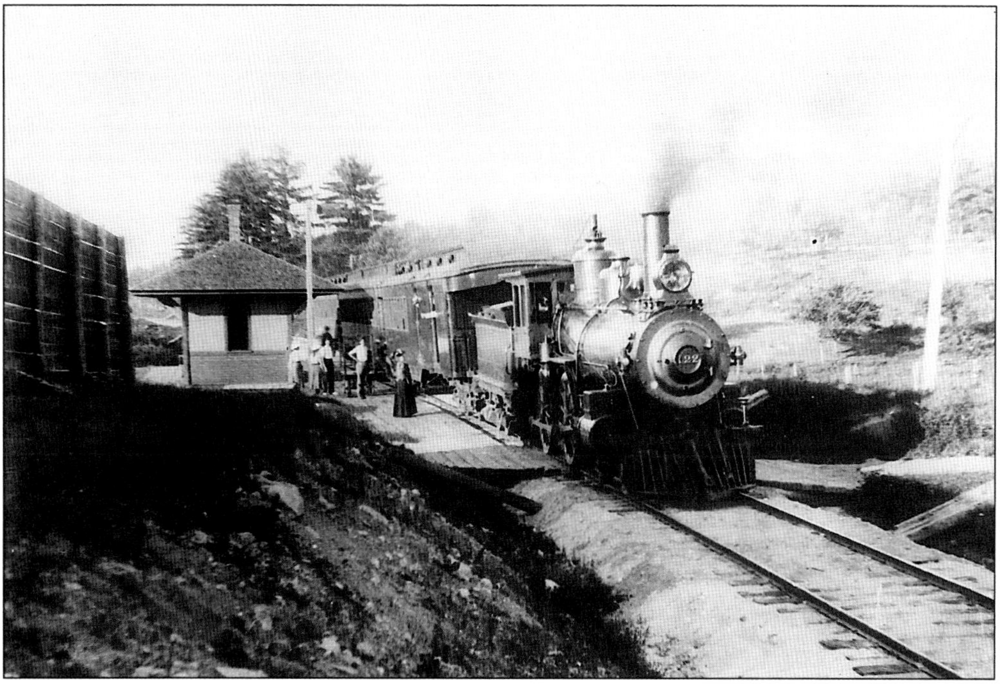

The steam train No. 122 of the Lake Shore Railroad at the Glendale Station, 1897. The railroad began operation from Alton Bay to Lake Village (Lakeport/Laconia) in 1890 and ended in 1930. In 1933 the tracks were removed.

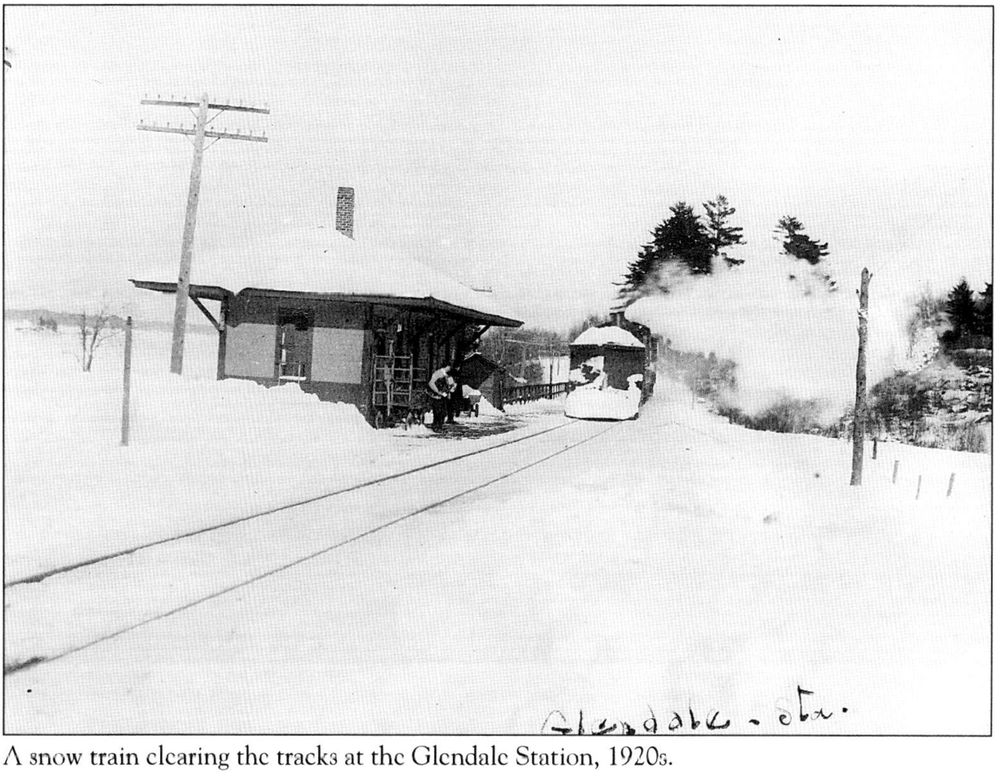

A snow train clearing the tracks at the Glendale Station, 1920s.

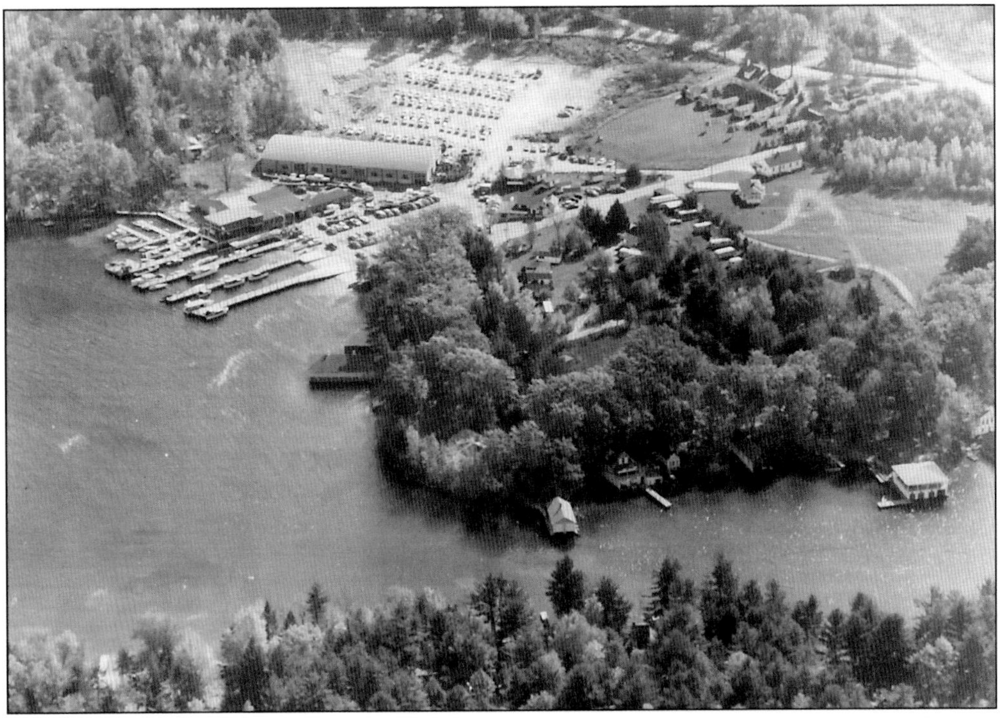

An aerial view of Glendale Bay in Gilford, New Hampshire. Just behind Locke's Island is the busy port and harbor of Glendale. Glendale is the home of the New Hampshire's Department of Safety's Marine Division. These people patrol the lake, keep navigation equipment in repair, and are an aid to boaters in distress. They have complete jurisdiction over all lakes in the state of New Hampshire.

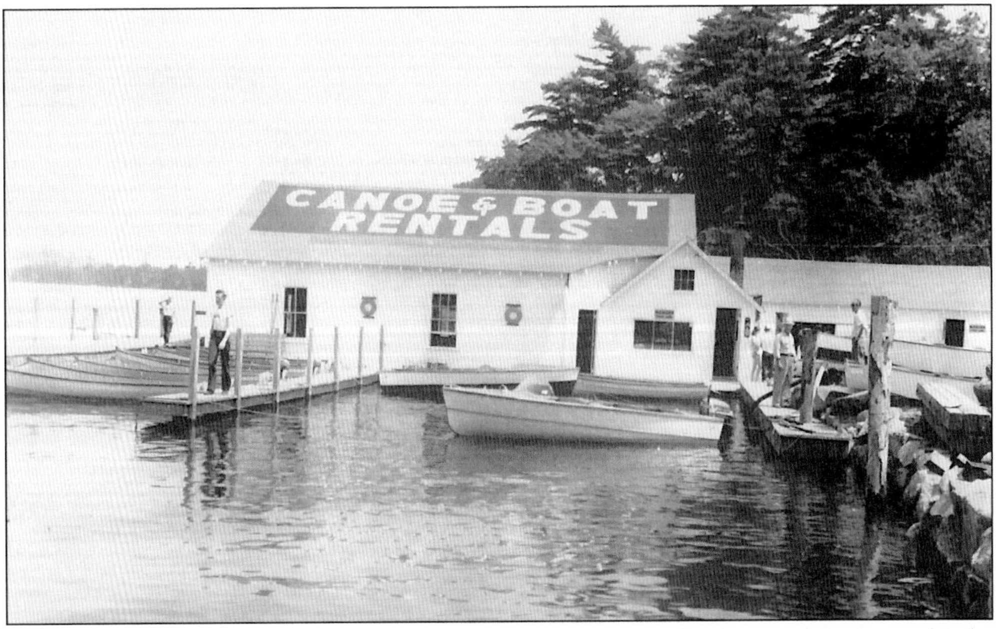

A typical canoe and boat rental dock as found in many of the bays and harbors of Lake Winnipesaukee. This one may possibly be located 1 mile north of Weirs Beach, 1950s.

Five

Moments to Remember

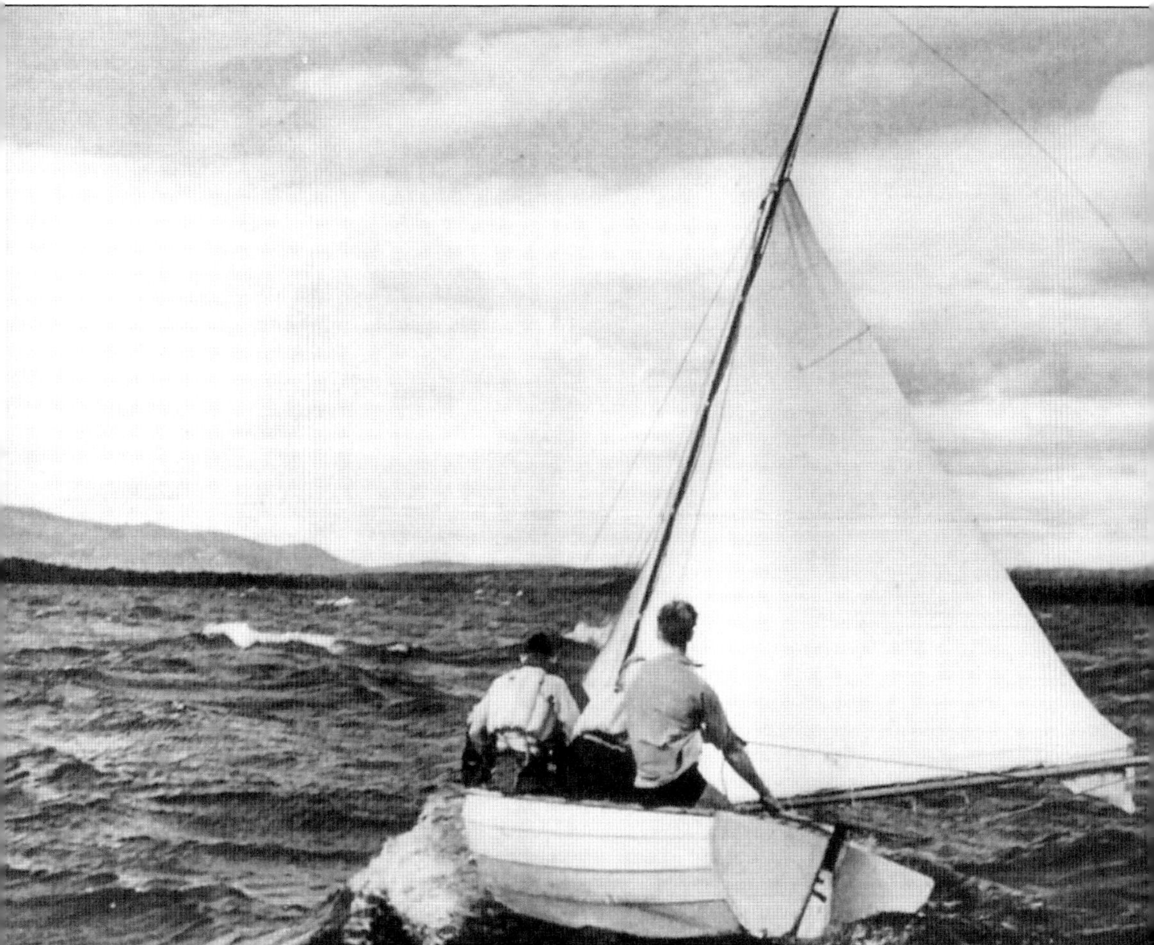

Sailing on the "Big Lake."

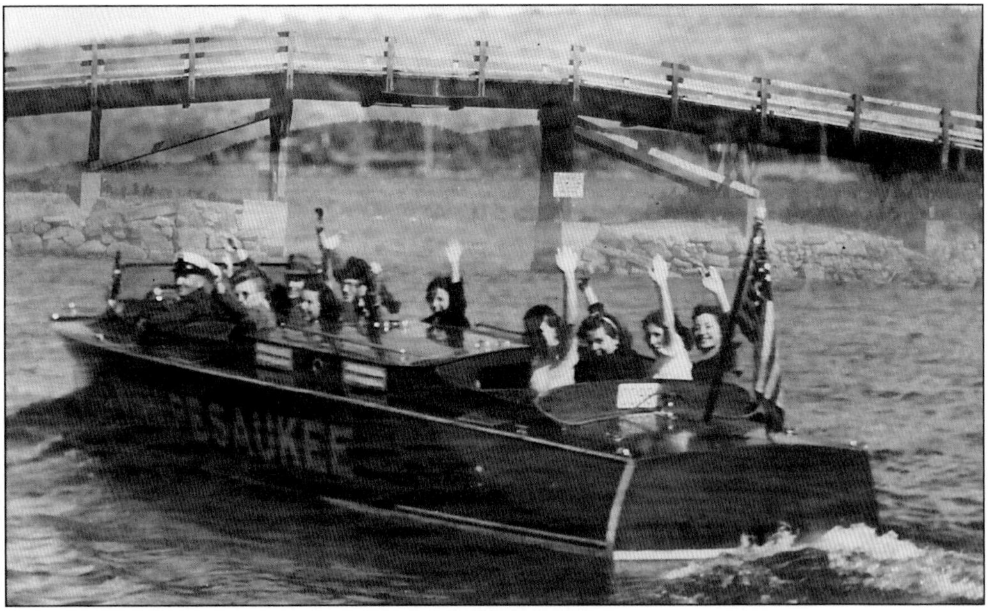

Miss Winnipesaukee approaching Governor's Island bridge. Cal Maloon is piloting the 26-foot Chris-Craft. Speed boat rides were very popular during the 1930s and 1940s.

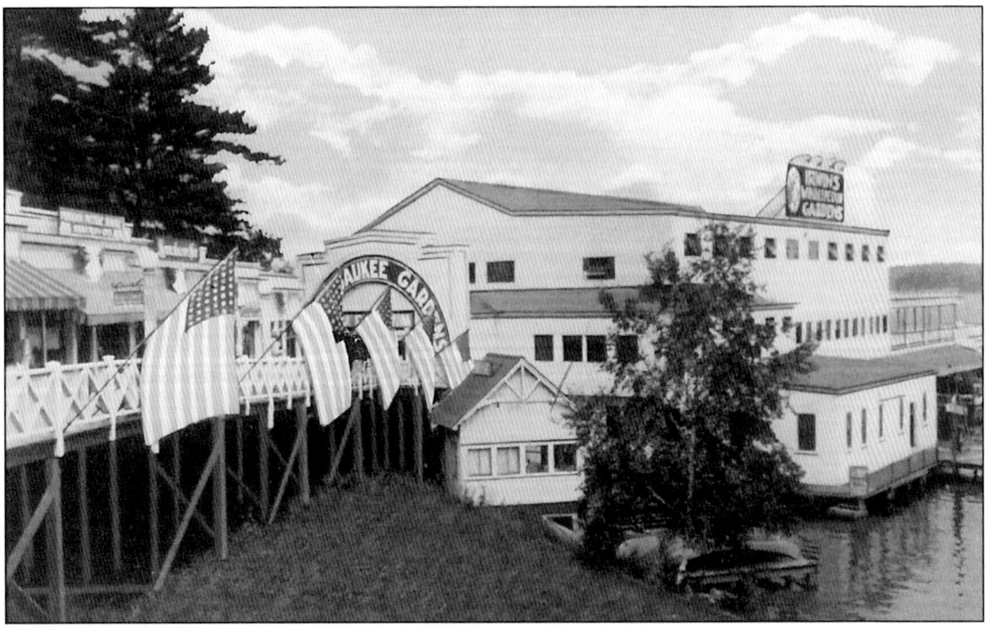

Irwin's Winnipesaukee Gardens. This was a very popular dance hall which featured many of the best big bands in the nation during the 1930s and 1940s. Jim Irwin built the hall and pier in 1925.

Water skiing stars Jack Beattie and Dick Binette. Both were members of the Weirs Water Ski Club. They are shown here discussing their friendly rivalry in water-ski jumping. Jack held the unofficial world's record of ski-jumping (at 94 feet), while Dick won both the New England and Eastern jumping titles in 1951.

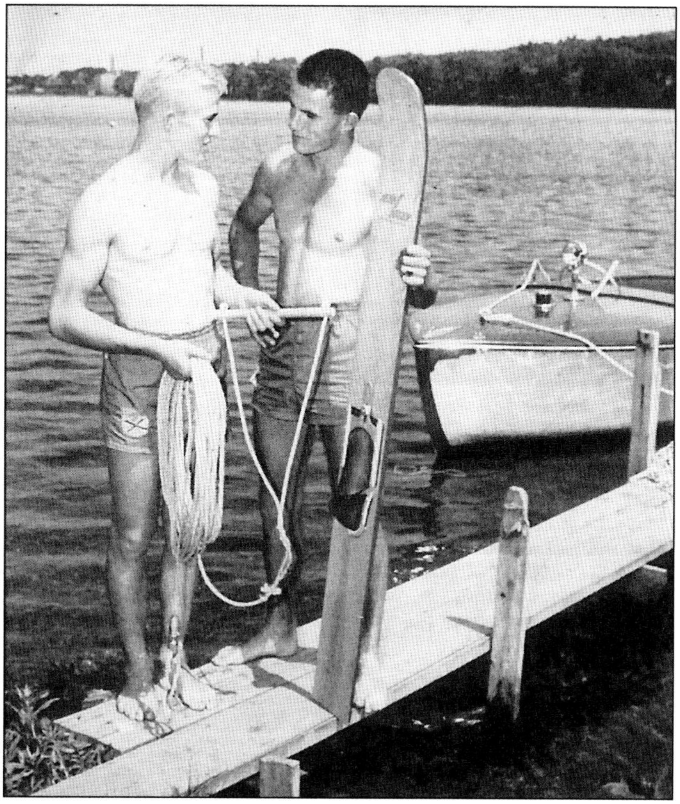

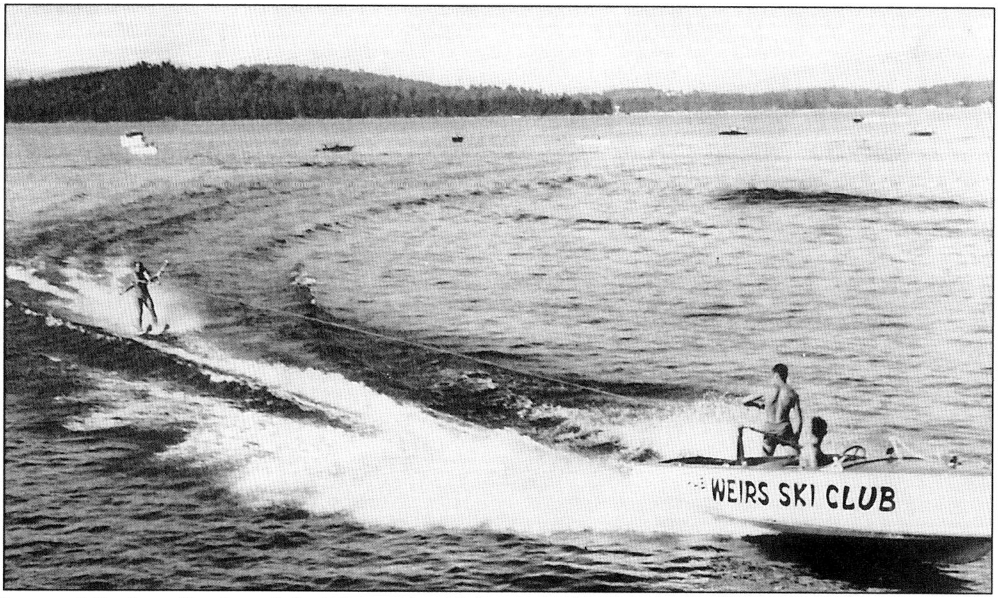

Jim and Pauline Stathis of the Weirs Ski Club. Here they perform a "double turn" in the 1951 New England Championship water-skiing contest.

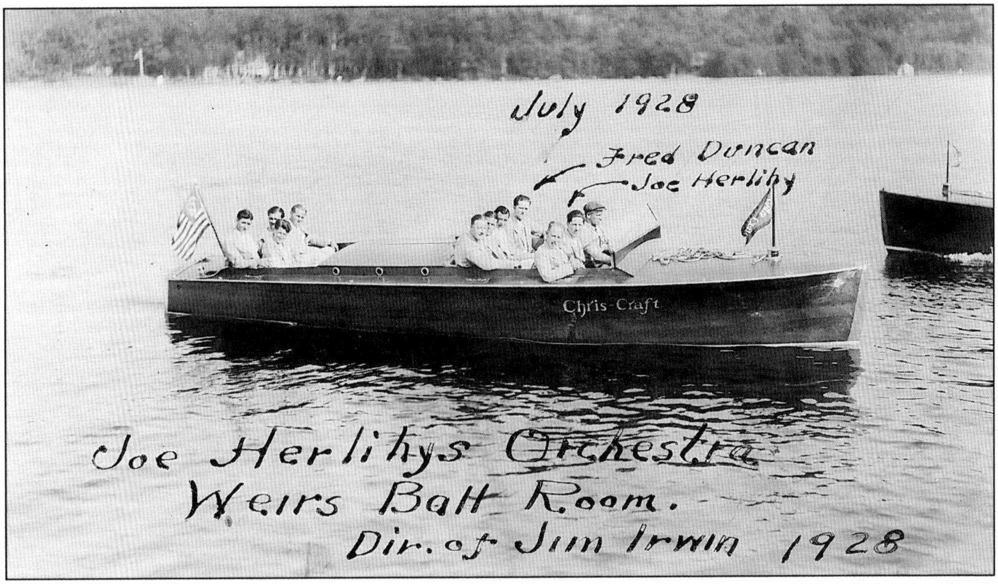

A 26-foot Chris-Craft, July 1928, with Frank Brooks, driver. Joe Herlihy's Orchestra, which was performing in Irwin Gardens Ballroom at The Weirs, is seen enjoying an afternoon ride on the lake.

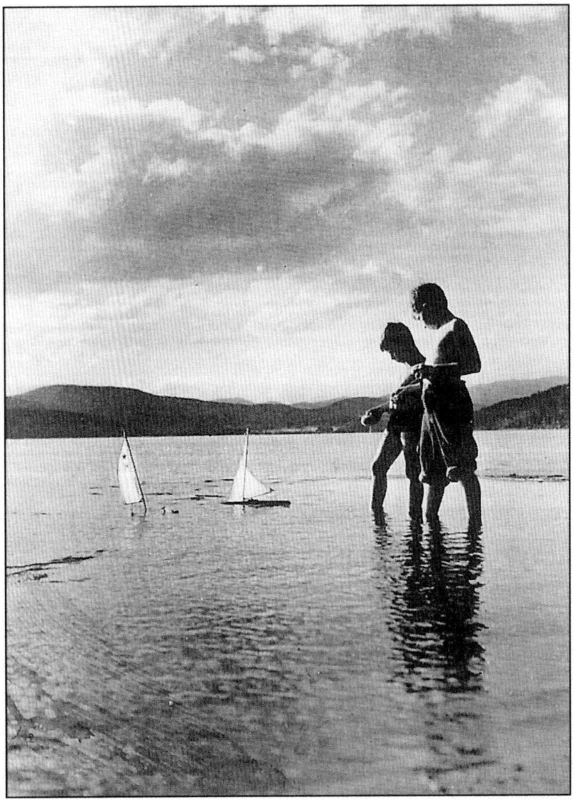

Youthful sailors at Lake Winnipesaukee. This photograph by Henry M. Bla was awarded first prize in the 1941 Lakes Region Photographic Contest.

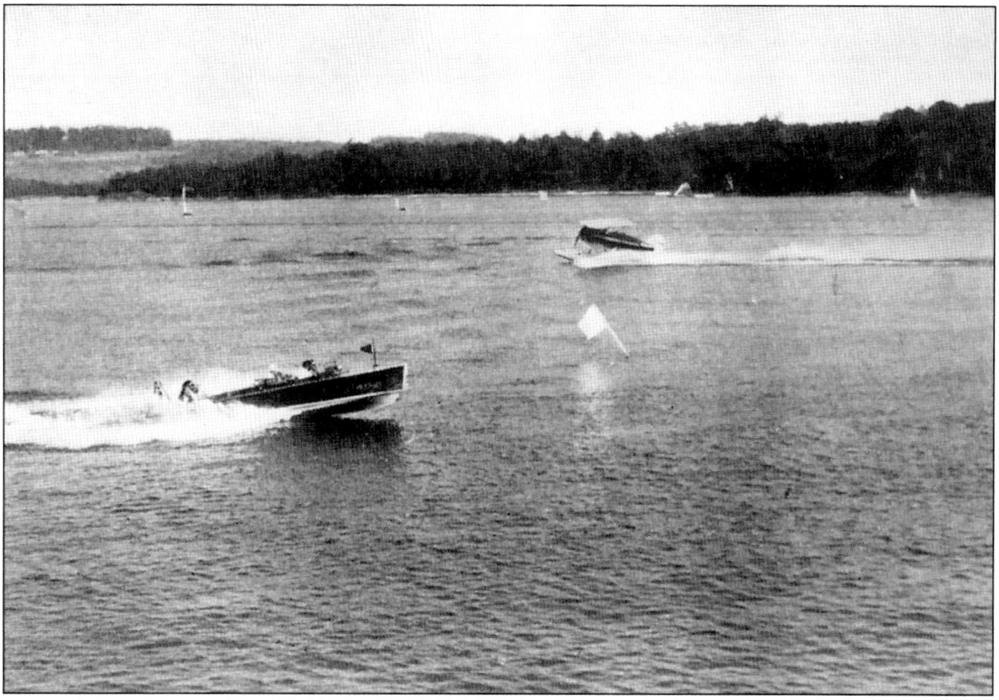

A speed boat race with a sea plane in the background.

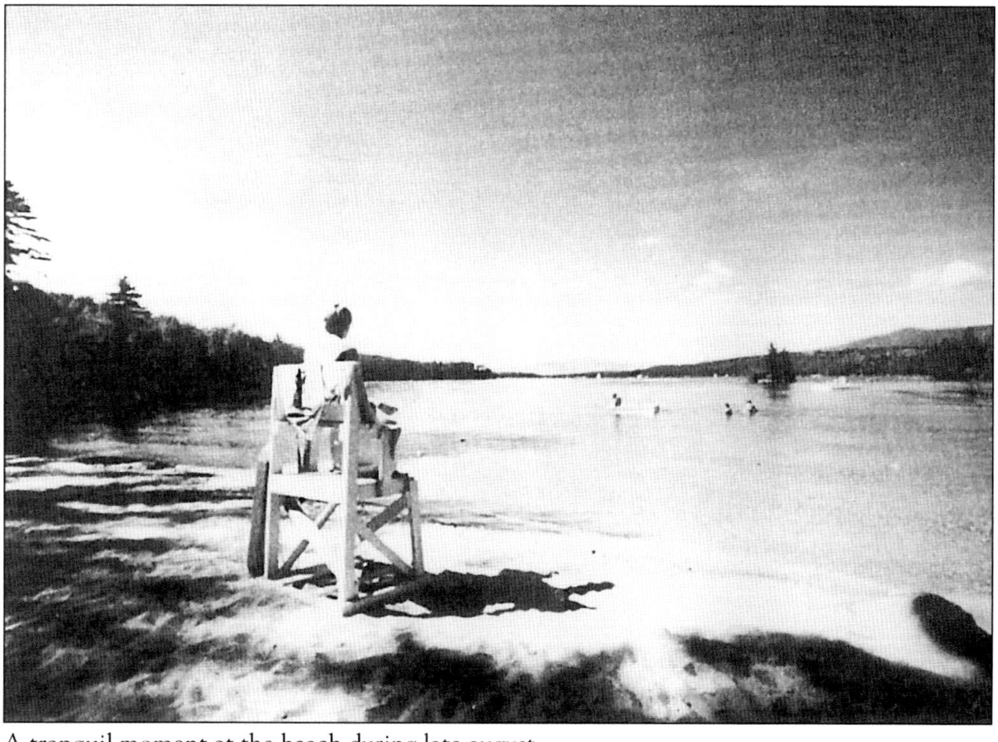

A tranquil moment at the beach during late august.

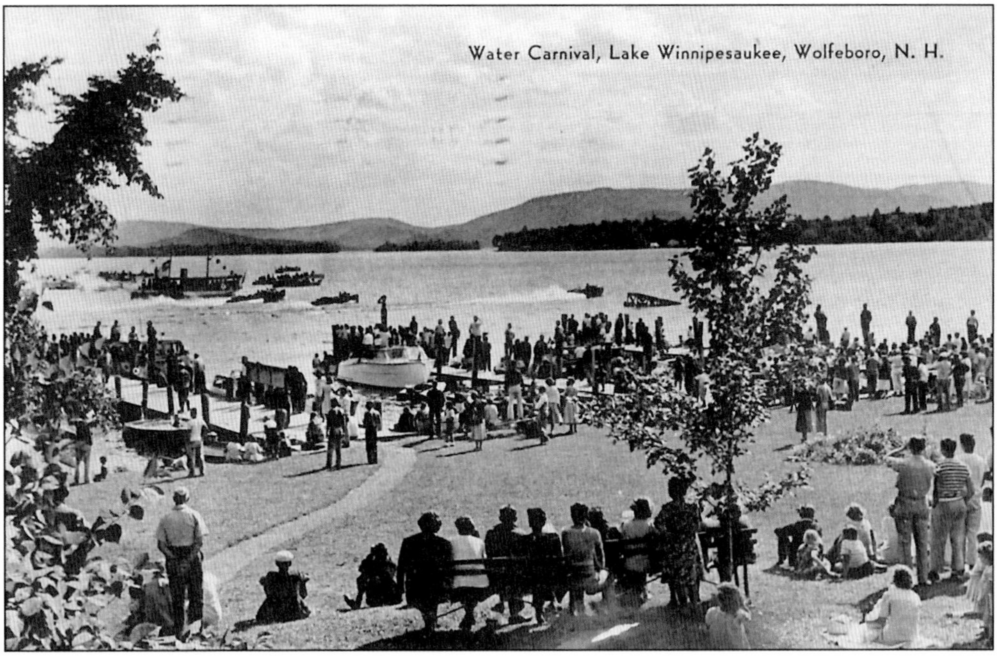

The 1951 Water Carnival on Wolfeboro Bay.

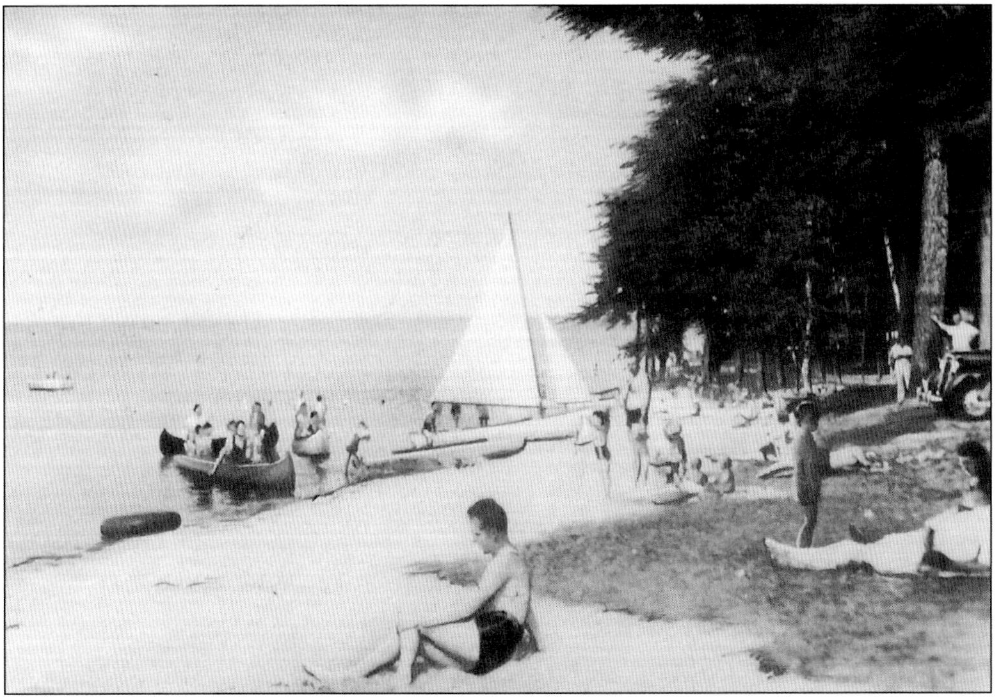
Vacation days at Lake Shore Park. The white beach and soft sands compile to make one of the most beautiful locations on the lake front, 1940s.

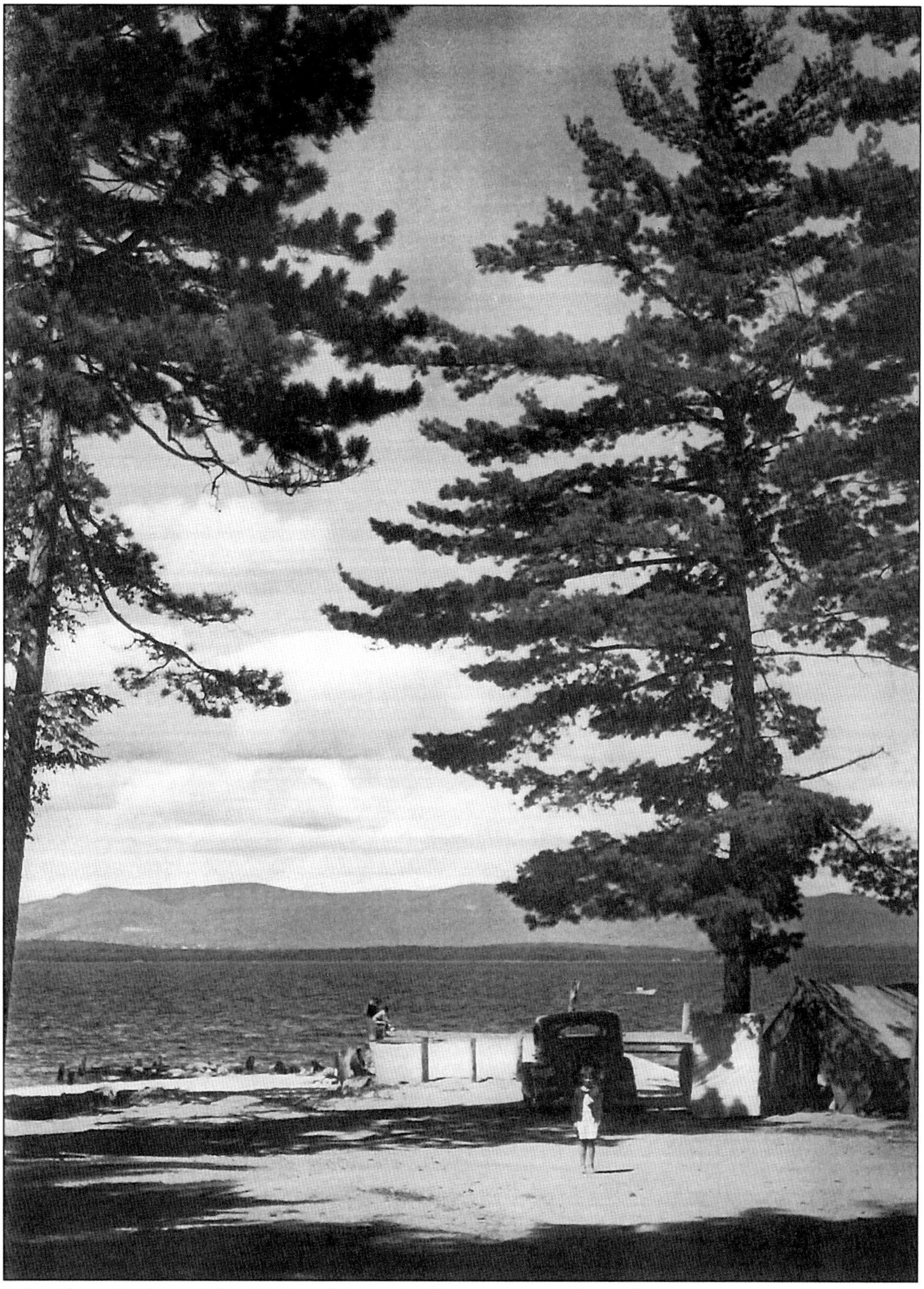

Lake Shore Park and the Ossipee Mountain Range as seen from the pine grove, mid-1930s.

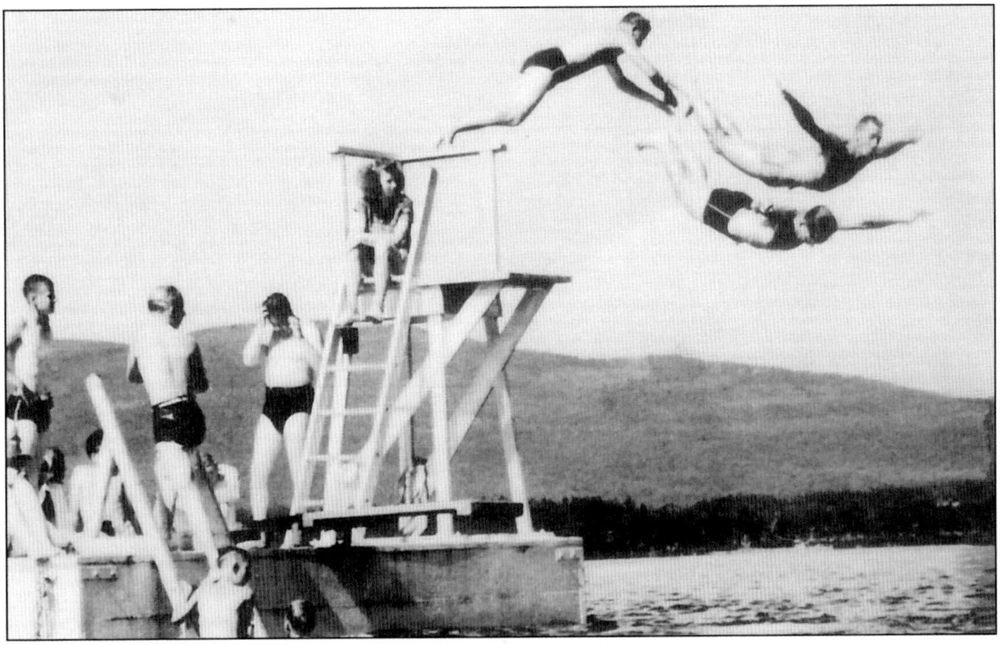

In the swim at Geneva Point Camp, Moultonboro, New Hampshire.

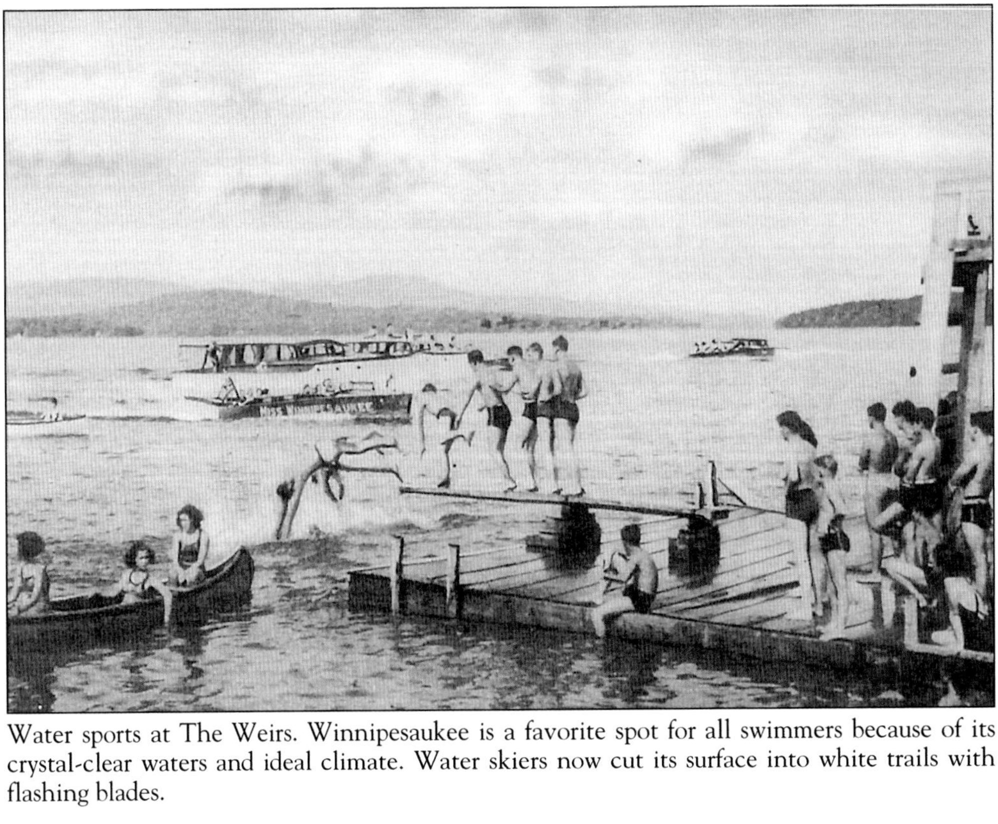

Water sports at The Weirs. Winnipesaukee is a favorite spot for all swimmers because of its crystal-clear waters and ideal climate. Water skiers now cut its surface into white trails with flashing blades.

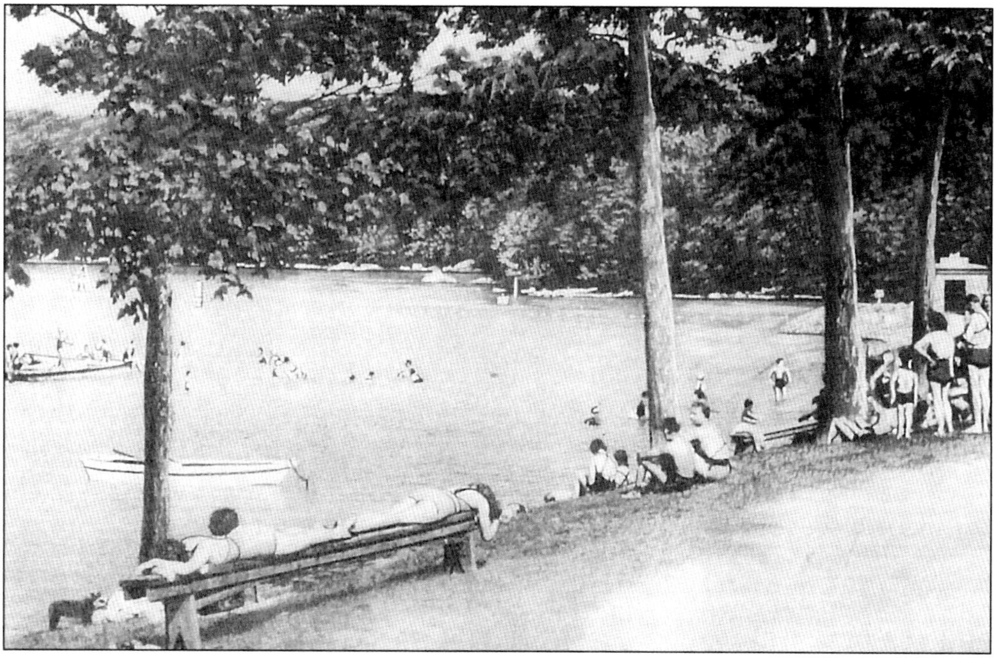

The Endicott bathing beach at The Weirs. This large bathing beach, with attendants, bath house, and excellent facilities, is owned and operated by the state, 1940s.

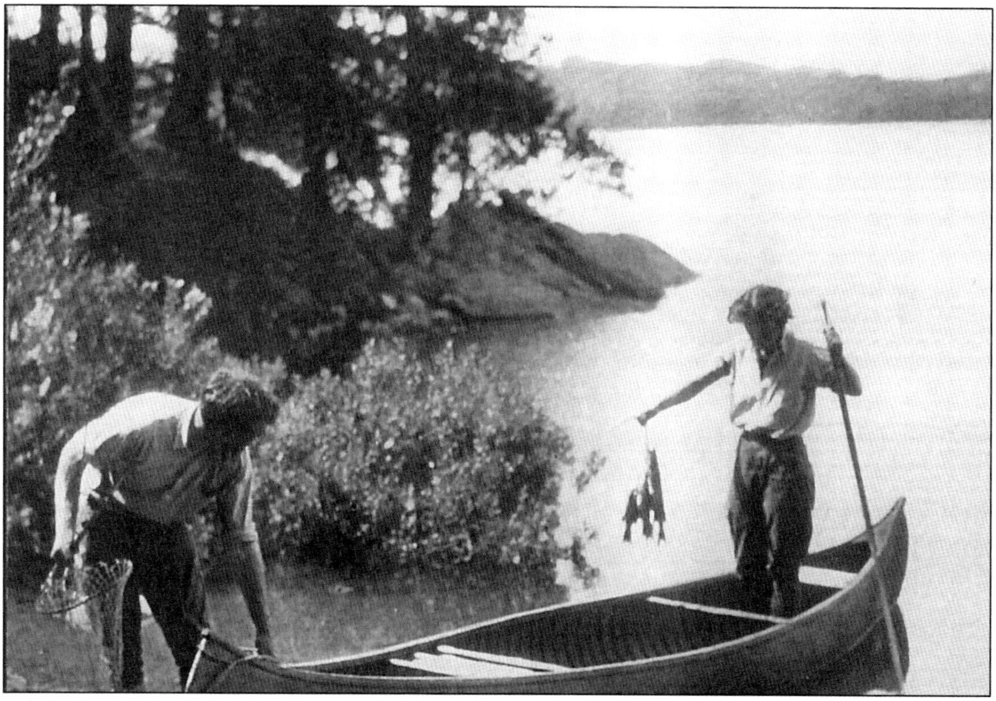

Lake past time. Fishing is very good in the lake with salmon being stocked and taken from early spring through the summer months. Lake trout are native and are taken from the first of January through September. Bass, pickerel, white fish, shad, and perch are all taken in their proper seasons.

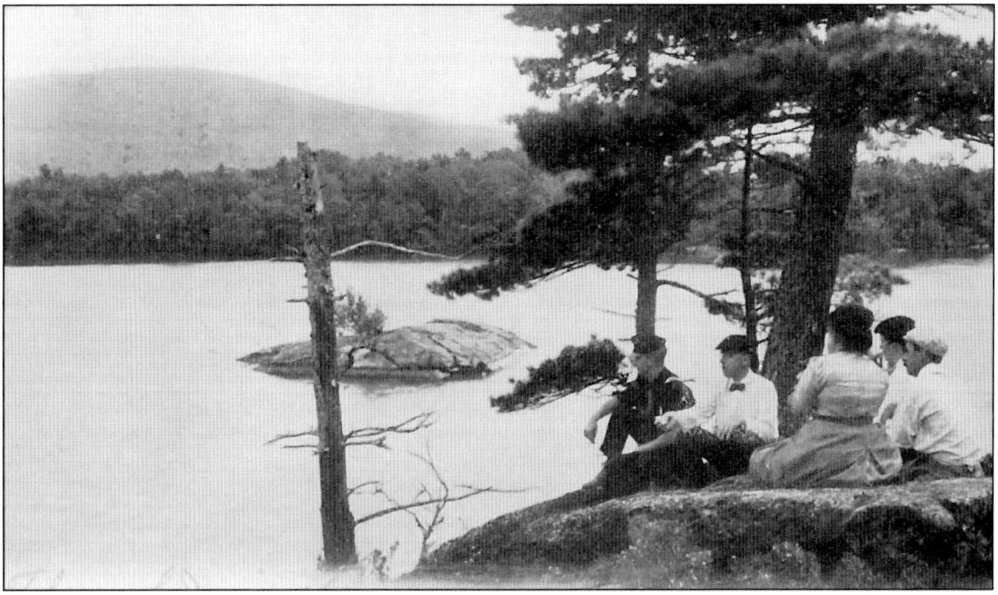

A picnic party at Green's Basin, Moultonboro, New Hampshire, 1910.

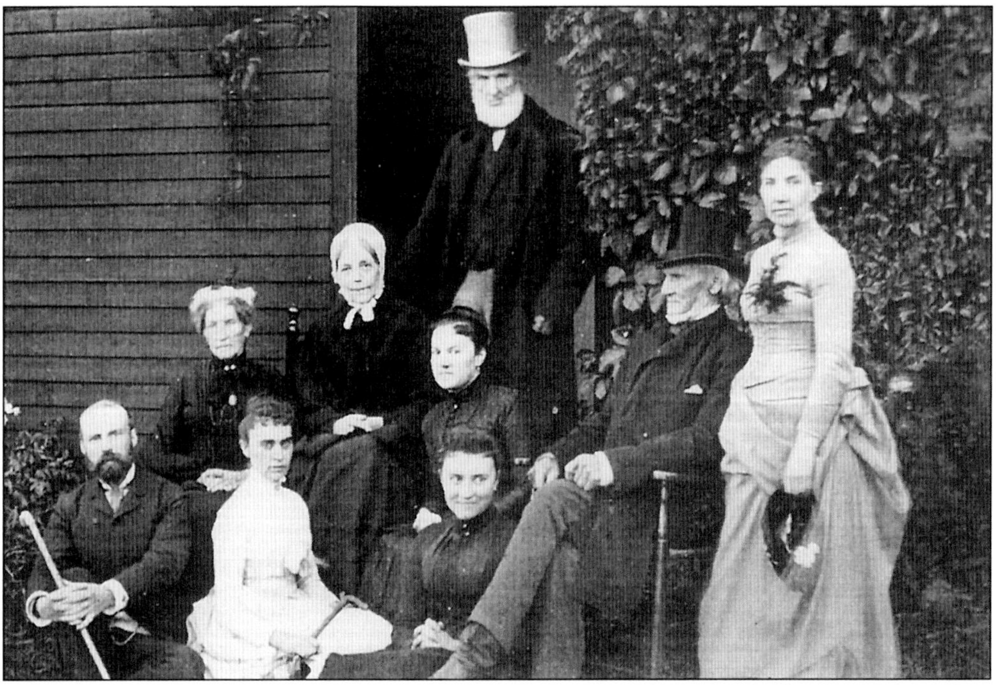

Friends and family gather in Center Harbor. This picture of John Greenleaf Whittier (standing in the doorway at the Sturtevant Farm) was taken in 1885.

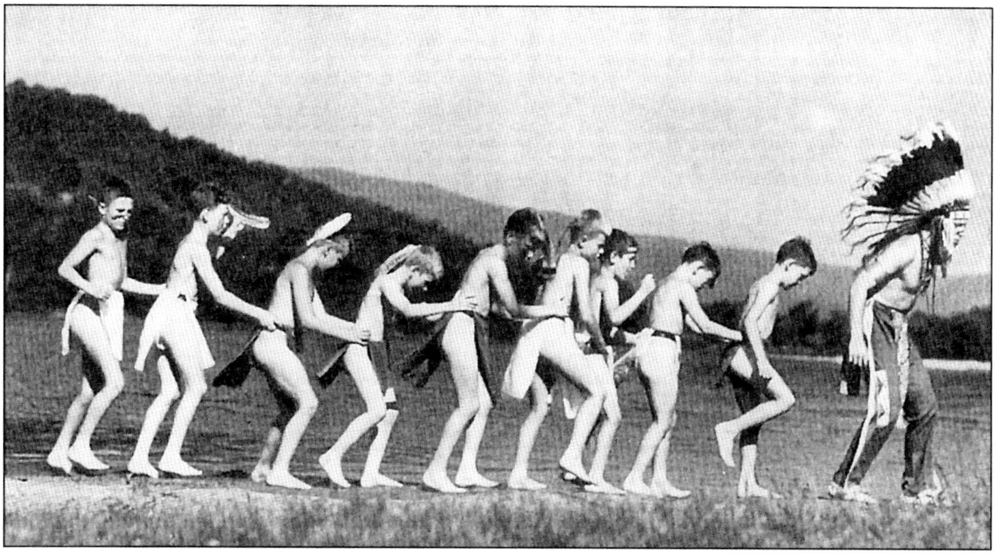

A group of camp boys learning to "play Indian" on the shore of Lake Winnipesaukee, 1940s.

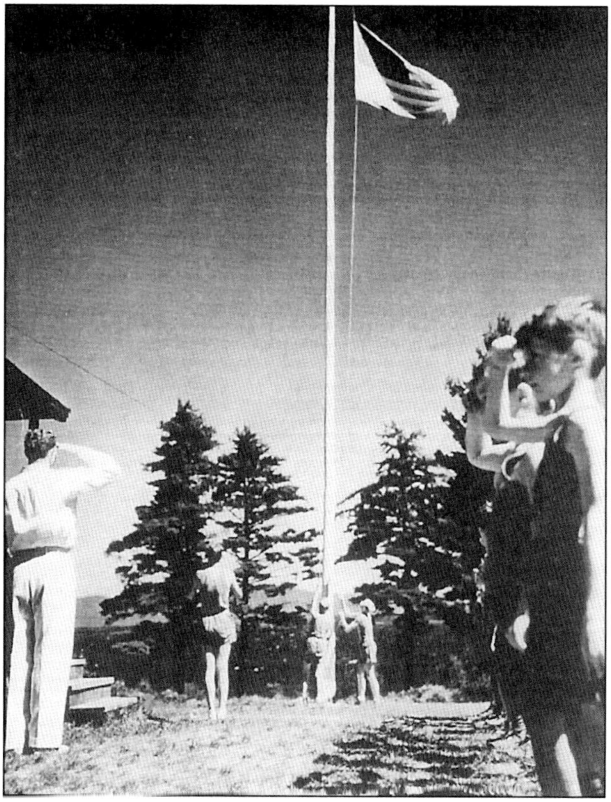

Raising the flag for another day at camp, 1940s.

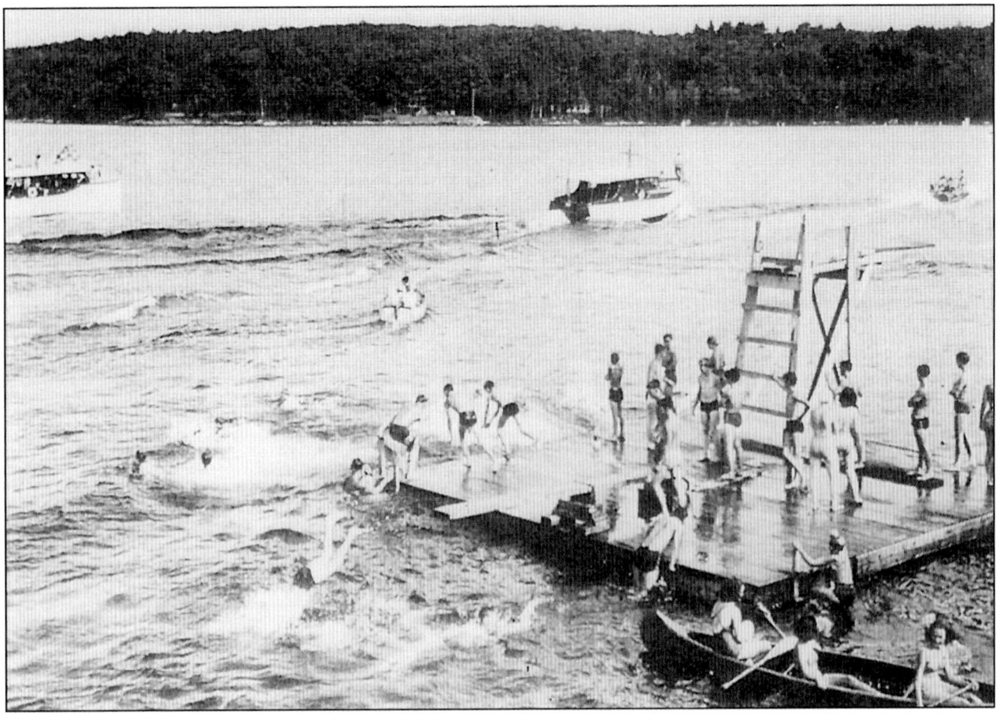

One of the many bathing beaches found on the lake, 1950s.

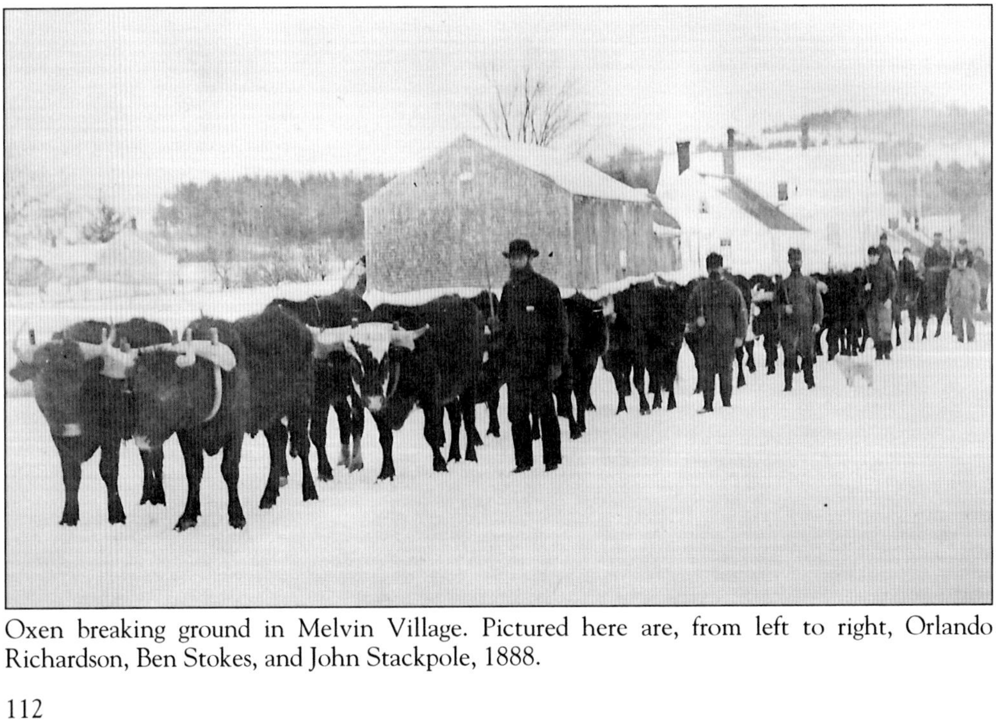

Oxen breaking ground in Melvin Village. Pictured here are, from left to right, Orlando Richardson, Ben Stokes, and John Stackpole, 1888.

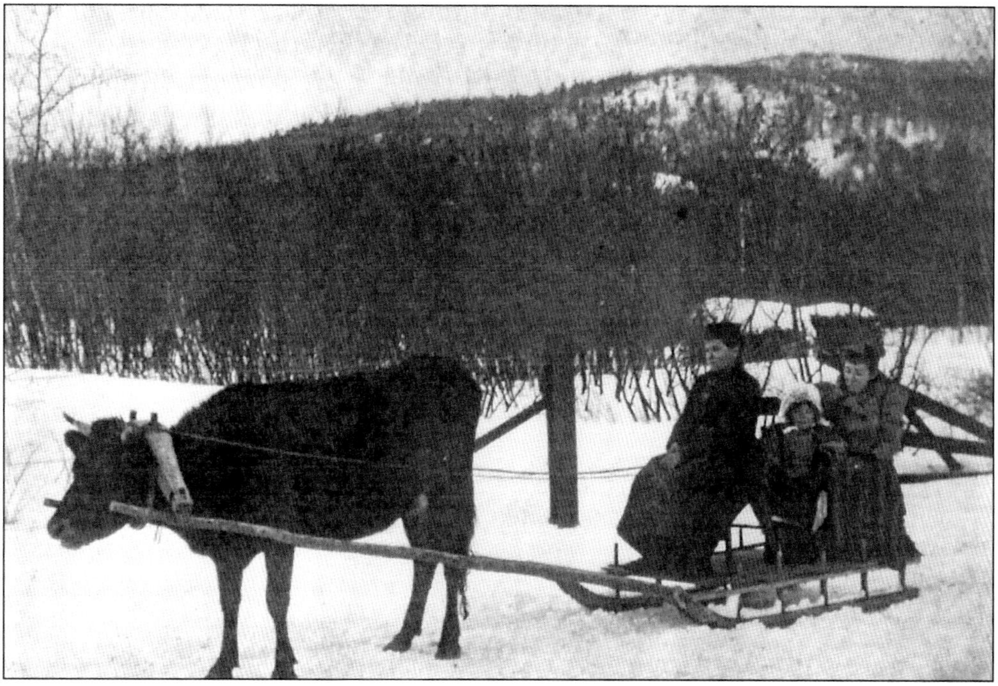

A quiet ride on the back roads in Moultonboro, New Hampshire, 1950s.

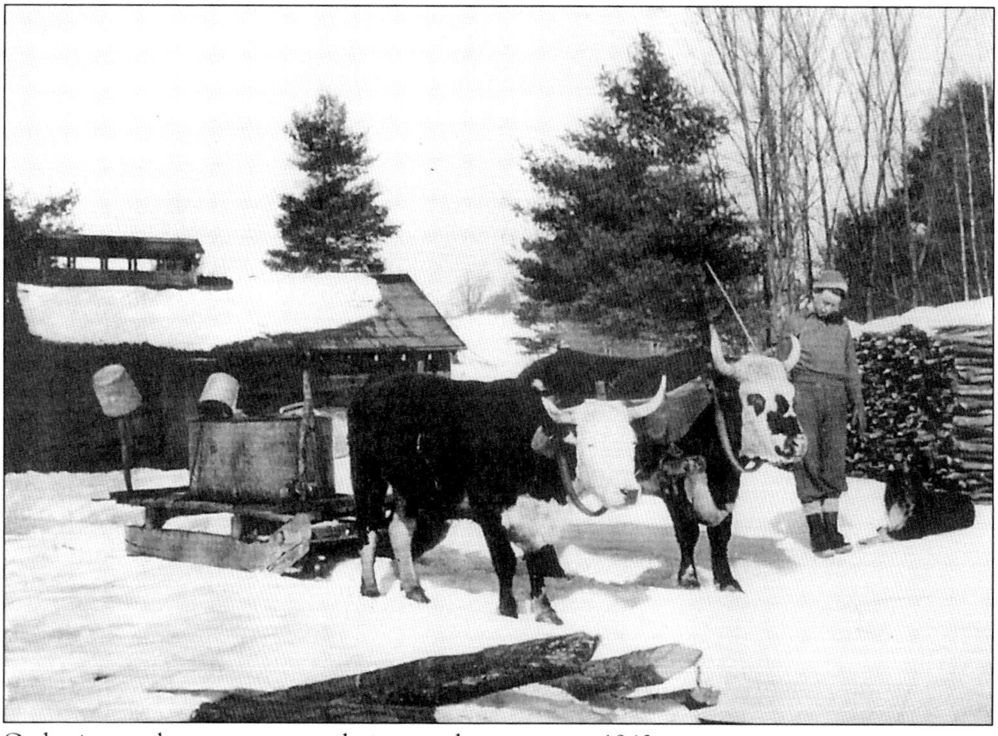

Gathering sap by an oxen team during maple sugar time, 1940s.

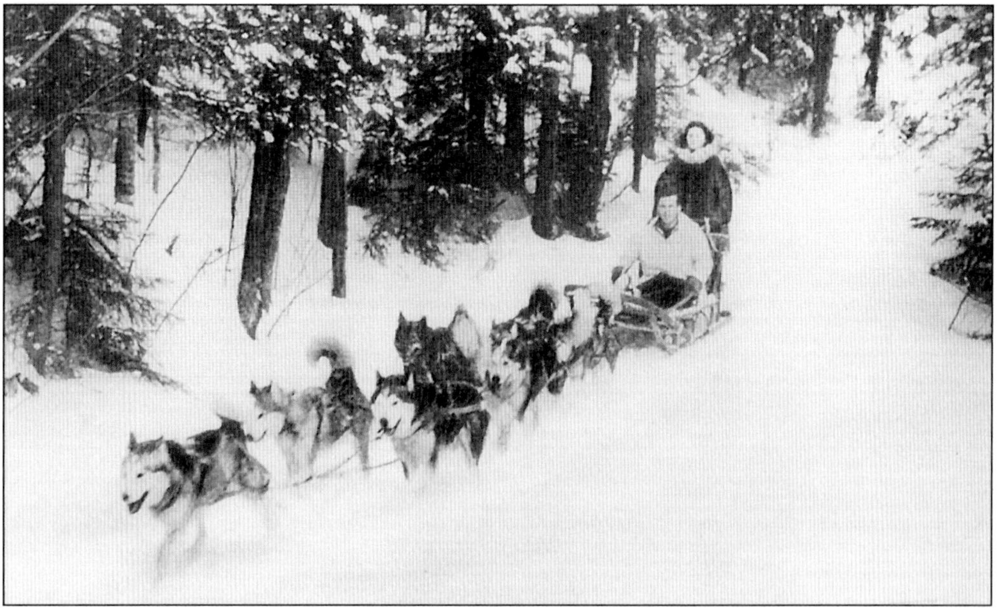

Mrs. Milton (Eve) Seeley and her Chinook Kennels sled dog team, 1940s. During the 1930s, many of her dogs were trained for dog-sled races, which were a main feature of winter carnivals held throughout New Hampshire and Canada in the winter months.

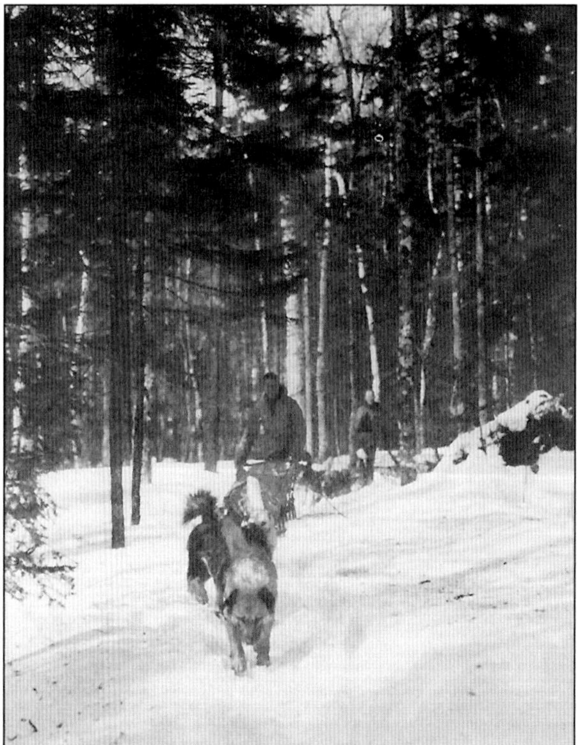

A dog sled team breaking the trail in the woods of Sandwich, New Hampshire, 1950s.

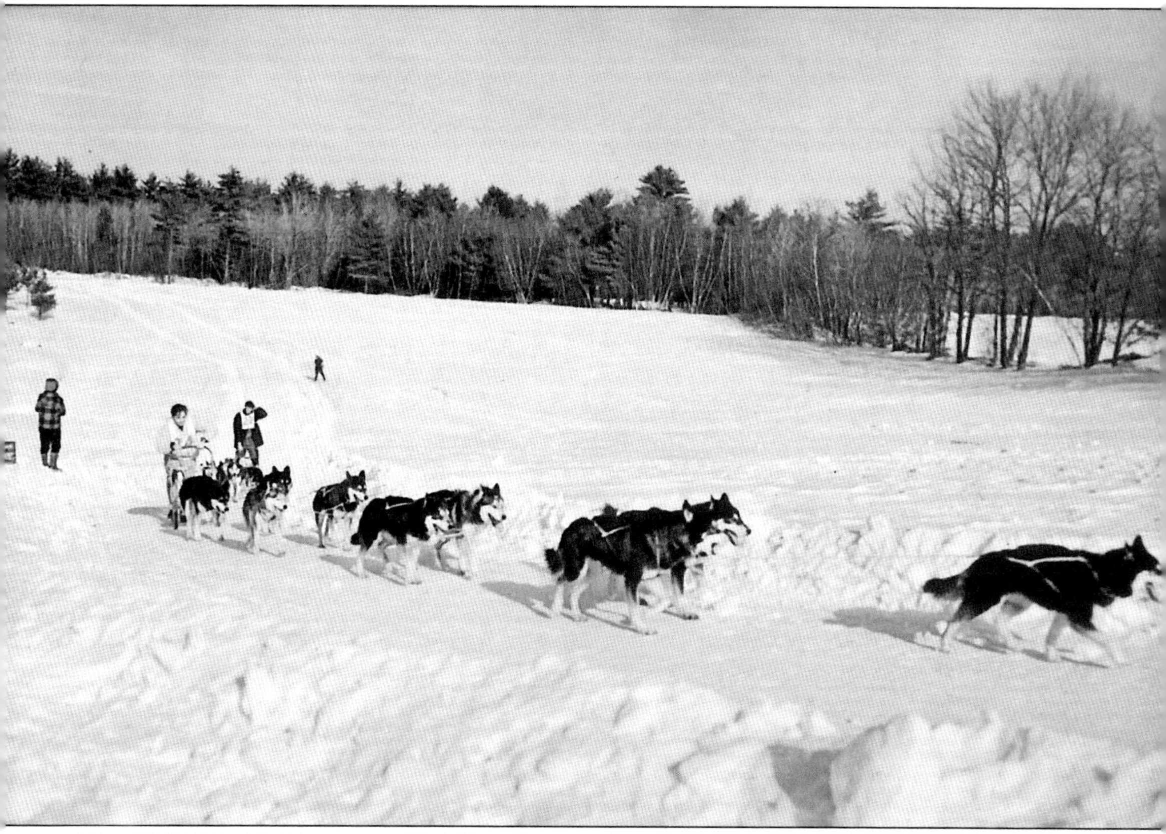

The 1968 World Champion Sled Dog Race in Laconia, New Hampshire. Sled dog races continue to be an exciting winter activity of the Lakes Region.

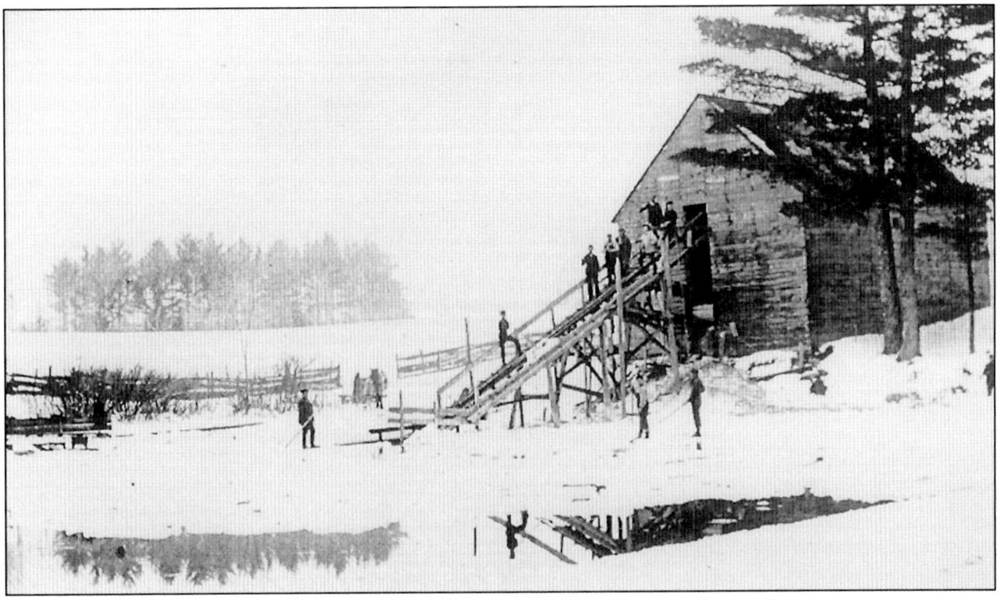

Ice harvesting at Pout Pond, 1905. Throughout the Lakes Region this industry was very active, even as late as the 1940s.

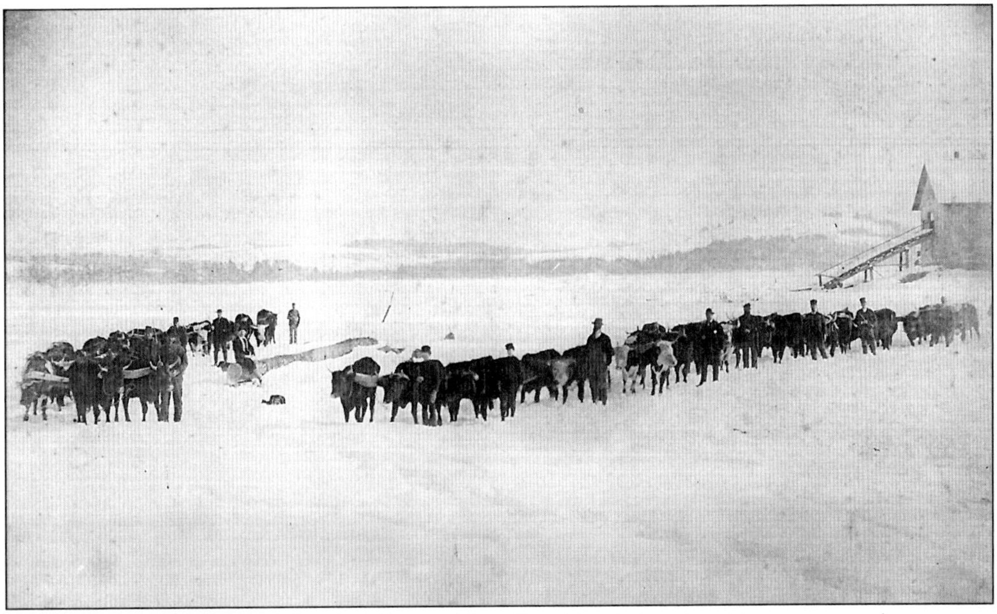

The Old Town Team on Meredith Bay, 1880s. The Shook Lumber Company can be seen on the right. The team was used to break roads throughout the town.

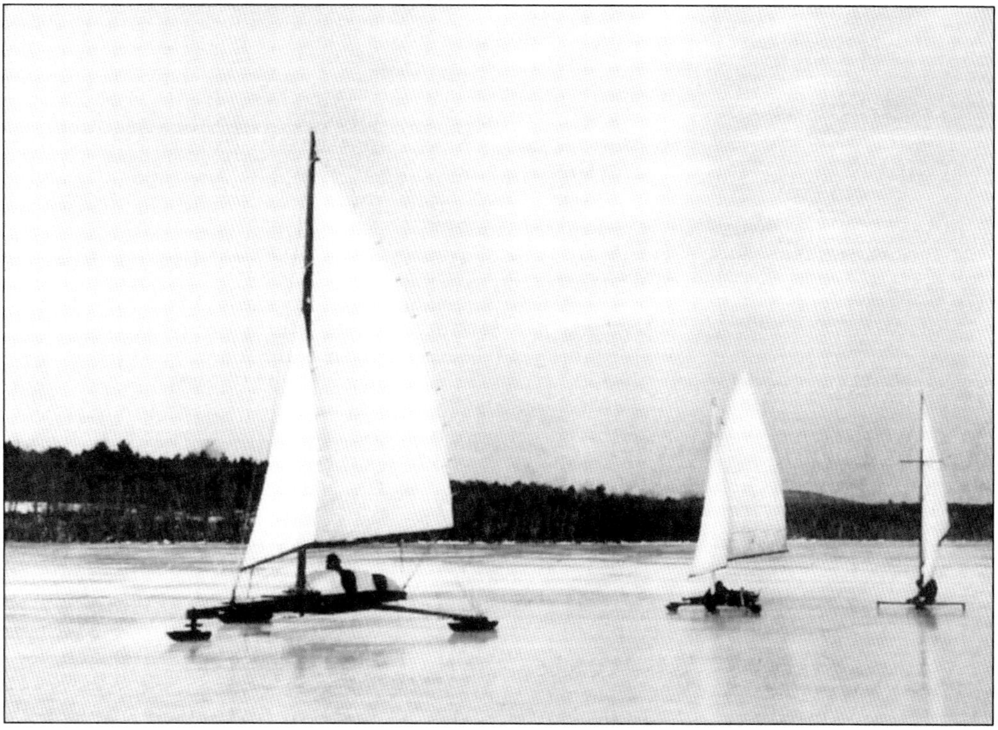

Ice sailing is still a favorite winter sport on Lake Winnipesaukee. This picture was taken in the 1940s.

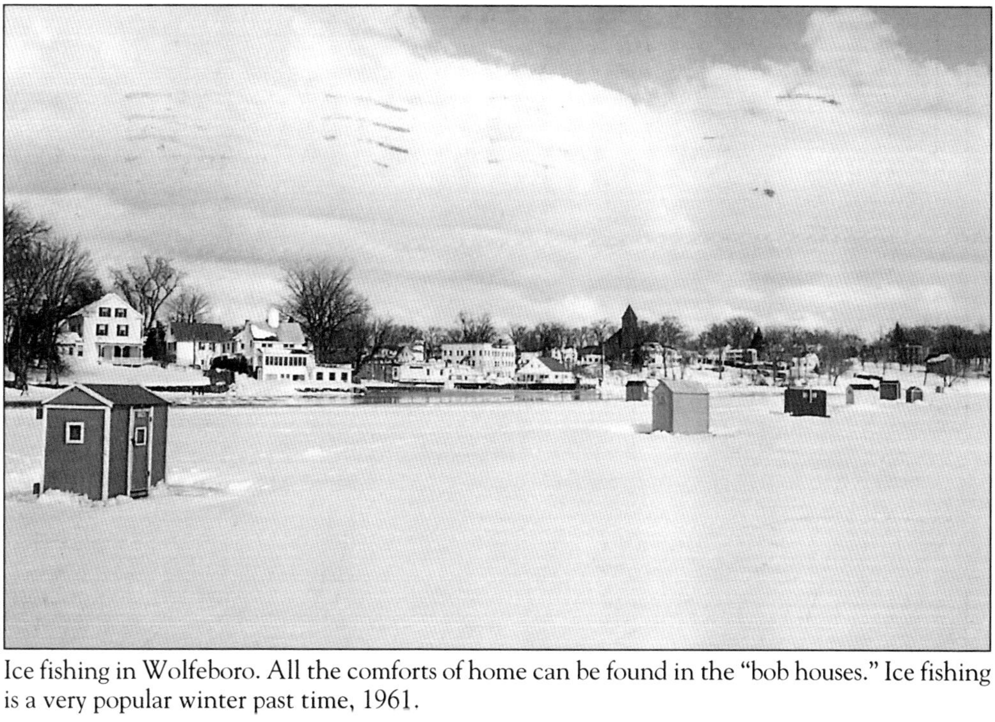

Ice fishing in Wolfeboro. All the comforts of home can be found in the "bob houses." Ice fishing is a very popular winter past time, 1961.

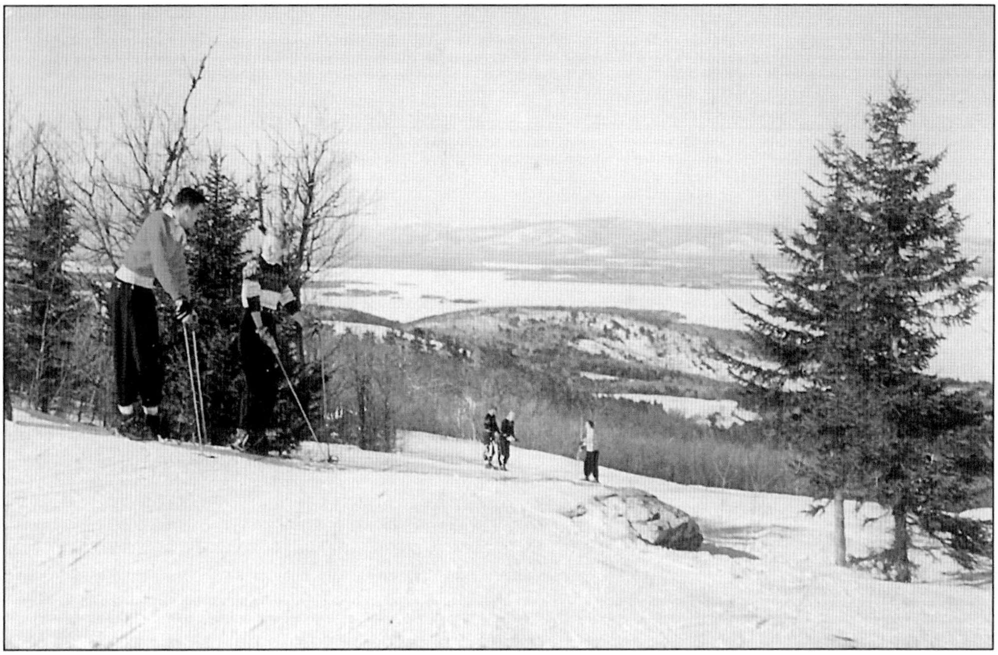

The Belknap Ski Area, Gilford, New Hampshire, 1968. A pause occurs in the day's skiing fun at the Belknap Ski Area. In the background is a panoramic view of the Broads in Lake Winnipesaukee framed by the Ossipee Mountain Range in the far distance.

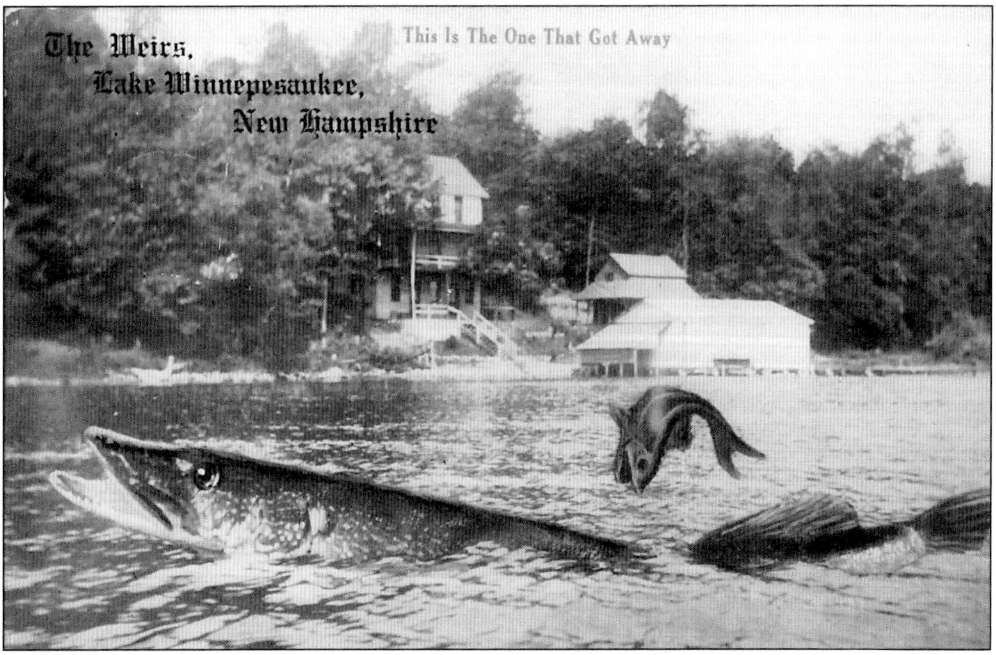

Fishing is very good here, but this is one that got away.

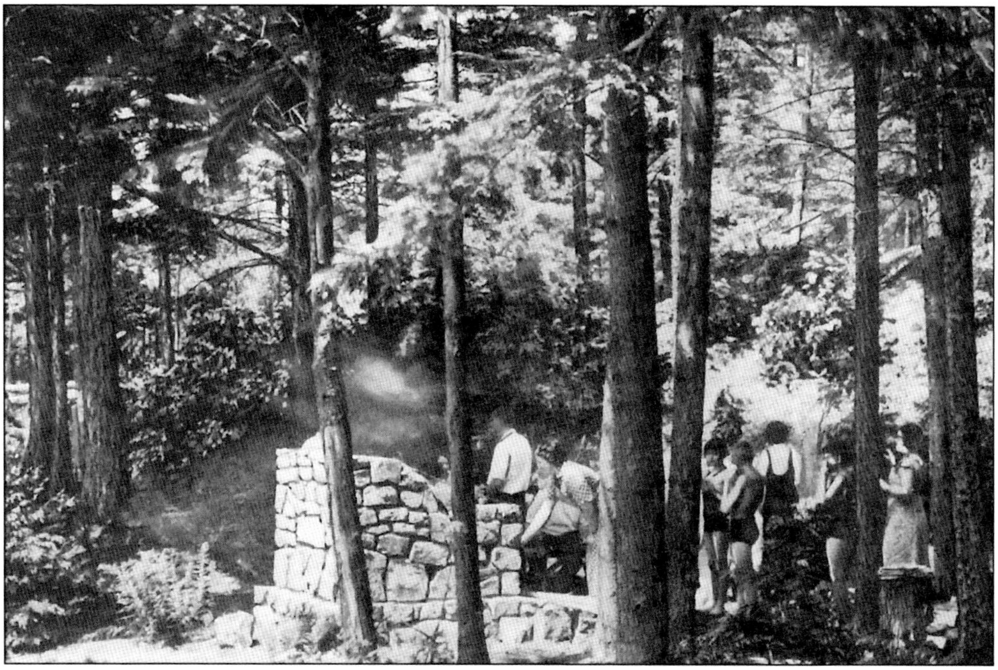

One of the many public fireplaces at the Belknap Recreation Area, Gilford, 1940s.

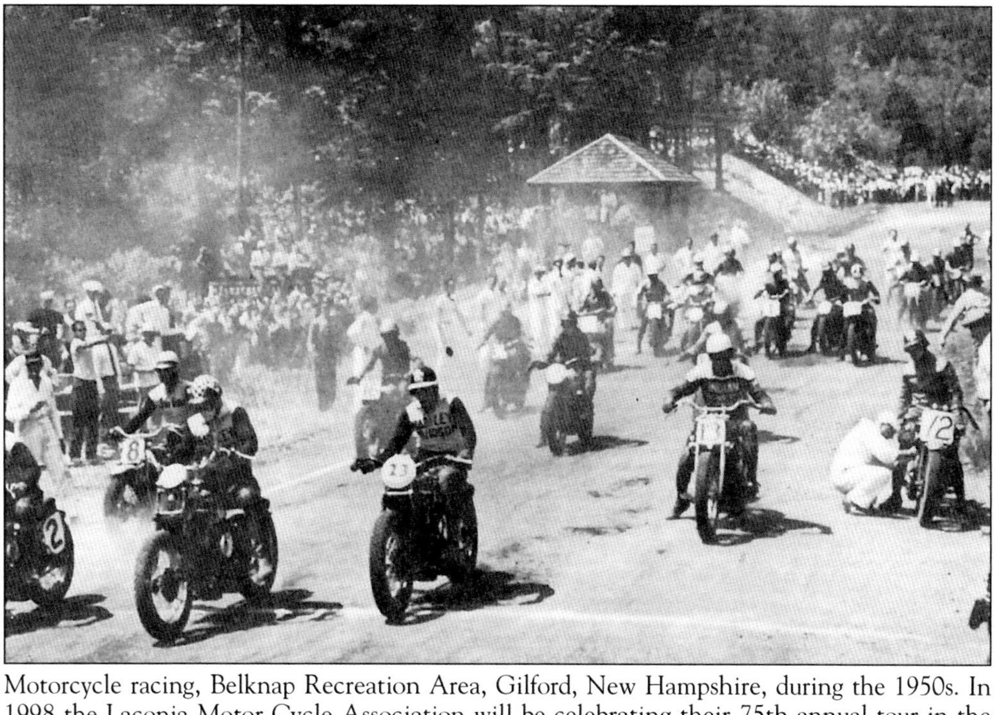

Motorcycle racing, Belknap Recreation Area, Gilford, New Hampshire, during the 1950s. In 1998 the Laconia Motor Cycle Association will be celebrating their 75th annual tour in the Lakes Region.

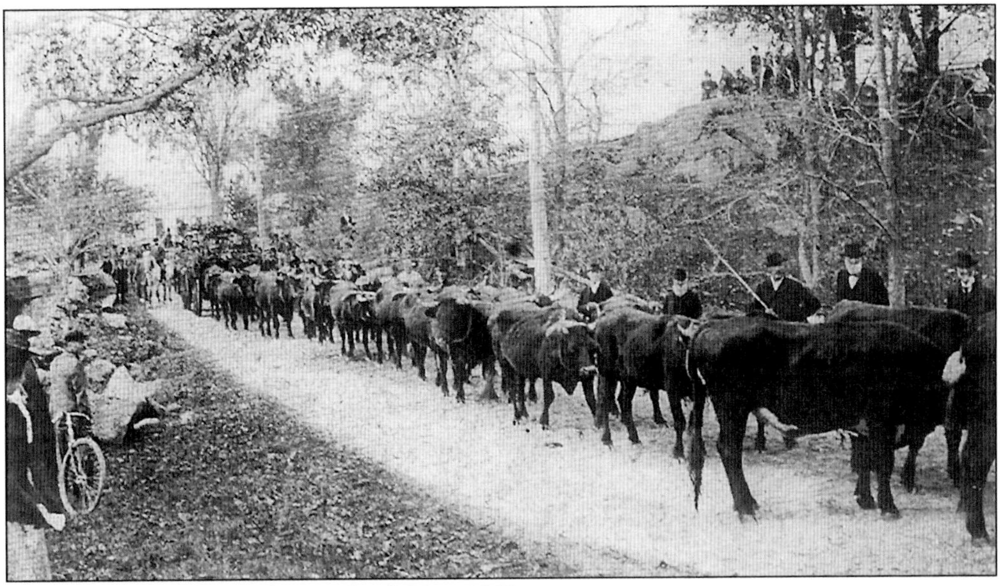

Cattle on parade during the Sandwich Fair, 1960s.

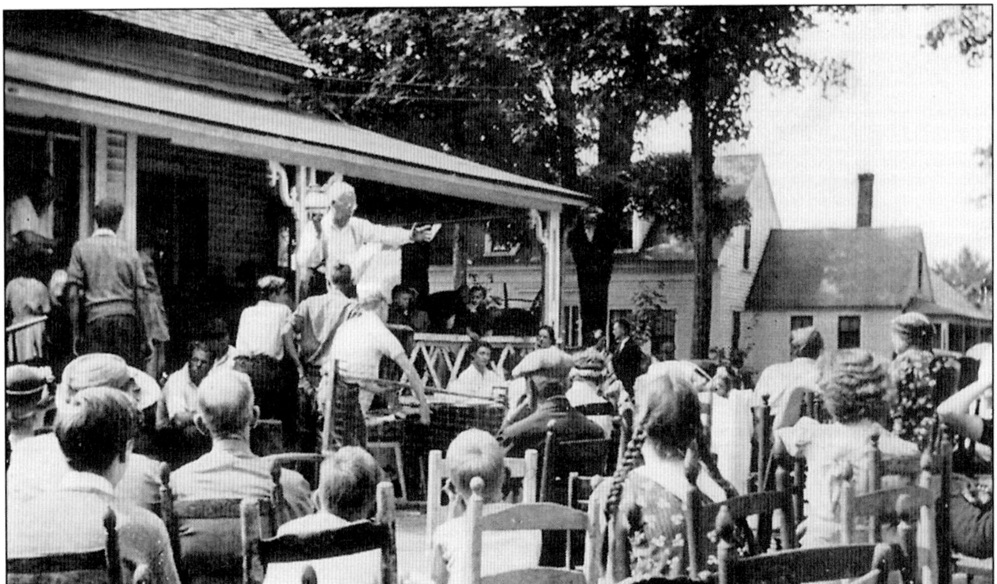

Auction time in the Lakes Region, 1960s.

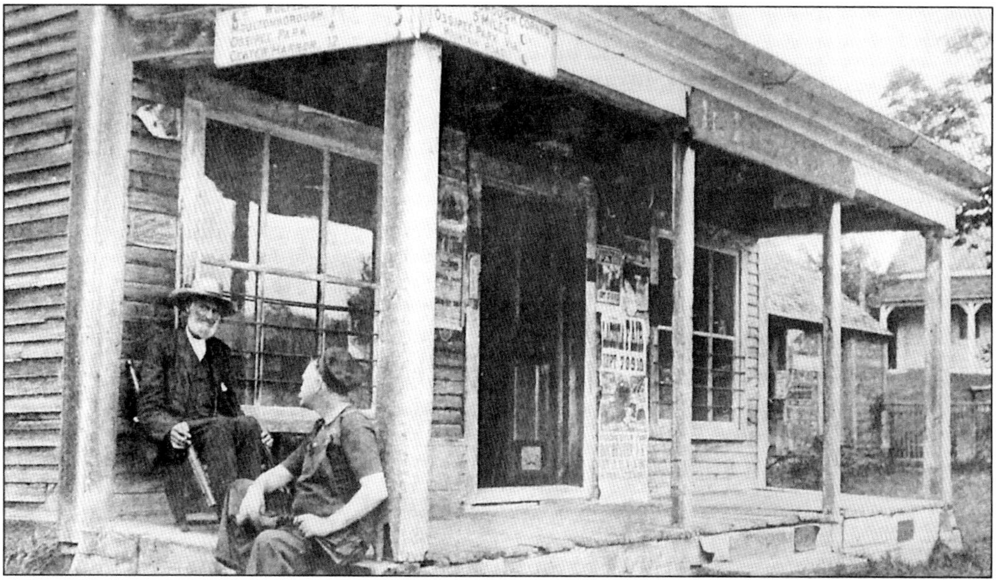

Dan Fernald's General Store at Melvin Village, Tuftonboro, New Hampshire, 1880s. The old-fashioned country store has always been the magnet for the curious shopper. This store, which once stood on the corner of Main and High Streets, was operated at one time by the Rev. Moorehouse. "On Sundays, after preaching his sermon, he would '...rush to the store to sell candy and soda pop' to the boys from Camp Tecumsah who had just attended church."

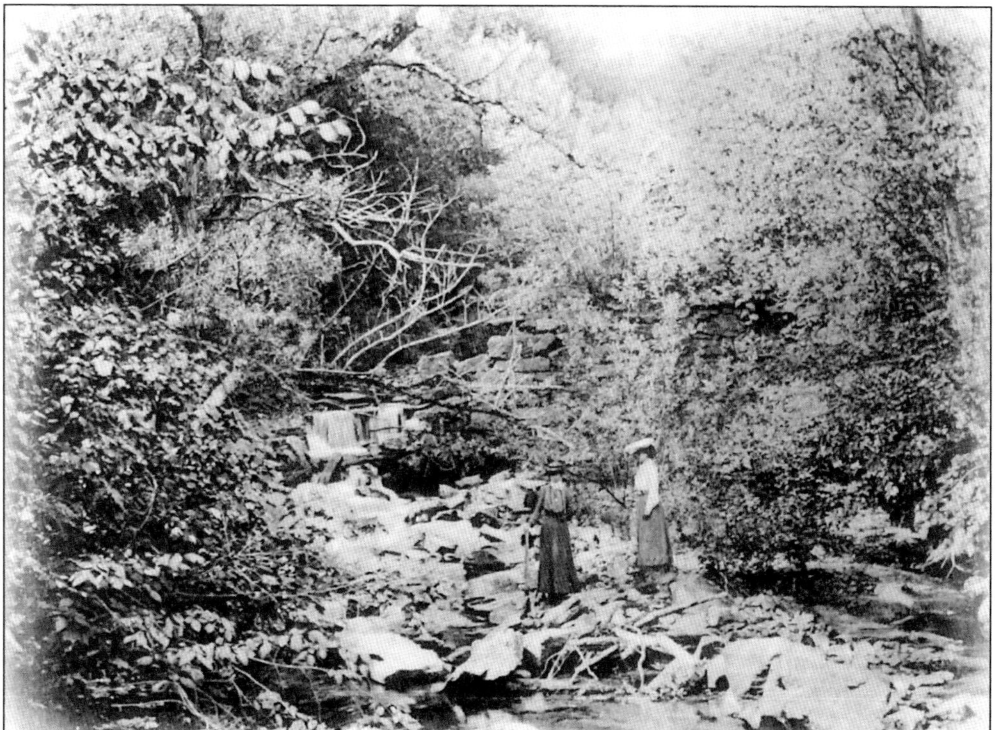

A quiet moment by a mountain stream to Lake Winnipesaukee, 1907.

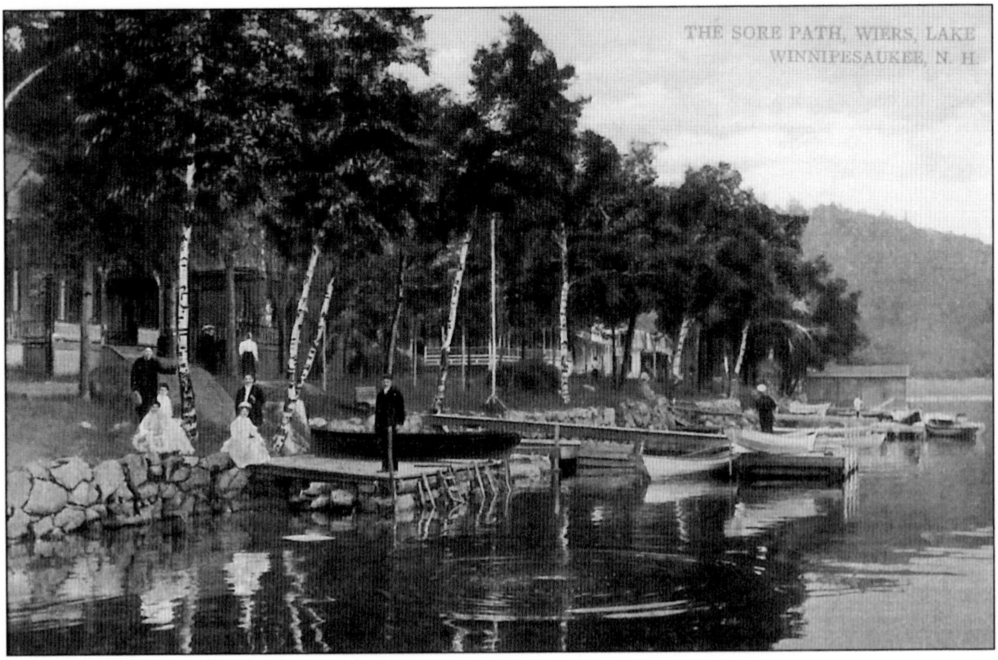

The Sore Path at The Weirs, early 1900s.

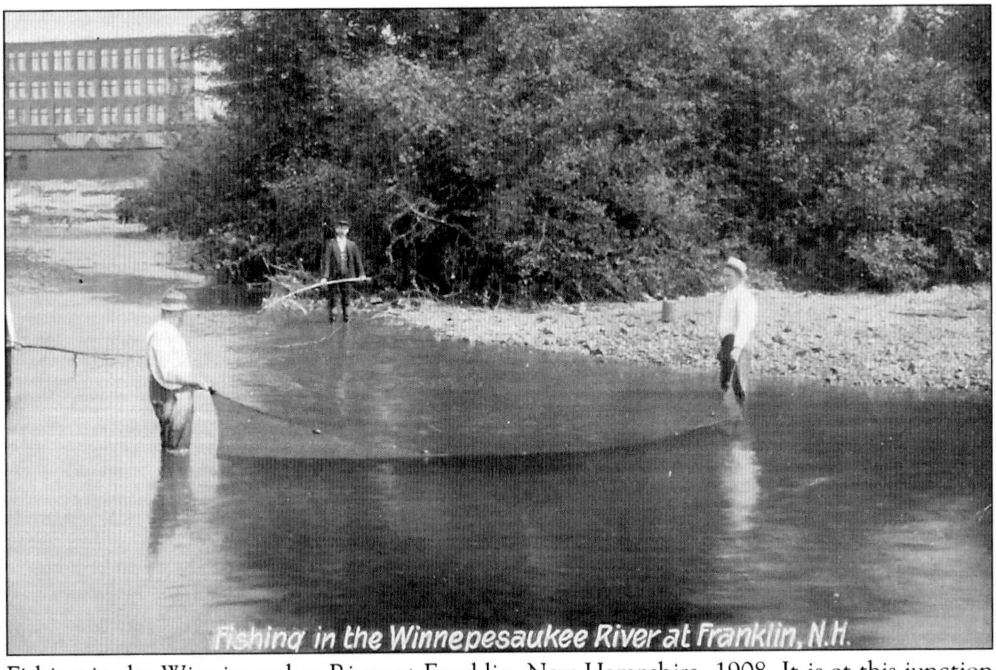

Fishing in the Winnipesaukee River at Franklin, New Hampshire, 1908. It is at this junction that the waters from Winnipesaukee join the Pemigewasset River to form the Merrimack River, which eventually flows through Manchester, Concord, and finally to the Atlantic Ocean off the shore of Massachusetts.

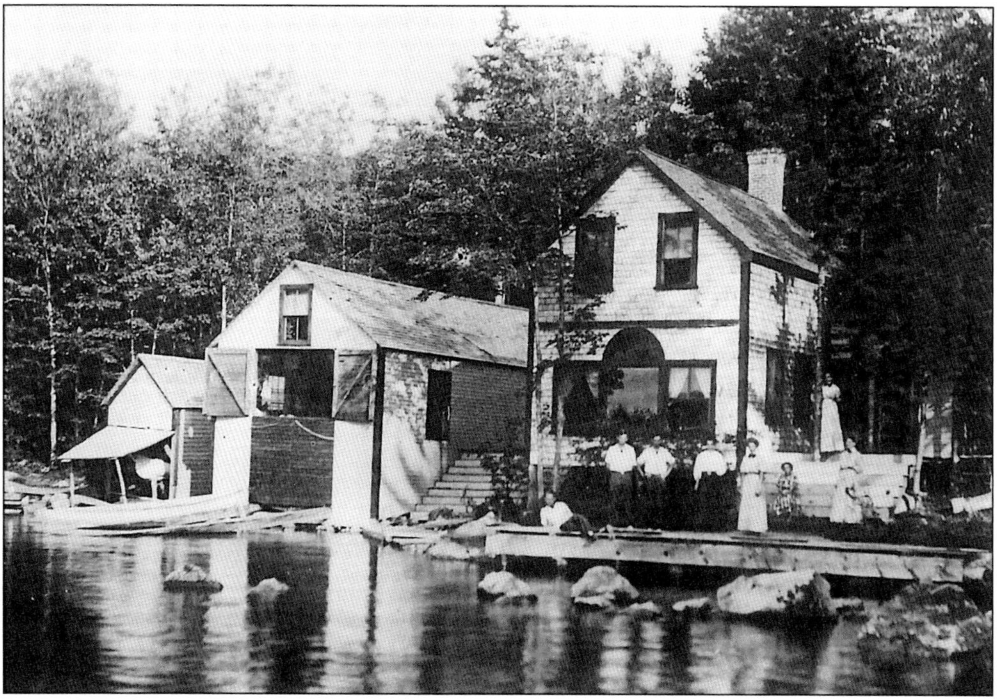

A family gathering at their summer cottage on the lake, early 1900s.

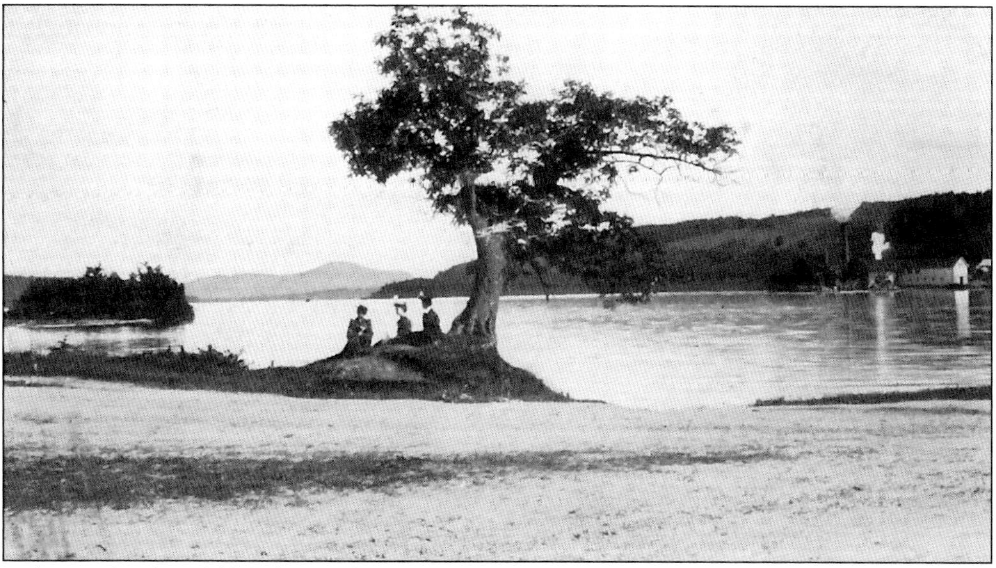

Ladies under the "Old Oak" at Clough's Park on the shore of Meredith Bay, New Hampshire, late 1800s. In the distance on the right is the old Shook Lumber Company where the present St. Charles Church now stands.

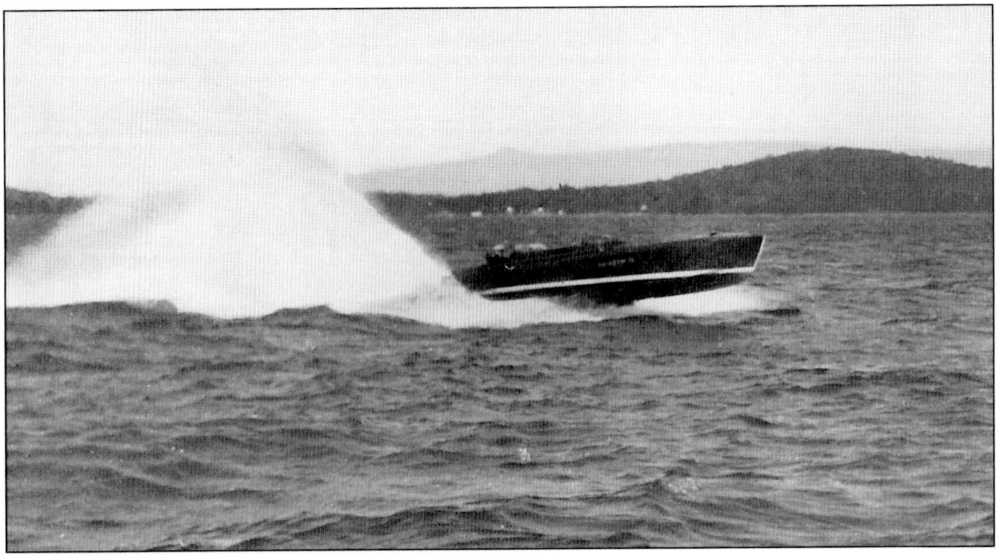

A solo speed boat at the race in the Broads, 1927.

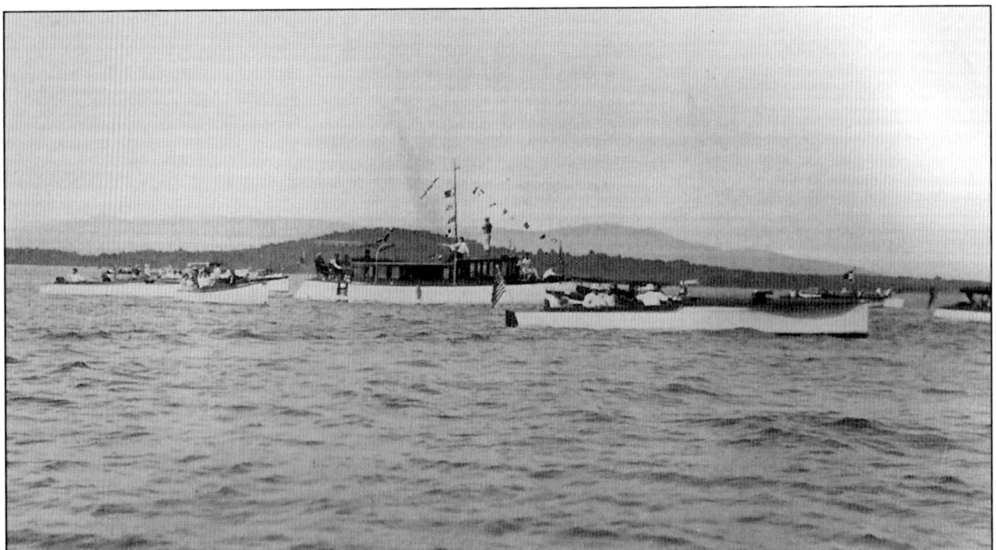

Spectators and the judge's boat at the race in the Broads, 1927.

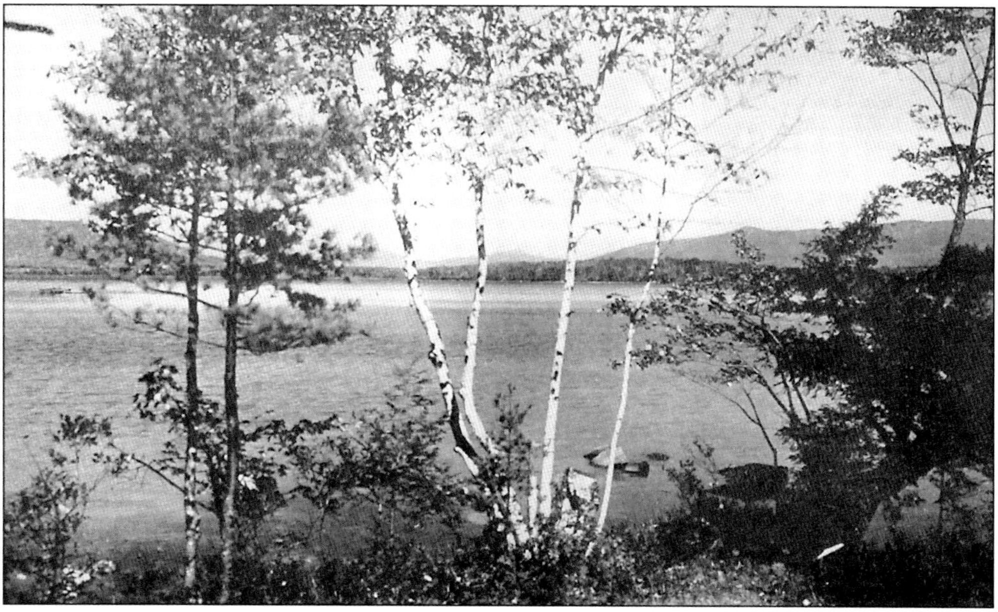

Lake Winnipesaukee looking north from Pine Island, Meredith, New Hampshire.

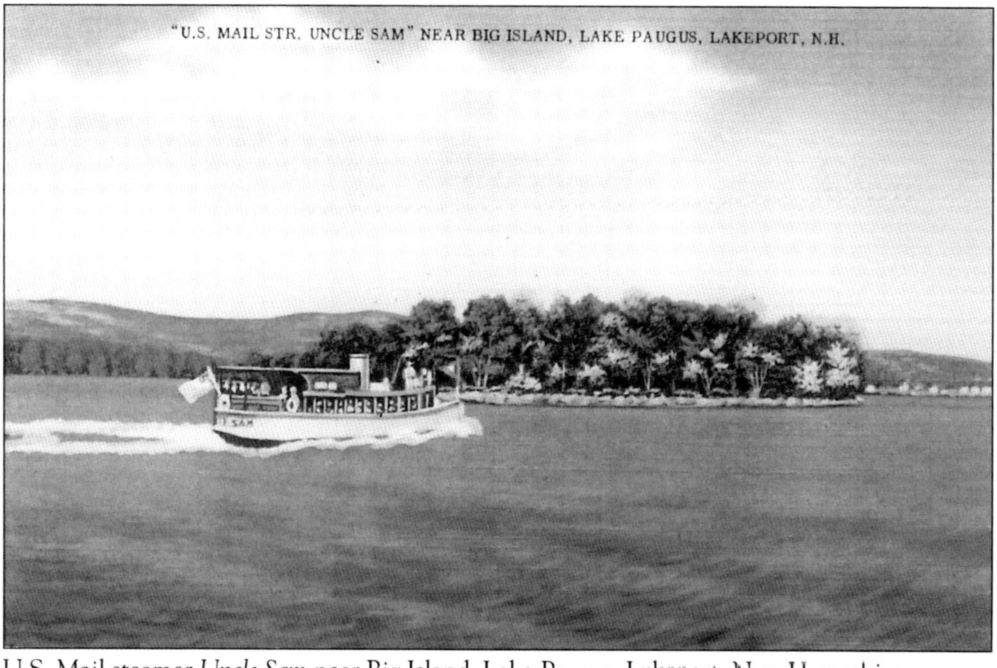

U.S. Mail steamer *Uncle Sam* near Big Island, Lake Paugus, Lakeport, New Hampshire.

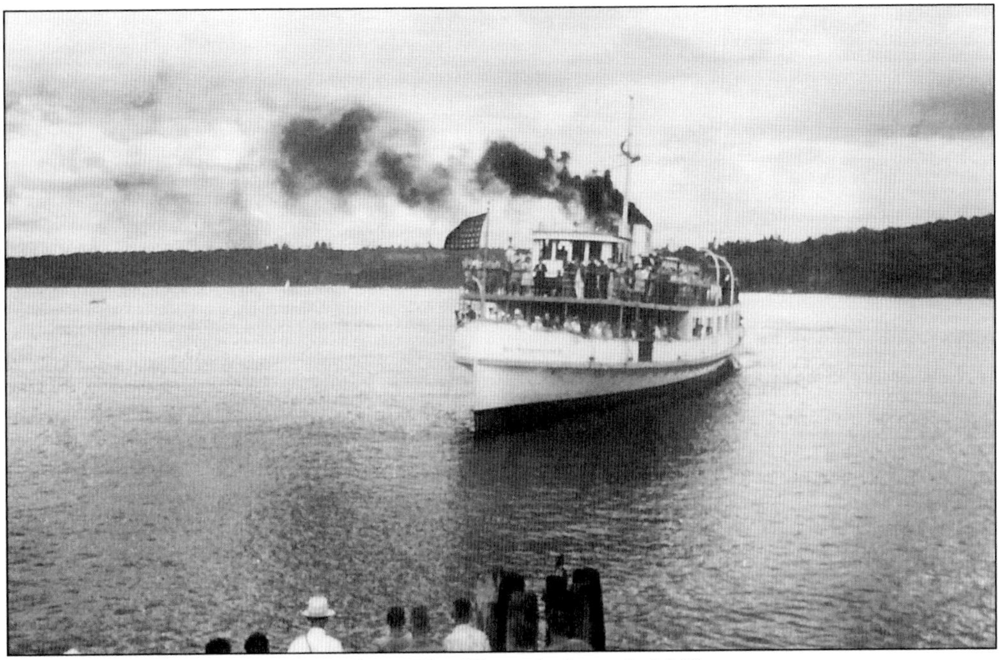

The *Mount Washington II* approaching The Weirs dock, early 1940s.

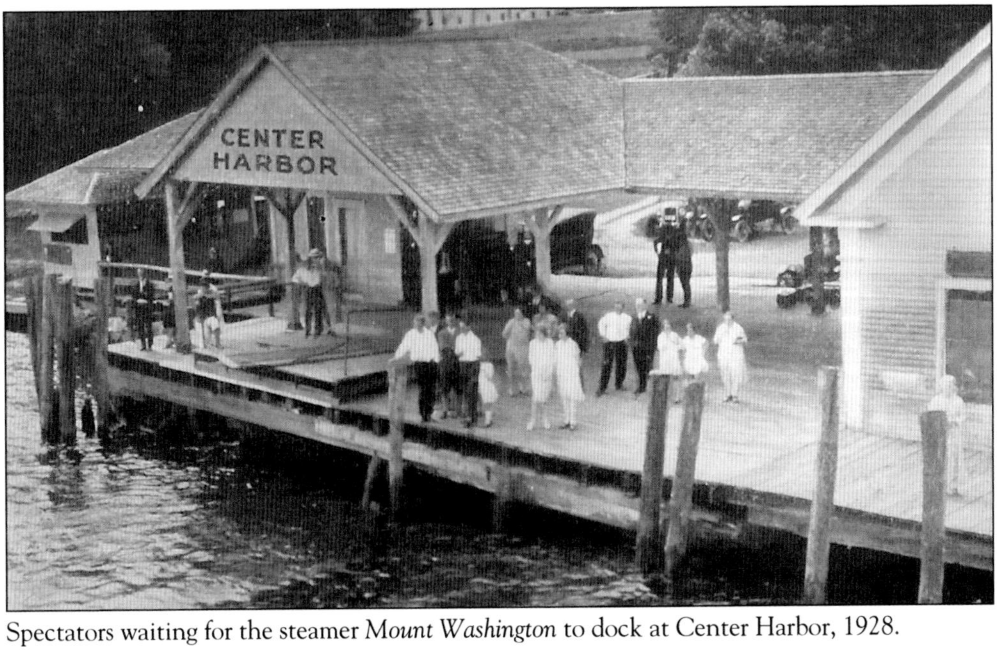

Spectators waiting for the steamer *Mount Washington* to dock at Center Harbor, 1928.

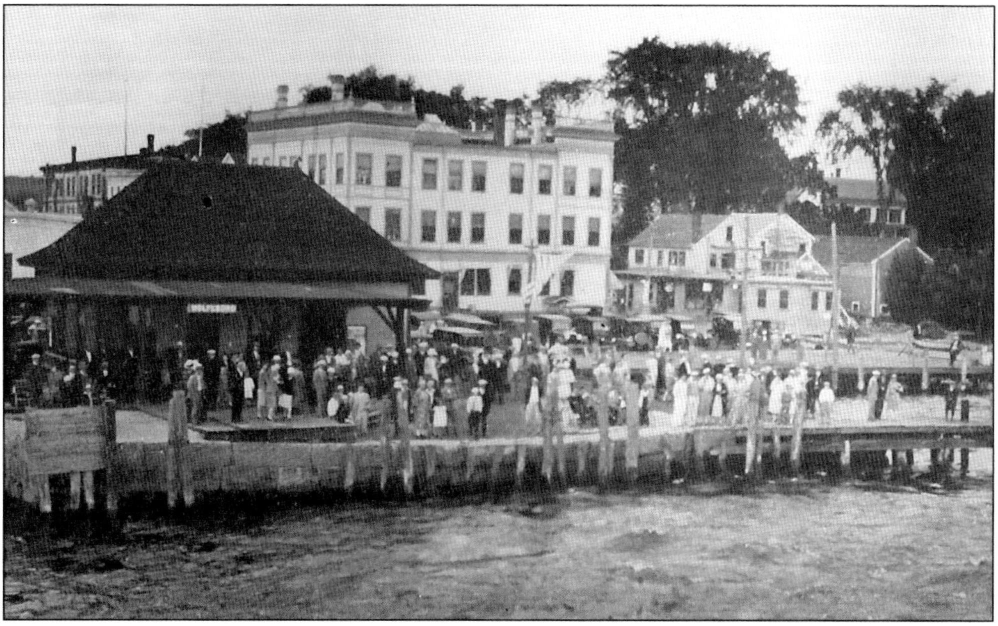

The public docks at Wolfeboro, a daily port of call for the *Mount Washington*, 1928.

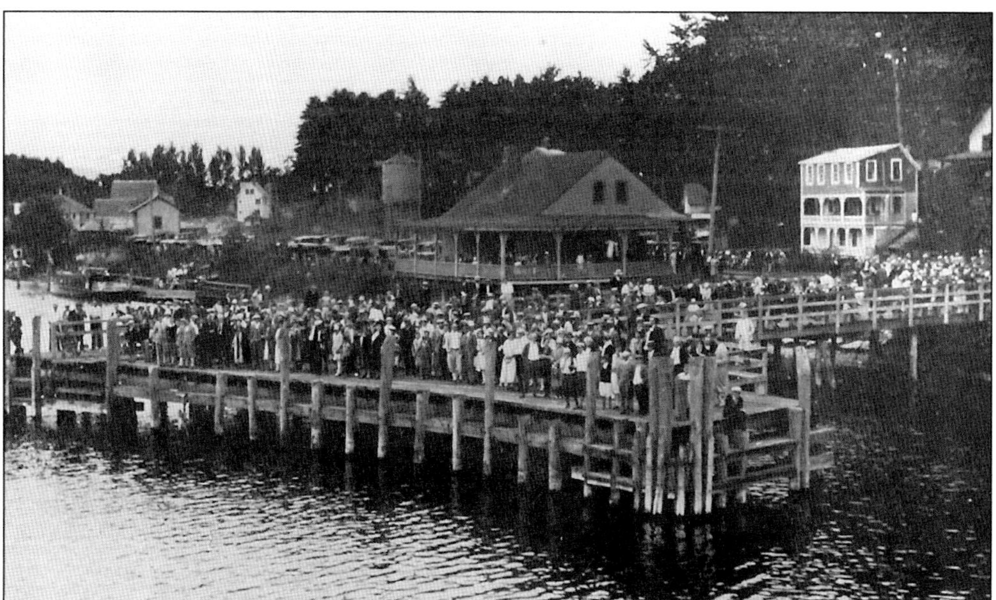

Hundreds of visitors waiting for the *Mount Washington* to dock at Alton Bay, 1928.

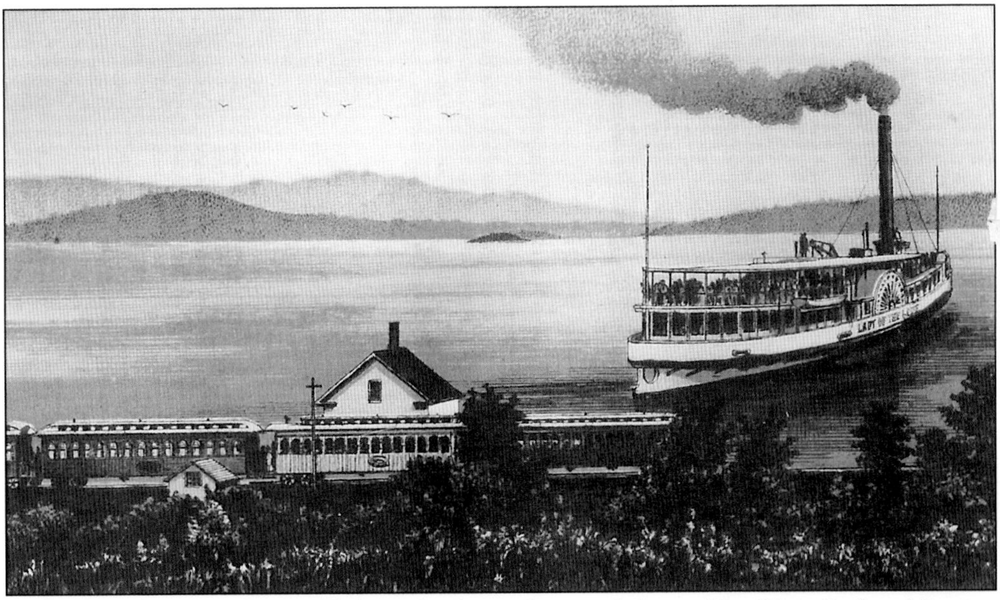

The *Lady of the Lake*. This vessel closes the day as she quietly leaves The Weirs Railroad Station for a final cruise around the lake.

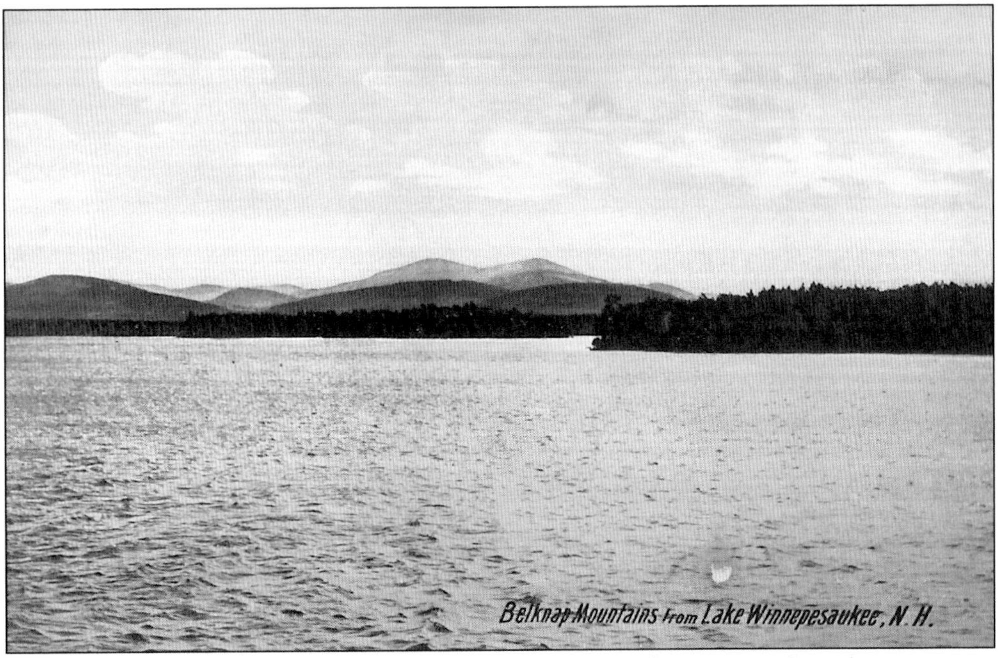

The Belknap Mountains from Wolfeboro at sunset with Sewell's Point on the right.